UNIVERSITY OF WINCHESTER
LIBRARY

D1351362

Social Media and Minority Languages

MULTILINGUAL MATTERS
Series Editor: John Edwards, *St. Francis Xavier University, Canada*
Multilingual Matters series publishes books on bilingualism, bilingual education, immersion education, second language learning, language policy, multiculturalism. The editor is particularly interested in 'macro'-level studies of language policies, language maintenance, language shift, language revival and language planning. Books in the series discuss the relationship between language in a broad sense and larger cultural issues, particularly identity-related ones.

Full details of all the books in this series and of all our other publications can be found on http://www.multilingual-matters.com, or by writing to Multilingual Matters, St Nicholas House, 31-34 High Street, Bristol BS1 2AW, UK.

This book has been developed within the framework of Mercator European Network of Language Diversity Centres funded by the European Union through the Lifelong Learning Programme of the European Commission in 2008-2011.

Education and Culture DG

Social Media and Minority Languages

Convergence and the Creative Industries

Edited by
**Elin Haf Gruffydd Jones and
Enrique Uribe-Jongbloed**

MULTILINGUAL MATTERS
Bristol • Buffalo • Toronto

Library of Congress Cataloging in Publication Data
A catalog record for this book is available from the Library of Congress.
Social Media and Minority Languages: Convergence and the Creative Industries/Edited by Elin Haf Gruffydd Jones and Enrique Uribe-Jongbloed.
Multilingual Matters: 152
Includes bibliographical references and index.
1. Minorities in mass media. 2. Minorities in the mass media industry. 3. Linguistic minorities. 4. Social media. 5. Web 2.0--Social aspects. I. Haf Gruffydd Jones, Elin, editor of compilation.
P94.5.M55S63 2013
302.2308–dc23 2012044138

British Library Cataloguing in Publication Data
A catalogue entry for this book is available from the British Library.

ISBN-13: 978-1-84769-904-6 (hbk)

Multilingual Matters
UK: St Nicholas House, 31-34 High Street, Bristol BS1 2AW, UK.
USA: UTP, 2250 Military Road, Tonawanda, NY 14150, USA.
Canada: UTP, 5201 Dufferin Street, North York, Ontario M3H 5T8, Canada.

The policy of Multilingual Matters/Channel View Publications is to use papers that are natural, renewable and recyclable products, made from wood grown in sustainable forests. In the manufacturing process of our books, and to further support our policy, preference is given to printers that have FSC and PEFC Chain of Custody certification. The FSC and/or PEFC logos will appear on those books where full certification has been granted to the printer concerned.

Typeset by DiTech.
Printed by MPG Printgroup, UK.

Contents

Part 3: Media Convergence and Creative Industries

Contributors

Josu Amezaga is a Professor at the Department of Audiovisual Communication and Advertising of the University of the Basque Country.

Rhodri ap Dyfrig is a PhD student at the Department of Theatre, Film and Television Studies at Aberystwyth University, Wales.

Edorta Arana is a Lecturer in Media Programming and Audience Research at the Department of Audiovisual Communication and Advertising of the University of the Basque Country.

Patxi Azpillaga is a Lecturer in Economics at the Department of Audiovisual Communication and Advertising of the University of the Basque Country, and is at present pursuing a PhD on Audiovisual Communication.

Aurélien Bénel is an Associate Professor in an interdisciplinary research team on 'Computer Supported Cooperative Work', Troyes University of Technology, France.

Donald R. Browne is Emeritus Professor of the Department of Communication Studies, University of Minnesota, Minneapolis, Minnesota, USA.

Douglas Chalmers is Caledonian Scholar and Senior Lecturer in Media and Journalism at Glasgow Caledonian University, Scotland.

Júlia Cordonet is a former researcher-journalist at the Centre Internacional Escarré per a las Minories Ètniques i les Nacions (CIEMEN), Barcelona, Catalunya.

Mike Cormack is Head of Lèirsinn and Senior Lecturer at Sabhal Mòr Ostaig, University of the Highlands and Islands, Scotland.

Daniel Cunliffe is a Reader in the Department of Computing and Mathematical Sciences, at the University of Glamorgan, Wales.

Mike Danson is Professor of Enterprise Policy at Heriot-Watt University, Scotland.

Nicole Dołowy-Rybińska is a Researcher-Lecturer at the Institute of Slavic Studies in the Polish Academy of Sciences, Warsaw, Poland.

Franck Eyraud is a graduate in Information Technology from the National Institute of Applied Sciences (INSA) in Lyon (France) and has been involved in the TraduXio project from its beginning.

David Forniès is Head of Research at the Centre Internacional Escarré per a las Minories Ètniques i les Nacions (CIEMEN), Barcelona, Catalunya.

Any Freitas is Senior Programme Manager at the European Union Institute for Security Studies.

Elin Haf Gruffydd Jones is a Senior Lecturer in Media and Creative Industries and Director of the Mercator Institute for Media, Languages and Culture, at the Department of Theatre, Film and Television Studies, Aberystwyth University, Wales.

Ian Johnson is Senior Communications and Research Officer for political party Plaid Cymru at the National Assembly for Wales.

Philippe Lacour is a Researcher at the International Centre for the Study of Contemporary French Philosophy (CIEPFC), Cirphles, Ecole Normale Supérieure de Paris, France, and President of the Zanchin NGO, which develops the TraduXio project.

Alison Lang is a freelance writer and former Corporate Affairs Officer for MG ALBA, the organization responsible for delivering Gaelic television services in Scotland.

Philippa Law is a PhD student at the School of Languages, Linguistics and Film, Queen Mary, University of London, England.

Ruth Lysaght is a Visiting Fellow researching Irish language cinema at An Foras Feasa in NUI Maynooth, Ireland.

Niall Mac Uidhilin is a Lecturer in ICT and Researcher in Learning Technologies with Acadamh na hOllscolaíochta Gaeilge, National University of Ireland, Galway, Ireland

Lindsay Milligan is a Lecturer at the School of Education in the University of the West of Scotland.

Tom Moring is Professor of Communication and Journalism at the Swedish School of Social Science, University of Helsinki. Finland.

Delyth Morris has retired from her post as Senior Lecturer in Sociology and Social Policy at Bangor University, Wales.

Bea Narbaiza is a Lecturer at the Department of Audiovisual Communication and Advertising of the University of the Basque Country.

Eithne O'Connell is a Senior Lecturer in Translation Studies at the Centre for Translation and Textual Studies in SALIS (School of Applied Language and Intercultural Studies) at Dublin City University, Ireland.

Amaia Pavón is a Lecturer-Researcher in Media Literacy at the Department of Communication at Mondragon University, the Basque Country.

Cynog Prys is a Lecturer in the School of Social Science at Bangor University, Wales.

Enrique Uribe-Jongbloed is Director of the research group on Audiovisual Culture, and Assistant Professor at the Faculty of Communication of Universidad de La Sabana, Chía, Colombia.

Laszlo Vincze is a doctoral student in media studies at the Faculty of Social Sciences, University of Helsinki, Finland.

Melanie Wagner is a Researcher at the Department of Luxembourgish Linguistics and Literatures at the University of Luxembourg, Luxembourg.

Diana Zambon is a computer scientist, graduated in 2009 from Politecnico di Milano, and works as freelance developer on the TraduXio project.

Aitor Zuberogoitia is Professor-Researcher in Media Literacy and Basque-Language History and Evolution at the Department of Communication at Mondragon University, the Basque Country.

Preface

The focus of this book is a response by a group of researchers to the changing landscapes of media and communication and in particular to issues and themes of particular relevance to 'minority' or 'minoritised'[1] languages.

It is, by now, a tired platitude to state that the ways in which individuals and societies communicate with each other have been radically transformed through the advent of the popular, interactive internet and that social media have revolutionized our use of language. Yet, research into policies and practices is still conspicuously scarce, especially in the context of 'minority', 'minoritised', 'lesser-used', 'regional' or 'less widely known' languages. For that reason, the Mercator Network – with the support of its home institutions and the European Commission – brought together some of the most prominent academics involved in 'minority language media studies' together with new entrants to the field in order to debate and exchange ideas resulting in this publication.[2]

It is true to say that this group of researchers identifies strongly with the language communities they are researching. Many feel a close allegiance to, or indeed are part of, a specific language community where there is both an everyday lived experience of the awareness of the fragility of one's own language and a manifest ambition to contribute towards its future. It may also be true to say that there is a shared concern with the survival and sustainability of other languages as well as one's own and indeed of belonging to a wider research community. In the closing chapter of this collection, Mike Cormack notes that minority language media studies must be concerned with 'how media can be used to help languages'. Significantly, he cautions that if 'it drifts away from this focus, then it becomes simply a part of mainstream media studies that happens to look at minority languages and loses any claim to be a distinctive and coherent area of study'. It is from this engagé approach that this particular field of study has emerged.

This book is divided into five parts: Browne and Uribe-Jongbloed's introductory essay explores the journey taken thus far in ethnic/linguistic minority media and suggests avenues for further research; Part 1 then proceeds with three chapters focusing on 'Theoretical Debates on Convergence and Minority Languages'; Part 2 presents eight chapters on the theme of 'Web 2.0, Social Networking Sites and Minority Languages'; Part 3 continues with six chapters focusing on 'Media Convergence and Creative Industries'. The book closes with Cormack's concluding remarks.

In their chapter, Browne and Uribe-Jongbloed's examine what they term as 'ethnic/linguistic minority media', highlighting the complex relationship between language and means of communication in societies where linguistic shift has happened to the detriment of the language of identification. Their overview of the history of these media identifies common threads that can be used to analyse the development of media policy, outlets and production – namely technology, economic support, government support, social movements, suspicion, perceived utility and finally convergence. The authors illustrate their arguments with examples from across the globe, while at the same time recognizing that the landscape is extremely varied from community to community. The second section of this chapter presents a history of the scholarly study of ethnic/linguistic minority media, a valuable insight into the key publications in this field, with particular focus on the period beyond the mid-1990s. In the third section of this essay the authors ask where we as researchers might go next and suggest the following topics: 'languages' (including language standards, the use of dialects and the relationship between media and language instruction), 'the conception of professionalism' (which Browne observes to be growing), 'financing and promotion' (including the complexities of serving more than one audience) and 'developing a sense of community' emphasizing the *interactional* aspect of community building and the increasingly important role that social media plays. The authors close their essay advocating two aspects of studying ethnic/linguistic minority media that are particularly relevant, namely *direct comparisons* and *cultural sensitivity*. They note that 'in order to make direct comparisons, we need comparable dimensions' and also argue the case for comparisons beyond Europe and North America. Cultural sensitivity, they claim, is imperative to ensure that the research and the conclusion are based on the soundest possible footings. Participatory research (which is explored further in Part 2) is recommended as one way of approaching cultural sensitivity in research.

In Part 1, three chapters present an engagement with different aspects of theoretical debates on convergence and minority languages. In the first of these 'Minority Language Media Studies and Communication for Social Change: Dialogue between Europe and Latin America', Enrique Uribe-Jongbloed makes the case for increased contact and exchange of ideas between these two schools of research. It advocates a 'contextual approach that studies the processes of identity negotiation and participatory agency defined under the concepts of *hybridity* and *convergence*'. In addition, and sharing the notion of *cultural sensitivity* as proposed in Chapter 1, it urges 'research to increase participation of its subjects of inquiry', in accordance with the practices of communication for social change. Given the contextualized and activist approach of much of the research that takes place in minority and minoritised language communities, it is anticipated that this approach will be embraced by many European researchers.

In their chapter, László Vincze and Tom Moring propose that ethnolinguistic identity can be a motivational variable for using specific media. They argue that this approach can lead to a better understanding of minority language media audiences. Their empirical study is based on Swedish-speaking and Finnish-speaking populations of Finland. Their results show that amongst Finnish speakers they saw small divergence from Finnish, yet among Swedish speakers – the minority language – there was a relatively large divergence from Swedish. They note that 'gratifications sought and obtained seemed to be met amongst Finnish speakers, but not amongst Swedish speakers'. Furthermore, the study concluded that 'some variables did not prove to be good predictors of minority language media use' and that there were considerable asymmetries between majority and minority; for example, 'local vitality' of Swedish is a very important predictor in media use amongst Swedish speakers, whereas it is a rather weak predictor of media use amongst Finnish speakers. Finally, the authors restate the importance of *supply* of media in minority languages as this affects not only the gratification obtained but also those sought. After all, 'nobody seeks media content that does not exist'.

The last chapter in this part examines some of the widely recognized indices that have been used to gauge linguistic vitality. It questions whether they are equally important in the context of convergence and in particular with regard to the position of 'media' in the various analyses of linguistic vitality and language revitalization. In the light of this, Jones presents a new reading of one of the seminal texts of this field of study, Joshua Fishman's Graded Intergenerational Disruption Scale presented in *Reversing Language Shift*. She suggests that the renowned sociolinguist's perceived 'unwillingness to recognise a positive role for the media' was 'largely rooted in the organizational power structures that control the media, which he (rightly) states are usually located beyond the minority language community and outside its influence and control'. However, an understanding of media in a converged, interactive environment as presented in social media and Web 2.0 makes it possible to argue that these too are part of 'real neighbourhood life' and as such should be high-priority tools and domains for language revitalization. Jones concludes her chapter by noting that 'attempts to integrate online communication into the existing frameworks of assessing linguistic vitality will require a substantial overview of the present indices and the concepts from which they are derived'. She notes that 'a simple assimilation of online communication within the indices associated with the old media paradigm of "one-to-many" distribution is not sufficient in itself'.

In her view, this 'restricts our understanding of online communication as a mere shift in technology and the invention of new appliances without recognizing that convergence culture has, according to Jenkins and others, more to do with changes in cultural practices and heightened levels of participation and interactivity. She underlines the importance of elaborating 'adequate and useful indices, especially if we want to do more than merely record and document the demise of linguistic diversity'.

Part 2 is entitled 'Web 2.0, Social Networking Sites, and Minority Languages'. In the first of the eight chapters, Daniel Cunliffe, Delyth Morris and Cynog Prys draw on empirical evidence in the online and offline linguistic practices of young bilingual people in Wales. Their study presented in this chapter shows that young people *do* use the Welsh language on social media albeit to a lesser degree than they use English. Their findings echo those of Moring and Vincze in that the local community language is a factor in the language used online, implying a strong resonance with the observation made by Ellison *et al.* (2007) that online social networks tend to replicate real-world social networks, rather than create new ones. They note that while English is the main language of surfing, Facebook represents a space on the web where they speak Welsh. This finding can be seen as an example of the interactive web – or Web 2.0 – and social media being better for minority language use than the less participatory aspects of the internet.

In the next chapter, Melanie Wagner draws particular attention to the importance of literacy and of writing in order to communicate in the online world. The field work provides an insight into language ideologies and attitudes towards the different languages spoken in Luxembourg, and the conflicting voices expressed. The author concludes that 'Facebook is being used as a platform to discuss these issues' and 'a platform for written Luxembourgish that did not exist before … which has brought attention to discussions never before available to the public eye'.

Next in Chapter 6, Ian Johnson draws our attention again to online literacy. Here, he studies the practices of a group of Twitter users within the framework of these two seminal sociolinguistic theories: audience design and communication accommodation theory. His findings suggest that there is much reciprocity between the online linguistic behaviour and the practice norms of Welsh–English bilingual communities. However, the research also points to 'a far greater difference between use of spoken and written Welsh than that implied in the Census returns', with a 'number of Welsh–English bilingual speakers, known to the author to use Welsh in face-to-face contexts, showed no bi-literate skills in their use of Twitter'. The lack of opportunities to read Welsh both online and offline may well have a bearing on users' 'textual cues' and thus affect their application of literacy. It is also suggested that private conversations conducted offline in Welsh are now being conducted online, but in English, performed with an 'eavesdropping' audience in mind. Furthermore, the author concludes that the non-use of Welsh is a matter of serious concern for language revitalization.

The next chapter takes us to quite a different community, especially in terms of literary and literacy traditions. Unlike Welsh, with its continuous tradition of written literature since the Middle Ages, the Kashubian language is, in fact, beginning its literary period alongside the internet as is highlighted by Nicole Dołowy-Rybinska. Once again, literacies and the practice of writing languages in the context of online activity are examined. In her survey, Nicole Dołowy-Rybinska observes 'the internet has provided the opportunity to use Kashubian outside the oral sphere – prior to the rise of the internet, Kashubian writing was reserved to a narrow band of experts'. The advent of the internet has created 'spaces where the use of Kashubian is "natural"'. Furthermore, she identifies three specific characteristics of the infrastructure provided by internet communication: it is 'elastic (it is simple to adapt to a local context), non-hierarchical (it allows people to meet and talk on equal footing) and scalable (new people are able to join projects to change and improve them)'. The observations and conclusions in this chapter suggest that the internet is indeed a vital form of communication to create a linguistic community for young users of Kashubian.

Cunliffe and ap Dyfrig's chapter focuses on another popular online site. They attempt both 'to characterize the Welsh-language media space on YouTube' and 'to explore some of the methodological issues and research questions raised' in this research project. Unlike previous chapters, where the focus has been clearly on social media where written forms of communication dominate, Cunliffe and ap Dyfrig explore different modes of communication and content. They note that the 'audiovisual nature of YouTube and the predominance of music content also permit language to be less of a critical issue in comparison to blogging'. Their observations infer that 'it is difficult to argue on the basis of this sample that there is a coherent Welsh language media space'. However, this may not be simply a matter of lack of material or a shortage of users. They argue that the 'limited use of social networking functionality on YouTube also suggests that coherent linguistically hermetic media spaces may not be an obvious feature in any of the languages which are not yet officially supported by the site'.

Niall Mac Uidhilin (Chapter 9) explores the use of online approaches in language learning. He draws on several sociocultural approaches to learning and literacies, such as 'collaborative learning' and Gee's (2008) notions of *Discourses* and powerful literacies. In discussing the application of Web 2.0 practices to learning communities, he observes that the 'participatory nature of these technologies can facilitate dialogue and collaboration on these literacies'. Once again, the author concludes that increased participation provides more opportunities for minority language communities to practice the language. His research in the Irish context showed that 'the learner's attitude towards Irish became more positive and the collaborative nature of the class resulted in a more cooperative, supportive environment'.

The penultimate chapter in this part by Philippe Lacour, Any Freitas, Aurélien Bénel, Franck Eyraud and Diana Zambon considers the case of a specific Web 2.0 tool and its application in media production contexts. Their chapter reminds us of the close relationship between language and convergence. The authors note that in 'a context of increasing media convergence, content may be conveyed not only in different ways but also in many different languages – to different audiences'. They emphasize that the 'spread of multilingual content sites and localization strategies have only reinforced such trend and considerably boosted the relevance of translation on, for and through the web'. They present an analysis of a linguistic diversity 'norm' (on and beyond the web) followed by observations on media convergence and technological development, such as the importance of 'collaborative technologies', Wikis, etc. In this context, the *TraduXio* project is proposed as 'an innovative platform for collaborative translation that offers an alternative approach to multilingual e-translation'. The authors conclude that the *TraduXio* environment offers a different approach to multilingual work contexts that can further empower social users and enhance linguistic diversity.

The last chapter of Part 2 draws on the author's own experience in media production. Philippa Law examines the practices of production teams and offers valuable insights from the perspective of the traditional media producers whose professional work environments are changing. Drawing on examples, she highlights some of the benefits of audience participation as perceived by the producers. She notes that for 'language activists and media practitioners to make the most of these opportunities, it is important to understand the expectations and attitudes of not only the audience but also the producers involved in creating the content.' These include the notion that participation 'provides evidence that someone is listening', it 'serves the audience', 'creates a sense of community' and it 'provides new or unexpected content'. She concludes by pointing to four specific considerations for language activists to reflect upon in the process of engaging with media producers in participatory production exchanges. She emphasizes that 'not all ... producers are alike in their approach to interactivity', reiterates that 'the needs of the linguistic community must be taken into account', proposes that 'communities should consider their policy on the "correctness" and fluency of the minority language permitted on-air' and finally warns producers and partners alike to 'keep a copy of all your audience feedback. Do not underestimate its value in motivating production staff and potentially providing evidence of "value" to funders'.

Part 3 is entitled 'Media Convergence and Creative Industries'. In the first of the six chapters, Eithne O'Connell examines the context and practices of minority language broadcasters in the light of convergence and the 'dissolution of the media domain paradigm'. She draws on the specific experiences of the Irish case, yet these reflections may indeed be applied further afield. O'Connell suggests that it may be possible 'to identify at least five distinct headings within broadcasting under which linguistic perspectives and/or practices could be usefully investigated: corporate mission, in-house communications, broadcasting language, translation and commercial dealings'. She presents an analysis of these headings, highlighting the key questions and observations of each part of the broadcaster's activity. In conclusion, she favours the option for 'media professionals involved in minority language broadcasting to recognize the media as a key element in broader language policy'. She notes that by 'focusing attention on the language element of minority language broadcasting and reflecting critically on current linguistic practice in all sectors of the industry, policies can be developed to maximise the contribution of broadcasting to the future of the minority language'.

In Chapter 13, drawing on the relatively strong case of the Catalan language, Júlia Cordonet and David Forniès examine the public debate and the legal aspects of cinema distribution in the language. They follow the legal proposals aimed at increasing Catalan language screenings in the Catalan Autonomous Community – the territory where the language is most vibrant, in comparison with the other Catalan-speaking territories. Although this case study examines an element of media practice that may be well beyond the aspirations of many minority language communities, the conclusions offered reflect many of the observations stated by contributors whose focus was on other language contexts. Cordonet and Forniès suggest that their evidence points to an opportunity to use the new law to 'substantially increase the screenings in Catalan, because there is a real market and a real demand for them', hence contributing to the debate on the relationship between legal impediments and minority language activity. They also propose that 'further study of the impact of this law ... would serve to prove the point that it was lack of availability, rather than lack of demand, what kept Catalan away from the cinema screens', echoing Vincze and Moring's observations on the importance of supply in minority language contexts.

In their chapter, Douglas Chalmers, Mike Danson, Alison Lang and Lindsay Milligan present the contemporary case of Scottish Gaelic. They contextualize the emergence of the revised BBC ALBA in the context of public policy towards the language. They note that 'television in a minoritised language is often regarded as having social benefit beyond sheer entertainment' and underline the expectation on BBC ALBA to 'have strong economic, social and linguistic contributions to make throughout Scotland'. The chapter proceeds to consider the 'early indicators of these effects'. The authors conclude that 'BBC ALBA is an important source of employment for the growing Gaelic creative class' and in addition it helps to 'create and disseminate high-quality products that can be enjoyed by many'. However, they also note that the contribution BBC ALBA will make to the learning and use of Gaelic in Scotland is 'less certain'. Yet, if these challenges and the interactive options offered by Web 2.0 are addressed, the authors are confident that the 'BBC ALBA channel offers to be a valuable instrument in reversing language shift'.

The next chapter in this part examines the 'multilingual practice of the EITB group and its TV provision for teenagers'. Young people feature prominently in many of the other chapters in this collection; however, Amaia Pavón and Aitor Zuberogiotia's focus is clearly placed on the media practices of young people and the Basque broadcaster's policies for provision aimed at them. Minority language studies have tended to emphasize children and education rather than young people and media. The chapter traces the early years of the Basque public broadcasting group and its development into a multilingual media conglomerate. It examines its Basque language television provision for teenagers and also develops a methodological proposal for the study of bilingual teenagers' habits of consumption in the era of digital convergence. The results of a pilot study on the methodology are presented in the chapter. The key questions asked are how many Basque media do teenagers use and what are their motivations to use them? The authors observe that the teen audience are 'digital natives' and are 'heavy users of the new audiovisual technologies' because 'they are the ones who have best adapted to the process and new era of the medium. Their study concludes that 'we should not be investigating the audiovisual content on the internet as an isolated phenomenon'. This discussion is taken up by Cormack in the last chapter of this book.

The penultimate chapter in this part compares two television series on traditional singing from opposite sides of the globe on national indigenous television stations. In Chapter 16, Ruth Lysaght explores two television programmes, one in Irish and one in Māori, both of which draw on performed song and poetry. She asks how traditions of performance translate to television and presents three important elements that are transmitted by the song in various ways to television: 'a sense of place, a sense of community and relationship with language'. She observes that in both cases 'these programmes therefore see television taking on the role of *seanachaí* (storyteller) or *tohunga* (expert)'. In these cases, she concludes that 'tradition is reinvented as the song moves from live performance to the "as live" medium of television'. The national indigenous broadcasters in presenting traditional songs on screen, 'draw on the power of a continuous oral tradition to create a new relationship between people and their language and culture'.

In the last chapter of Part 3, Bea Narbaiza, Josu Amezaga, Edorta Arana and Patxi Azpillaga argue that we are living in a moment of change, characterized by three factors: 'the multiplication and transnationalization of the provision of media content', the 'significant decrease in the presence of the minority languages in the media in quantitative terms' and 'the multiplicity of meanings acquired by communication' – people who were traditionally only receivers have also become producers and distributors of content. The chapter presents a possible categorization of 'television channels and television content in minority languages in the European Union' in order to tease out the substantial differences between varying degrees of provision available to language communities. It then addresses the question of 'minority language media or media in minority languages?' and reports on eight in-depth interviews with managers and executives from minority language television broadcasters. In their conclusions, the authors say that the 'interviews with some of the minority language television managers pointed to the suggestion that language normalization has ceased to be the main objective of the television service'. The authors observe that the 'media organizations see themselves as producers of audiovisual content, rather than being social instruments for language normalization, revitalization or preservation' and 'content becomes the substantive part of the process, language becomes an adjective or a descriptor'.

The last part of the book comprises of Mike Cormack's concluding remarks. The chapter examines the state of play in the field of study and the key issues in the relationship between media and language in the converged environment. Cormack focuses his discussion on 'language planning' and the 'challenge of new media' drawing on many of the observations, comments and conclusions of other contributors to this volume. His own conclusions recall the role of the engagé approach to minority language media studies. In his closing remarks, he notes that 'if we want to use the media to help language development, we need to understand the processes by which people interact with language in the media'. Calling for innovative and relevant ways of studying the relationship because 'immediate reactions do not tell us much' and 'broad language trends are too long-term to be useful', he cautions that minority language media 'need to show what benefits they are having for the languages concerned'. Academic researchers in this area, he states, must be clearer 'about the processes by which media help in the maintenance of a language community'.

Finally, a word of thanks to all those who have contributed to this specific publication and to all those whose work has played a part in creating and enriching an international discourse in favour of minority languages and linguistic diversity.

Notes

1. The field of study (indeed like many others) is characterized by a vibrant debate on appropriate terminology. Some researchers readily adopt the term 'minority language', by far the most commonly used, to denote the field, others reject it, preferring 'minoritised' to convey a sense of process and many pragmatically use both terms interchangeably. Other terminologies, such as 'linguistic minorities' 'autochthonous', 'lesser-used', 'less widely known', 'regional', etc. are also used in the field. Our approach with this collection of essays has been to allow the authors to use the terminologies they expressly prefer. For that reason, there is variation in the volume, both across chapters and occasionally within them. This is one way in which the intricacies of the variant forms can be respected.

2. The Mercator Network was created – originally in four themed centres – following the Kuijpers Resolution of 1987, also concerned with the situation of such languages, to facilitate dialogue and encourage debate and to extend and deepen knowledge and research in the field of minority languages. Since its creation in 1988, the Mercator Network's philosophy has been based on the following principles:

    i. an *engagé* approach: to engage in research projects with a focus on applied research with the aim of improving the conditions of minority languages; research based on critical distance and rejecting attempts at a false neutrality of observationalism;

    ii. a bridging approach: to engage in academic research but in contact with practitioners in the field; creating a dialogue between the scholarly study of minority languages and the real-world context of professionals, policy makers, advocates and activists;

    iii. a grounded approach: to locate itself in the geopolitical areas where minority languages are a lived experience, to use the languages as widely as possible and to recognise the specificity of the locality in which activity takes places, encouraging connections to be made between the 'local' and the 'international';

    iv. a multidisciplinary approach: to recognize that the study of minority language media, for example, cannot be created through media studies alone, that it has to develop from a wider base of knowledge and include other disciplines such as sociolinguistics, politics, etc. and to be open to new and varied methodologies;

    v. a comparative approach: to aim to produce research paradigms that can usefully link theory and practice across a range of different social realities, to illuminate the specific and the local through connection with a broader picture and with other specificities;

vi.   a networked approach: to create and develop sustainable networks of organizations and institutions active in this field and to enhance contact between people by hosting and supporting events and fora that facilitate discussion and the exchange of knowledge and ideas in order to create new discourses that engage with minority languages beyond the confines of state borders.

The Mercator Network's activities for almost a quarter of a century have consisted of a programme of conferences and seminars, publications and newsletters, aimed at facilitating exchange of information and dialogue across communities with the aim of contributing to the greater project of the sustainability of linguistic diversity in Europe and across the world. It has been supported through various programmes of the European Union. The events that led to the creation of this volume were financed in part by the EU Life Long Learning Programme and supported by Mercator's host institutions:

Mercator European Research Centre on Multilingualism and Language Learning at the Fryske Akademy, Ljouwert/Leeuwarden, Fryslân (the Netherlands); Mercator Legislació i Drets Lingüístics at CIEMEN (Centre Internacional Escarré per les Minoríes i les Nacions) in Barcelona; Mercator at the Research Institute for Linguistics of the Hungarian Academy of Sciences in Budapest; Mercator at the Centre for Finnish Studies of Mälardalen University and at Stockholm University; the Mercator Institute for Media, Languages and Culture (Mercator Media) at the Department of Theatre, Film and Television Studies of Aberystwyth University in Wales.

In addition to the debate developed in the chapters of this book, discussion during the 'Experts' Seminar' and 'Media Convergence and Linguistic Diversity' conference prompted the elaboration of an online report which included specific policy recommendations. These discussions were based upon the six principles outlined above (engagé, bridging, grounded, multidisciplinary, comparative and networked approaches) through which the Mercator Network seeks to operate.

These recommendations can be summarized as follows:

a.   Research Recommendations

•   Linguistic preference studies in a variety of languages and language situations may provide extra information about how these decision-making processes take place.
•   The use of internet peer-to-peer and social media still requires lengthier and more elaborate studies, which allow for models to be developed and linguistic situations to be evaluated and compared.
•   Innovative ways of measuring linguistic impact of media output are needed in order to understand the ways in which new tools can provide spaces for language maintenance and development. Despite advances made in this area, there is still a need for more research on the interlinking relationship of media and language usage.
•   New possibilities for internet-based translation and collaborative work have arisen, and new studies on their quality, impact and creative potential can provide different perspectives to issues of linguistic exchange and translation.
•   The increasing participation of users in media production raises questions about the concepts of professionalism and quality that can have an impact on the perception and reception of media content and media outlets. There is a need for research on how these concepts are valued by producers and audiences alike, and what relevance they are likely to have, if any, in future years.

b.   Policy recommendations on all levels

- Media provisions *need to open their spaces to audience participation* and enable their input to have a bearing on production.
- The new spaces of media require language planners to understand *media as an integral part of all social activities* rather than just one domain or a separate context, measurable on its own right. Narrowing down media influence on linguistic vitality to output hours or audience numbers does not provide an adequate picture of the linguistic situation in the media.
- The new relationship with media requires *a new way to measure linguistic vitality*, taking into consideration that it permeates all spheres of social interaction.
- Facilitating an *increased space for multilingualism* and support for linguistic diversity across the media must be part of all public broadcasting remits.
- Production of media in various languages provides jobs and economic boosts to specific regions. However, media production demands better digital infrastructure in order to enable high-quality output. *Improved digital connectivity* is, therefore, a major requirement to ensure that said specific regions generate new and valuable capital.
- The *establishment and maintenance of minority language media production outlets* is a precondition to ensuring an economically viable alternative in which the media can help provide a space for language maintenance.
- The media in minority languages should be *assisted in disseminating content across borders*. Media can help fragmented communities to contact each other and can contribute to creating community relationships that are not state bound. Attention should be paid to *legislation that obstructs cross-border media* especially for radio stations and TV channels.

Adequate financial measures should be ensured for media that operate in a regional or minority language. Training media professionals for bilingual and multilingual environments can be more difficult than for monolingual situations.

Introduction: Ethnic/Linguistic Minority Media – What their History Reveals, How Scholars have Studied them and What We might Ask Next

Donald R. Browne and
Enrique Uribe-Jongbloed

Introduction

Ethnic, indigenous and linguistic minority media have been present, if not all that visible, for more than 200 years. After the unsuccessful *Tlysau yr Hen Oesoedd* in 1735, various periodicals in the Welsh language appeared in the late 18th century and early 19th century in Wales (Jones, 1993: 1–2). The Cherokee *Phoenix* first appeared in 1828. African-American newspapers in the United States go back to 1827, when *Freedom's Journal* first appeared. Many of the media services had very brief lifetimes, while others have managed to survive, and some have managed to prosper, without interruption. Some featured minority languages, some did not. Scholarship on minority media also has a long history. Much like the minority media services themselves, it has grown over the years, and particularly since the 1960s, thanks in part to civil rights movements, increased migration and the greater availability of less expensive technologies and licensing opportunities (low-power radio and TV, internet, etc.). Simply put, the existence of more and more minority media, combined with a growing recognition of the minority presence in various societies, has alerted scholars to a form of communication that demands greater attention.

What we present here is intended as a summary of minority *language* media (MLM) development – the central subject of the conference that inspired this book – and of published and possible future scholarship dealing with that activity. We believe that most aspects of MLM activity are relevant to minority media in general, as has been already pointed out before (Cormack, 2004, 2007).

Ours is not a comprehensive survey. Thankfully, there now is far too much available to cover in a single chapter – a statement we could not have made two decades ago. We limit ourselves mainly to book-length studies, since books seem to be particularly effective in bringing a mixture of facets and viewpoints on a given subject to the attention of potentially interested scholars. Minority media in industrially developed nations do receive book-length treatment more often than do minority media elsewhere, but happily MLMs in developing nations are catching up in that regard. Also, most of those books already contain lengthy bibliographies listing journal articles, dissertations, government and other reports, newspapers and magazines, among other references. We do not cover presentation of linguistic minorities by non-MLM outlets unless the focus is on minority language media producers. Finally, we devote more attention to 'Western' experiences than we would like, although we do provide examples from Latin America, Africa and Asia. We would be delighted if this chapter and book were to spur more investigation of what is taking place in those and other regions.

We begin with a very brief history of MLM, which is intended to provide a general picture of what developed when, where and why. We then present a snapshot view of MLM scholarship in the foundational years (1980–1995), highlighting the chief characteristics of most contributions, and follow this with a chronological listing of subsequent books. The third section of the chapter deals with understudied aspects of MLM and why in our view they merit more attention. The closing section proposes greater collaboration among MLM researchers as it could be applied to various facets of MLM activity.[1]

The Historical Development of Minority Language Media

When one examines the historical development of MLM, it becomes apparent that they often owe their existence to educational and societal (e.g. 'Sons of Norway') groups, and particularly to numerous individuals who regarded themselves as minority language (ML) community leaders. Those leaders tended to be quite goal-oriented and saw 'their' ML services as links with ancestral homelands, preservers of languages, guardians of histories and defenders of minority rights, particularly when 'their' minorities were émigrés rather than indigenous populations. They were predominantly male. Some of the MLM outlets employed combinations of 'mainstream' and 'minority' languages. Others used only their particular MLs. In many cases, they subsidized media services through their earnings in businesses, since few of the early ML services received much income through advertising or subscriptions.

Until a few decades ago, ML *newspapers* commonly appeared weekly or less often, and in editions of four–eight pages. News from the homeland was a common feature, though less so at present. The reporting of community activities, personal profiles of prominent ML community leaders and announcements of births, weddings and deaths also received much attention. Those newspapers have continued to be popular with linguistic minorities, and the newer (Hmong, Somali) émigré populations in particular have been quick to employ them, even though a fair share of those populations may be illiterate, since there are enough of their members who can read.

For the past few decades, and particularly in Europe, minority language newspapers increasingly have moved to daily editions, most often with one to two dozen pages, and a few with more. Many of them cover international and national 'mainstream' events, sometimes including minority angles, sometimes not. The European Association of Daily Newspapers in Minority and Regional Languages (MIDAS) lists over 100 such papers on its website (www.midas-press.org). Less expensive print technologies appear to have played a significant role in this expansion. Online-only minority language newspapers have begun to appear with some frequency, as well. It remains to be seen how prevalent such papers become, but there already are a number of far less 'professional' online papers.

ML *radio* initially was limited to small chunks of airtime (15 or 30 minutes once or twice a week, if any, and often at less popular time slots), usually 'leased' from a local commercial radio station and subject to cancellation at any time. If there was a single, national radio service, ML appearances generally were by invitation only and often for cultural or historical occasions and events, such as the celebrations of the signing of the Treaty of Waitangi (between Maori and 'whites') in New Zealand (Browne, 2008; Davies, 1994; Lemke, 1996). Once states began to open up licensing to include more 'community' stations (mainly in the 1970s and 1980s), opportunities increased for more minority groups to acquire or expand time slots and even to operate their own radio services, albeit sometimes within the structure of the national PSB. Common features resembled those mentioned for newspapers, with the addition of music from the ancestral homelands and, for some of the services, brief newscasts and political and social commentary. Transistor radios made it possible for many economically challenged minority households to listen to. And in the 1990s, the spread of radio by satellite enabled those households to hear broadcasts directly from their ancestral homelands. That had been possible earlier, but largely through shortwave radio, where reception quality was often poor and good receivers were expensive.

The development of ML *television* was very slow because of the high costs of production and transmission, as well as the practice on the part of many nations to broadcast through a single national outlet with modest if any regional or local production. That worked against the interests of linguistic minorities, many of which were (and still are) living in specific locales, and thus weren't 'nationally prominent'. It also discouraged the creation of local ML television services. However, linguistic minority populations increased in many nations starting in the 1970s (Turks in Germany, the Netherlands and France; South Asians in the United Kingdom; Latin Americans in the United States). By the 1980s, satellite television services from the homelands became more and more available, even though those services carried little or nothing that portrayed the 'new homeland' lives of those émigré viewers. The decreasing cost of TV equipment and the development of 'access television' channels in many of the industrialized nations also helped numerous linguistic minority groups to express themselves through TV, often through weekly or less frequent programs, from 30 minute to 1 hour, that emphasized cultural aspects of their lives. That situation also encouraged a few businesses, notably those wishing to serve Spanish speakers in the United States, to establish commercial networks.

More recently, some MLMs have created their own networks, although few of them have *affiliated* stations. But size of population is a problem if a network is seeking commercial support. And when combined with size of *territory* – the few hundred thousand Aboriginal Australians, the few million Native Americans in Canada and the United States or the various small indigenous groups that inhabit the Amazon basin in South America – the odds would seem daunting for radio and overwhelming for TV. Yet several populations do have national or regional distribution systems, including a few with local contributions. Canada's Aboriginal Peoples' Television Network is doing reasonably well, with a national newscast, discussion programmes and some entertainment, much of it produced by individual Canadian and other indigenous services. The US Native American Public Telecommunications Service distributes a fair range of Native American-produced TV programming but lacks daily newscasts. Australia's Aboriginal regional service, Imparja TV, carries a weekday children's programme entitled 'Jamba's Playtime', which has enjoyed much critical acclaim. However, it struggles to produce other Aboriginal-oriented material. The

Taiwan Broadcasting System launched Taiwan indigenous Television in 2008.

Summing up history

MLM activity is far greater now than it was at the turn of the 20th century or than it was 20 years ago. The creation of ML services, radio in particular, in 'Third World' nations over the past two decades has been spectacular (Alia, 2010; Wilson & Stewart, 2008). Given the precarious state of financial support for many MLMs, it is amazing that the *failure* rates throughout this period appear to have been quite low, although the electronic media have fared considerably better than their print counterparts in that respect. However, the 'convergence' movement that began to characterize the 'mainstream' media industry in general from the 1990s onwards largely bypassed the MLM sector. One exception was Mana Maori Media in New Zealand, where a single enterprise published a monthly magazine dealing with Māori life and at the same time produced national radio newscasts in Māori and in English (Fox, 1993).

Looking back on the past century, we note five major factors that have shaped traditional MLM development, all relevant today: *technology, economic support, social movements, suspicion* and *perceived utility.*

Technology was particularly important in the growth of MLM in two forms: the expansion of the number of outlets and the expansion of reception capability. UHF/FM radio transmission multiplied the number of stations that could be licensed, helping to break the PSB monopoly in many parts of the world, since the 'scarcity of spectrum' argument no longer was quite so sustainable. Satellite technology played a key role in the ability of radio and TV services for minorities to distribute signals to local outlets for re-broadcast. US American Indian Radio on Satellite's (AIROS) highly popular live call-in daily discussion programme 'Native America Calling' never could have been created without satellite's ability to furnish uplinks and downlinks. Also, the satellite brought AIROS to the many widely scattered reservations across the United States (including Alaska). The invention of transistors aided the manufacture of relatively low-cost radio and TV sets. This development made it possible for those with modest incomes, which often included many linguistic minority households, to own sets.

Much the same holds for a Quechua network (Red Kiechwa Satelital, RKS) serving Andean Quechua speakers, in this case assisted by both satellites and computers, along with a network of radio stations (Luykx, 2001; see also Uribe-Jongbloed, Chapter 1). Recording and playback technology, in the form of video and audio tapes, was also fundamental in the spread of ML production developed and distributed within the communities, both in the case of traditional tales in Mali (Leguy, 2007) and in creating an indigenous video movement in Latin America (Salazar & Cordova, 2008). The World Wide Web has enabled the creation of online newspapers, radio and video services by and for ethnic minorities. The 'personal' media have thrived with the expansion of Web 2.0 systems such as social networking sites (e.g. Facebook – which is the topic of two of the chapters in this collection) and have enlarged the possibilities for those communities to enter into a wide range of public forums, with more interactions over large spaces. The following chapters highlight some of the multilingual challenges of those technological changes.

It should be no surprise that *economic support* would be a major factor in the development of traditional MLM. The history of ethnic/linguistic minority *newspapers* indicates that many of them were short-lived, with lack of funding as a frequent culprit. The same holds true for *radio*. Even the production of specific ML programmes often suffered from unreliable financial support. Until *television* became a more affordable medium technologically speaking (less expensive equipment, and the spread of cable, which sharply brought transmission costs down), it was beyond the means of most linguistic minority service operators. Only when such a minority became 'economically attractive' thanks to its size – Turks in Germany, Arabic speakers in France, Spanish speakers in the United States – were advertisers interested in supporting it, and even then at levels sufficient for little more than programming relayed from the ancestral homelands. As noted later, that situation is beginning to change.

Over the past few decades, we have seen an increase in *government support* for ethnic and linguistic minority newspapers and, even more so, broadcasting, sometimes in the form of government 'advertising' of positions available, notices on health campaigns, military recruitment, etc. In addition, legislative bodies have supported, usually through annual appropriations, such entities as Ireland's Raidió na Gaeltachta and Māori Television. Various government agencies such as the Irish Bord na Gaeilge and New Zealand's government-created and -supported Māori funding agency Te Māngai Pāho also have provided such support. In Colombia, the then Ministry of Communications promoted a programme called 'Comunidad' for the support of radio stations for indigenous minorities (Murillo, 2008), and in Vietnam, the government supported the creation of a television service through an ethnic minorities' channel (van de Fliert & Hien, 2009). There is a possible downside to government funding, however: the more prominent it becomes, the more vulnerable it may be to increased scrutiny both from within and from outside the government. Legislators in particular may raise questions as to the continuing need for such support on various grounds: 'it isn't supposed to be forever, and if it's really worthwhile, it should be able to attract other sources', or 'are such services really of value to society?' Also, government support usually is limited to full-time media services or provides only the initial costs of infrastructure, leaving the community responsible for supporting the operation. Neither does it help the small-scale linguistic minority ventures that need or can manage to produce only limited numbers of programmes.

Social movements have been of great importance in their support for the development of media outlets for 'the voiceless', which has included linguistic minority groups. The establishment of community radio services in the 1970s and 1980s frequently was brought about in part through pressure applied by various 'power to the people' groups, which had become disenchanted with the scant and often (in their eyes) biased coverage of their activities by the mainstream media. Simultaneously, the social movements for improved media coverage in minority languages also took hold in Europe, with the Welsh, the Catalan and the Basque leading the fray (Hourigan, 2004). But undoubtedly, the most striking example of such pressure was the campaign by Plaid Cymru, and in particular its leader Gwynfor Evans who vowed to fast unto death unless the Channel Four service for Wales were to be a Welsh language channel. The very modest scale of BBC broadcasts in Scottish Gaelic received a boost in 1976 with the creation of BBC Radio Highland, prompted in part by protests from Scottish Gaelic activists. Aboriginal Australian activists helped both to bring the first full-time Aboriginal radio station (8KIN Alice Springs) into existence and to spur the creation of Aboriginal television. Supporters of a dedicated Canadian Inuit television service persisted in making the case for it until 1982 when the Inuit Broadcasting Corporation began its daily satellite-delivered programming (Alia, 1999; Roth, 2006). Media presence and related demands were always part of indigenous resistance movements in Colombia, finally achieving some level of access after the 1991 Constitution (Murillo, 2008; Rodriguez & El Gazi, 2007).

One of the more interesting lessons yielded by a study of the history of MLMs is the *suspicion* with which many of them have been regarded at various times. There were minor indications of it in the United States in the early 1930s, as fears of the spread of communism led to suspicions regarding Russian language radio programmes, although none was forced off the air. Similar suspicions arose in the early 1950s, and this time pressure from a variety of sources led to Polish, Russian and other Communist nation language broadcasts being dropped from several Detroit and New York City radio stations. When the producers of some of those programmes sought airtime on other New York City-area radio stations that carried 'foreign' language broadcasts, they were told that no airtime was available (Konecky, 1948: 41).

In more recent times, individuals and groups have voiced their anger to the mainstream media and the US broadcast regulatory agency, the Federal Communications Commission, regarding the presence of 'foul' language on some Spanish language stations and 'unpatriotic sentiments' in the form of Chinese-Americans protesting the NATO bombing of the Chinese Embassy in Belgrade during a call-in programme on a Chinese language station in San Francisco (Michaels, as noted by Browne, 2008: 36–37). Norman Tebbit, while serving as Chair of the UK Conservative Party in the mid-1980s, was said to have been responsible for halting the government's plan to license community radio services, in part on the grounds that some of the 'foreign' language groups who would be sure to use such services would utter seditious statements, which the government might not be aware of because they were in a 'foreign' language (Browne, 1996: 187).

Wars are quite likely to provoke such suspicions if only because of the fear that broadcasts in 'enemy' languages could contain veiled or coded utterances that encourage unpatriotic acts on the part of diasporas. Certainly, the World War II experiences of the United Kingdom and the United States illustrate that condition. Not long after the War had begun, the controller of home broadcasting at BBC headquarters became concerned that its Welsh language broadcasts, few as they were, might contain unpatriotic material and considered demanding advance translations of all Welsh language broadcasts, although in the event nothing materialized (Davies, 1994: 133).

The US Congress in 1943 considered legislation that would require stations broadcasting in 'foreign' languages to provide full translations of their content and make those translations available to a 'screening' agency before actual broadcast. No such legislation was passed, but the FCC did require such stations to supply full translations if requested (Grame & American Folklife Center, 1980). The American Legion, a US private organization for ex-military, even passed a resolution in 1941 condemning foreign language broadcasting (Browne, 2008: 25). The US National Association of Broadcasters (NAB) created a 'watchdog committee' to monitor foreign language broadcasts for 'unpatriotic' broadcasts, and acting on the committee's recommendation, directed a Chicago radio station to 'remove' two Italian language broadcasters if it expected to have its license renewed. The NAB did not license stations, but it could inform the FCC of what it had discovered and recommend non-renewal.

In Colombia, internal conflict has always prompted power brokers to regard ML broadcasting as potentially dangerous. The Left-wing guerrilla group FARC threatened the indigenous Awa community in southern Colombia for broadcasting in their language, arguing that their broadcast included coded messages that would assist the government military forces (Caracol TV, 2009). In the early-1980s, the government forbade broadcasting in the creole, or bendé, language of the archipelago of San Andrés, for providing secessionist ideas to the local population of African descent (Uribe-Jongbloed & Peña Sarmiento, 2008). Agosta (2009) notes similar actions during the civil war in El Salvador.

Perceived utility includes both linguistic communities and the larger, 'mainstream' society, and can be summed up by the phrase 'What's in it for us?' It's doubtful if the 'mainstream' society in most nations even considered the issue of 'utility' throughout most of MLM history, since relatively few of its members were exposed to any MLM activity. But the very growth of MLM services in recent decades, accompanied by claims from its supporters for public (usually government) financial assistance, has raised public awareness of its existence and has led to questions regarding the need for such support. Such questioning often appears to rest on two assumptions: that the services reach relatively few people and that minority languages themselves are of little use in the 'modern' world – especially the economic world. Furthermore, the availability of such services might actually hinder the 'assimilation' of ML groups. And if the children of émigrés or of indigenous parents receive little or no exposure to minority languages at home, in school, in the workplace and even among the media outlets available to them, they themselves may wonder why they should bother to learn their 'ancestral tongues'.

Mainstream broadcasters themselves at times have cast doubt on the utility of MLM services. For example, in 1931 the BBC's Regional Director for Scotland requested that the BBC consider broadcasting lessons in how to speak Scottish Gaelic. The BBC Programme Director replied, 'I personally disagree with the idea, as I should have thought that it was better not to do anything which would stimulate the spread of "native" languages at a time when we are doing all we can for the English language' (Programme Director BBC, 1931). Dialects have drawn criticism as well (1980s), as noted below.

Francois Grin and some of his colleagues (see, for instance, Grin, 2003; Grin & Vaillancourt, 1999) have advanced a number of economic arguments for the utility of minority languages. Those arguments seem valid when they are applied to many MLM activities in industrialized societies. Whether they apply quite so well to Third World nations, or to economically challenged linguistic communities in nations such as Australia and New Zealand or Canada and the United States, where Māori, Aboriginal Australian and

Native American populations are concerned, remains to us an open question. That would appear to be a worthwhile subject for research.

Finally, what does the history of MLM tell us about *convergence* – a major theme of the chapters in this book? First, most of those services received relatively little support from governments, national commercial and PSB networks or newspaper chains until the 1970s at the earliest, and even now that assistance often is relatively small, with the qualified exception of BBC support for Welsh, Scottish Gaelic and South Asian services, RTÉ (Ireland) likewise for Irish language radio and TV, Māori funding agency Te Māngai Pāho for Māori broadcasting and Australian government funding of the multilingual Special Broadcast Service (SBS). Certainly, there are few instances where mainstream bodies themselves took the initiative in creating MLMs. Rather, most MLM services resulted from the great and persistent effort of 'activist' individuals and groups, drawn particularly from the ranks of minority language teachers, labour unionists and various advocates of 'power to the people'.

Activist support usually does not take the form of large sums of money, so it shouldn't be surprising that, as we enter the second decade of the 21st century, most MLMs remain financially challenged, to say the least. But that condition hardly is conducive to economic convergence. The Murdochs, Viacoms and Berlusconis of this world aren't that anxious to buy up local MLM services, and for the most part aren't interested in the relatively few minority broadcast networks that exist. General Electric, the NBC network's 'parent', did purchase the No. 2 Spanish language US TV network, *Telemundo*, even though the sale was strongly protested by various Hispanic-American groups. They feared most of all that it would lead to a decline in *Hispanic American*-oriented programming (National Association of Hispanic Journalists, 2006).

The creation of MLM networks would appear to hold some promise where convergence in *production* is concerned and cooperative arrangements for sharing material between radio and TV news and public affairs producers are beginning to develop. The Scottish Gaelic TV service BBC ALBA has shared content generated by BBC Radio nan Gàidheal. The local production of radio programmes to be broadcast by their different member stations has been a staple of RKS in the Andean cordillera, and they are now available for download on the ALER website (www.aler.org) with bilingual comments and description in Spanish and Quechua/Kichwa.

One also could imagine cooperation between radio, television and internet *entertainment* production teams. Developing a sense of a national ethnic minority culture through entertainment is in many ways a laudable goal. However, it's much harder to bring that about if numerous minority language populations are present. Australia's SBS attempts to do so for dozens of such groups but rarely produces entertainment programmes for them. The cost is far too great. Also, tribal cultures such as Māori, Native American and Australian Aborigines sometimes feel threatened by an increased emphasis on a 'national' culture if it might diminish the relevance of local cultures. But convergence through economic forces may be even more threatening, in that it carries with it the possibility that an MLM acquired through merger is likely to be regarded as the 'junior partner', with possible negative effects on the amount and orientation of minority programming. It can be very tempting for the senior partner to 'bend' programming in ways that will make it more appealing to a mainstream audience, thus helping to increase revenue for the corporation, but perhaps resulting in a less culture-specific service for minority audiences.

Foundational Research in Minority Language Media Before 1995 and After

From 1980 to 1995, books focusing largely or entirely on MLMs were few in number, although there were several others that covered community broadcasting, and a few provided examples of minority language programming. It was even rarer to find works that considered issues of media usage of a minority language. Theodore Grame's (1980) US Library of Congress report 'Ethnic broadcasting in the United States' appears to be the earliest detailed work that *emphasizes* MLMs. Its author visited most of the stations and services he discusses to collect his data, rather than relying heavily upon secondary sources. Risteard Ó Glaisne provided a critical appraisal of Raidió na Gaeltachta over its first decade in his 1982 book of the same title. In 1984, what appears to be the first PhD dissertation on indigenous peoples and the media was written by Scott Olson: 'Devolution and indigenous mass media: The role of media in Inupiat and Sami nation-building'. Littlefield's (1984) *American Indian and Alaska Native Newspapers and Periodicals* furnished a comprehensive if not analytical account of that activity.

Mark Stiles and Associates reported on 'Broadcasting and Canada's Aboriginal Peoples' for the Canadian Radio-Television and Telecommunications Commission in 1985, and raised certain language issues. Eric Michaels' 1987 *Aboriginal Invention of Television* featured an anthropological perspective on how a linguistic minority population used and thought about television, in the tradition of the Wirth and Adair (1972) study of Navajo use of film. Michaels' long-term residency among central Australian tribes gives his carefully qualified conclusions particular weight. Also, he devotes considerable attention to *visual language* – a dimension several other anthropologists have examined. The journal *Visual Anthropology* is a good source for such studies, especially Vol. 11(2) from 1995, while Jennifer Deger's 2006 book *Shimmering Screens* is a worthy successor to Michaels' work. Kurt Hein addressed language usage at a largely Andean Indian-operated Baha'i radio station in his 1988 book *Radio Baha'i Ecuador: A Baha'i Development Project*. Miquel de Moragas Spà and María Corominas' 1988 book *Local Communication in Catalonia (1975–1988)* traced the formative period of media activity in a minority language (Catalan) that eventually became the co-official (with Spanish) language of Catalunya.[2]

Durk Gorter and associates (1990) highlighted linguistic minority media in their edited work *Fourth International Conference on Minority Languages*. While there had been numerous conferences on linguistic minorities before that time, they paid relatively little, if any, attention to media. The variety of disciplinary perspectives reflected in the individual contributions is also commendable, in that edited collections of papers on MLM activity often tend to reflect just one or two research traditions. Kate Madden's 1989 PhD dissertation, 'To be nobody else: An analysis of Inuit broadcasting attempts to produce culturally sensitive radio programming' took notice of the vital role such programmes played in strengthening indigenous languages.

Steven Riggins, in his edited 1992 book, *Ethnic Minority Media,* was particularly careful to ensure a broad global representation among his contributors, who were both academics and practitioners (a trend that continues in this book). Some of them treated linguistic minority services in lesser-known languages such as Kabyle *(tamazight)*. Charles Husband took somewhat the same path in his edited 1994 book, *A Richer Vision: The Development of Ethnic Minority Media in Western Democracies*, in the sense that academics and non-academics (including at least one practitioner) are represented. Michael Meadows (1992) stressed *policy* issues in *A Watering Can in the Desert: A Study of Australian Indigenous (Aboriginal) Broadcasting*. While he did not emphasize the connection between policy decision and minority languages, it isn't difficult to conceive of the implications of such policies where language survival issues are concerned. Robert Karam and Arlene Zuckernick (1992) reported to the Canadian Ministry of Culture and Communication in *A Study of Audiences for Aboriginal Community Radio* possibly the first detailed examination of linguistic minority media *audiences*. Hamid Naficy described the largely Los Angeles-based media activities of émigré Iranians in his 1993 book *The Making of Exile Cultures*. Luisa del Carmen-Marquez' 1993 dissertation 'The uses of ethnic minority radio by ethnic minorities in Mexico' emphasized the participatory dimensions of such usage. Patrick Ismond studied production practices in his 1994 dissertation 'Ethnic minority media production in relation to British media policies'. John Davies created a rich portrait of BBC policies regarding broadcasting in Wales in his 1994 *Broadcasting and the BBC in Wales*, with ample reference to problems associated with broadcasting in Welsh. Juergen Busch treated one of the early multicultural/multilingual radio services in his 1994 account of Berlin's *Radio Multikulti: Moeglichkeiten für Lokalen Ethnofunk Berlin – Deutschland – Grossbritannien*.

The first 15 years show not only fairly slow growth up to 1994 but also a considerable range of subject interest and academic perspectives, with anthropology, sociology, communication, linguistics and 'practitioners' represented. Western Europe and North America received the lion's share of attention, and there was somewhat more emphasis on indigenous than émigré language media, even though those populations were growing quite rapidly. Media services for and by them were slower to develop.

The next 15 years of MLM scholarship began with a major outpouring – at least eight titles. Nannette Greiff examined another diasporic media manifestation in her 1995 book *Tuerkische Medien in Deutschland*. Lucila Vargas' 1995 book *Social Uses and Radio Practices* was unusual for its methodology: a very revealing observer/participant approach. Michael Keith's 1995 book *Signals in the Air: Native Broadcasting in America* was the first book-length treatment of Native American radio and consisted mainly of accounts of practitioners, some of whom addressed language issues. The contributors to Claire Frachon and Marion Vargaftig edited *European Television: Immigrants and Ethnic Minorities* (1995) provided examples of self-expression by ethnic and linguistic minorities in the western European nations. Marie Gillespie probed the viewing habits of South Asians in London in her 1995 book *Television, Ethnicity and Cultural Change*. Claudia Lemke provided an unusually detailed account of the early development of Māori radio activity in New Zealand in her 1995 MA thesis 'Maori involvement in sound radio broadcasting, 1915 to 1958'.

The list has grown considerably since 1995, as the following chronology indicates. While a few dissertation titles are listed for the foundational period, we have not attempted to do so for the post-1995 period, during which – happily – they have become far more numerous. Notice, however, that although we do not claim for this list to be exhaustive, we admit it is mostly confined to English language publications.

1996: Donald Browne, *Electronic media and indigenous peoples: A voice of our own?*

1997: Simon Cottle, *Television and Ethnic Minorities: Producer's Perspective*

1998:   Steve Cisler (ed.), *The Internet and Indigenous Groups, Special Issue of Cultural Survival Quarterly.*

Chris Lawe Davies, Multicultural broadcasting in Australia: Policies, institutions and programming, 1975–1995.

1999:   Valerie Alia, *Un/Covering the North: News, Media and Aboriginal People.*

Miquel de Moragas Spà, Carmelo Garitonandía and Bernat López (eds), *Television on Your Doorstep.*

Francois Grin and Francois Vaillancourt, *The Cost-Effective Evaluation of Minority Language Policies: Case Studies on Wales, Ireland and the Basque Country.*

Frank Horn (ed.), *Sami and Greenlandic Media.*

America Rodriguez, *Making Latino News: Race, Language, Class.*

2000:   Virginia Mansfield-Richardson, *Asian-Americans and the Mass Media.*

2001:   Joerg Becker and Reinhard Behnisch (eds), *Zwischen Abgrenzung und Integration: Türkischer Medienkultur in Deutschland.*

Charles Fairchild, *Community Radio and Public Culture: Being An Examination of Media Access and Equity in the Nations of North America.*

Alfonso Gumucio-Dagron, *Making Waves: Participatory Communication for Social Change.*

Helen Kelly-Holmes (ed.), *Minority Language Broadcasting: Breton and Irish.*

Helen Molnar and Michael Meadows, *Songlines to Satellites: Indigenous Communication in Australia, the South Pacific and Canada.*

Christopher Moseley, Nicholas Ostler and Hassan Ouzzate (eds), *Endangered Languages and the Media.*

Christine Ogan, *Communication and Identity in the Diaspora: Turkish Migrants in Amsterdam and Their Use of the Media.*

Clemencia Rodriguez, *Fissures in the Mediascape: An International Study of Citizen's Media.*

Beverly Singer, *Wiping the War Paint Off the Lens: Native American Film and Video.*

2002:   Faye Ginsburg, Lila Abu-Lughod and Brian Larkin (eds), *Media Worlds: Anthropology on New Terrain.*

Unidad de Radio, *Memorias del Encuentro Internacional de Radios Indígenas de América.*

2003:   Tania Bosch, *Radio, Community and Identity in South Africa: A Rhizomatic Study of Bush Radio in Cape Town.*

N.B. Christiansen, *Inuit in Cyberspace.*

Bruce Girard (ed.), *The One To Watch: Radio, New ICTs and Interactivity.*

Iarfhlaith Watson, *Broadcasting in Irish: Minority Language, Radio, Television and Identity.*

2004: Brigitta Busch, *Sprachen im Disput: Medien und Öffentlichkeit in Multilingualen Gesellschaften.*

Amelia Cordova and Gabriela Zamorano, *Mapping Mexican media: Indigenous and community video and radio – Native Networks.*

Patrick Daley and Beverley James, *Cultural Politics and the Mass Media: Alaska Native Voices.*

Niamh Hourigan, *Escaping the Global Village: Media, Language and Protest.*

Tom Moring and Unni Malmgren (eds), *Minority Languages, Media and Journalism.*

Alan O'Connor, *Community Radio in Bolivia: The Miner's Radio Stations.*

2005: Valerie Alia and Simone Bull, *Media and Ethnic Minorities.*

David Barlow, Phillip Mitchell and Tom O'Malley, *The Media In Wales: Voices of a Small Nation.*

Donald Browne, *Ethnic Minorities, Electronic Media and the Public Sphere.*

2006: Jennifer Deger, *Shimmering Screens: Making Media in an Aboriginal Community.*

Kyra Landzelius, *Native on the Net: Indigenous and Diasporic Peoples in the Digital Age.*

Luis Nunez, *Spanish Language Media After the Univision-Hispanic Broadcasting.*

Alan O'Connor, *The Voice of the Mountains: Radio and Anthropology.*

Lorna Roth, *Something New in the Air: The Story of First Peoples' Television Broadcasting in Canada.*

Abiodun Salawu (ed.), *Indigenous Language Media in Africa.*

2007: Mike Cormack and Niamh Hourigan (eds) *Minority Language Media: Concepts, Critiques and Case Studies.*

Kira Kosnick, *Migrant Media: Turkish Broadcasting and Multicultural Politics in Berlin.*

Ritvi Levo-Henriksson, *Media and Ethnic Identity: Hopi Views on Media, Identity and Communication.*

2008: Michael Evans, *Isuma: Inuit Video Art.*

Jeffrey Himple, *Circuits of Culture: Media, Politics and Indigenous Identity in the Andes.*

Pam Wilson and Michelle Stewart (eds), *Global Indigenous Media: Culture, Poetics and Politics.*

Tom Moring and Robert Dunbar, *The European Charter for Regional or Minority Languages and the Media.*

2009: Diana Agosta, *Naming the Future: How Salvadoran Community Radio Builds Civil Society and Popular Culture.*

Susan Forde, Kerrie Foxwell and Michael Meadows, *Developing Dialogues.*

2010:   Valerie Alia, *The New Media Nation.*
Jamie Medhurst, *A History of Independent Television in Wales.*

2011:   M.D. Matsaganis, Vicki Katz and Sandra Ball-Rokeach, *Understanding Ethnic Media: Producers, Consumers, and Societies.*

Comparisons between the pre-1995 and 1996 to the present lists of books clearly reveal a marked increase in numbers of books published over a comparable 15-year period, along with a similar increase in numbers of single-nation and single-language books as well as the dossiers of specific MLM situations in Europe issued by the Mercator Institute for Media, Languages and Culture at Aberystwyth University. North America and western Europe, as well as Australia, continue to dominate, but there is increased post-1995 attention, both in edited collections and in single nation/language works, to 'non-European' populations living in Europe: Turks, South Asians, Arabs and others. Edited books more often include chapters dealing with minority activities within Latin America, South Asia and occasionally Africa, where the rapid growth of community radio over the past 15 years has provided increased opportunities for those speaking languages rarely if ever heard over the state-run broadcast services to now do so.

Disciplinary perspectives also have broadened. A number of books and book chapters in the post-1995 period have been written by anthropologists, linguists, sociologists, geographers and others. The internet's role in providing yet another outlet for MLM activity is receiving attention of authors and editors of books. Visual communication, as an aspect of MLM activity, also attracts somewhat more attention, although far less than verbal communication. However, there remains a tendency in much of the work listed above to limit consideration of minority language media expression to recounting numbers and identities of languages, the presence of minority languages in popular music played by MLM services (and, less often, to its possible impact on the languages themselves) and, albeit rarely, to the place of 'traditional' forms of expression such as storytelling in MLM output. Economic perspectives such as Francois Grin's remain rare, so do studies of audience reaction to MLM services. Some of those 'under-covered' facets do appear in scholarly articles, often in specialized journals such as *Mercator Media Forum, Visual Anthropology, AlterNative* (a Māori scholarly journal) and *Cultural Survival Quarterly* (with at least four issues devoted to media and minorities), and in the increasing numbers of dissertations on MLM activity. But there remain a number of such facets that have received little or no attention from scholars.

Where Might We (as Researchers) Go?

Languages: Three aspects

Language standards

What roles should MLMs play in developing and maintaining standards of correctness in language usage and how strict should those standards be? After all, a living language *is* a changing language. Also, the authors wonder whether many of the 'language standards' organizations, both government and non-government, may consider language first and foremost in its *written* form, and not necessarily realize how different oral expression can be, and usually is, for most people (for a further debate, see O'Connell, Chapter 12).

Some questions that could be answered at least in part through academic research might be as follows: Since radio and TV are oral media, how should and do they interpret standards set by such organizations? How might/how *do* the media play a role in the actual development of standards, including the very important dimension of creation of new terminologies for various phenomena? How might the linguistic community become a part of that development? For example, Raidió na Gaeltachta at times not only has invented Gaeilge words on the spot in cases of immediate need (a late-breaking news item) but also has elicited suggestions from its listeners regarding the best Gaeilge term for a new phenomenon (Browne, 1996: 177). In Nigeria, the standard for written Igbo remains a controversial topic (Salawu, 2006), whereas in Aotearoa/New Zealand, Māori radio stations have created and solicited words, as well, often using two terms to create a third, unassociated term, for example uniting *rore* (electric) and *hiko* (brain) to signify 'computer' (Hippolyte, 1996).

Dialects

MLM radio and TV programmes featuring dialects certainly are not unknown. There are three major dialect regions in the West of Ireland; there are two in Wales. In both cases, radio (and to a lesser extent, TV) provides programming containing those dialects. We realize that there is no universally accepted definition of a dialect, and resort to using the term in light of what MLM staff themselves have referred to as dialects. Some of those staff have indicated their unease with the use of dialects; others have indicated that, if the media service is to bond with the community, a measure of the use of dialects (where present in a given linguistic community) is an excellent way to do so, provided that the practice isn't used often for *comic* portrayals. Māori tribal radio stations often feature local and regional dialects, as well, even though dialects can be a sensitive matter: for instance, the largest Aotearoa/New Zealand tribe, the *Tainui*, refused for several years to participate in furnishing material to the national Māori language newscast, since it didn't feature Tainui activities and Tainui dialect (Fox, 1993). Elsewhere, the extent of the standardized variant – euskara batua – by station ETB-1 in the Basque Country also works against the dialectal identification of some of its audience (Moriarty, 2007).

Jim Black, a BBC Radio 4 Editor, observed of accents and dialects that 'if [a language] is incomprehensible to the majority of people, then we are failing in our job' (Ariel, 1986: 3). He was not enamoured of accents and dialects, possibly because of the debut of BBC-TV's primetime soap opera 'EastEnders' in 1985. That series was somewhat controversial for many reasons, including the use of cockney dialect. (The BBC *did* make available a 'cockney dictionary' of sorts not long after the show's debut.) But another criticism is related to the issue of language correctness, where some critics have contended that the use of dialects by the broadcast media provides a negative model for language use.

There is an interesting argument *for* dialects that they may assist in increasing mutual understanding and perhaps respect among/between members of different dialect groups. Davies (1994: 187–188) notes Aneirin Talfan Davies's 1947 observation that a southern Welsh dialect play 'has been enthusiastically welcomed in the north, and "Hedd Wyn" [a radio play in northern Welsh dialect] has proved acceptable in the south (...) which perhaps indicates that radio may be the means of breaking down barriers of dialect'. Browne encountered the same sentiment when speaking with radio station staff in Ireland and Wales in the late 1980s–mid-1990s. Raidió na Gaeltachta staff in all three Gaeltacht areas noted how many complaints the service received in its early years ('Why do you broadcast in that awful Kerry/Connemara/Donegal dialect?'), but eventually those comments were far outnumbered by 'Well, I don't care for the dialect all that much, but you know, she/he has something worth saying'. Concomitantly, according to the staff of Radio Nasa, in the Andean mountains of Colombia, Uribe-Jongbloed and Peña Sarmiento (2008) found that the community's concerns about having trouble comprehending different dialects of the Nasa language – Nasa Yuwe – led to a meeting of community leaders to develop an acceptable compromise for standardization of their radio output.

The positive and negative aspects of dialect in ML radio and TV would seem to be well worth further study, as would programmes including Wenglish ('Welsh–English') or other minority/mainstream hybrids that seem to be increasingly prevalent (see the contributions by Cunliffe and ap Dyfrig, Cunliffe *et al.* and Johnson, in this volume), as Spanglish certainly is in the United States. Among the questions to answer are how widespread are those practices, how do audiences react to their presence and does that presence influence minority language usage in important ways?

Instruction

Strange as it may seem, the level of cooperation between MLMs and preschool, primary and secondary teachers of MLs for the most part appears to be quite low, and in some cases non-existent. One of the most common motivations that supporters of MLM have expressed is the hope that the media would assist materially in supporting language instruction. Browne has spoken to far more media staff than teachers about the lack of cooperation, so any tentative conclusions are somewhat one-sided, but the two most common explanations are that 'it takes too much time to establish and maintain cooperative relationships' and 'we don't sense much interest on the part of "the other side" in developing such relationships'. Other explanations, while less common, are quite interesting: 'colleges and universities don't educate teachers-to-be to be aware of the value of working with the media' and 'to the extent that teachers-to-be learn about the media, the "lesson" appears to be that the media often are a negative influence on students' language usage'.

When one considers the potential value of a strong working relationship between language instructors and MLMs, it would seem that this is a topic that almost demands rigorous research. Might case studies of successful relationships help to alter the situation? Might MLMs and researchers combine their efforts to assist educators by researching and developing such instructional tools as 'pop music' videos for language instruction? For example, instructors of the Zapotec (Mayan) language encouraged a rock group to record songs in the language that would encourage children to learn numbers, letters and words (available at http://www.youtube. com/watch?v=gz8JWED-HxA). Is it possible for researchers to work with educators and MLMs to develop a more thorough and detailed set of explanations for lack of cooperation, along with a set of concrete suggestions for how to turn things around? Proposals that aim to answer some of these questions are presented in this book in the contributions by Dołowy-

Rybińska; Mac Uidhilin; Law; Lacour *et al.*, and they may inspire further debate about how instruction can benefit from MLM.

'Professionalism'

One of the more noticeable changes in MLM and ethnic minority media that Browne has observed over the nearly 25 years that he has been conducting research on such media in various parts of the world is media staff conceptions of 'professionalism'. Those MLM and ethnic media services that are components of national public service broadcast (PSB) organizations – Welsh-language radio and television with the BBC, Sami Radio with Norway's NRK, Finland's YLE and Sweden's Sveriges Radio, Raidió na Gaeltachta and TG4 with Ireland's RTÉ and several others – have followed the professional practices of their respective 'parents'. Newscasts are presented in a formal manner, interviews perhaps slightly less formally, 'taste' in choice of subject matter is expected (even in the absence of specific rules or guidelines), etc. Correctness of speech, while not universally required, often is expected.

However, many electronic MLMs are not part of a large national PSB, and may create their own rules and guidelines for 'professionalism'. Those rules and guidelines sometimes resemble those widely followed by PSBs and national commercial networks if only because (a) many MLM journalists are 'trained' in schools or programmes operated by PSBs, (b) those who aren't have grown up listening to and viewing 'mainstream' radio and TV and are likely to have absorbed at least some sense of 'professionalism' as practised by those services and (c) non-journalists are very likely to have been influenced by 'mainstream' practices as well, so that their expectations of what should go into informational and entertainment programming.

The surprising thing about this situation is that, in the earlier years of Browne's research on ethnic and linguistic minority broadcast media, there appeared to be a greater readiness on part of the 'non-PBS' MLMs to assume that 'mainstream' media concepts of professionalism didn't always apply to minority media practices. It was particularly marked in the case of indigenous services, where it was the rule and not the exception to find announcers delivering the news more slowly than did 'mainstream' announcers, interviewers giving their interviewees ample time to pause before responding and other practices that made such services notably different from 'mainstream' media.

Such practices still exist, but in visits to similar stations over the past 10 years or so, Browne has found a growing tendency on their part to sound more like mainstream operations, with somewhat faster pacing, shorter pauses and a greater degree of 'cult of personality', with clever (often 'mainstream') on-air names for music programme hosts. How this has been received by listeners and viewers is difficult to determine, since relatively few 'non-PBS' MLMs conduct audience research. It's part of a larger question, which might be phrased as 'How "different" do MLM readers, listeners and viewers expect those services to sound, and what sorts of differences are most important in helping them to identify the services as "ours" – that is, intended particularly to serve "us" and not be imitations of mainstream media'. Evidence from some of the Scottish Gaelic broadcast research conducted by Lèirsinn indicates that listeners and viewers do make such distinctions, in both style and genres of presentation, and that they are important (MacNeil & MacDonald, 1999). This seems worthy of research on a broader scale, since it clearly relates to the development of linguistic communities, which are covered next.

Financing and promotion

The changes in practice just described may be driven as much as anything by perceptions of financial necessity. Government appropriations and donor support often have decreased in recent times, and particularly in the face of the great recession. Even before that occurred, some MLM managerial staff have observed that their services had moved in a more commercial direction, where attracting young mainstream listeners was an important priority (Goodwillie, 2007). That in turn seemed to lead to a perception that the services needed to sound more 'mainstream professional' in general, affecting how the news was delivered (and perhaps its content) and how interviews were conducted (likewise).

This change seems to be a potentially significant development. Some MLM 'non-PBS' services – not many, in our experience – have identified 'reaching out to the mainstream audience' as one of their priorities. That can be valuable in helping mainstream populations to better understand minority populations, but it would seem necessary to keep it in very careful balance with an MLM's primary responsibility: to serve one or more minority audience. Research on shifting patterns of MLM style and content would help determine whether that primary goal was being well met.

There is another administrative matter that could be important where MLM administrative practices are concerned. We all know how radically the media landscape has changed over the past 20 years, with increasing number of services available over the air, through cable and satellite, on the internet and on social media. Certainly, the MLM administrators with whom both of us have spoken are well aware of this. What they seem to be less aware of is what strikes us as the obvious need for MLMs in particular to work harder to ensure that the largest possible number of potentially interested audience members for MLMs be made aware of the existence of such services and their various offerings – in other words, service and programme promotion. There is a wide range of possible approaches that need to be clearly identified. Bush Radio in Cape Town, South Africa, illustrates many of them, ranging from monthly open meetings with audience members to development of programming produced by children (Bosch, 2003; Browne, 2005: 165–166). Some of these issues, about how the creative industries integrate with these changing audiences and their economic import, are addressed in the chapters by Chalmers *et al.*, Pavón and Zuberogoitia, Cordonet and Forniès and Narbaiza *et al.* in this book.

Developing MLM 'sense of community'

Alan Watkins, writing in the UK newspaper *The Observer,* opined that 'Whenever I hear the word "community," I become suspicious and feel that no good is afoot' (Watkins, 1981). Yet academics who study communication are quite fond of the term, and community radio and television have been important as outlets for minority language programmes for some time now, so it's appropriate to pose the question: What is a *linguistic* community and what might that mean where MLMs are concerned? Everything covered in the second section of this chapter is connected with that question.

Defining the term itself is difficult enough. Definitions offered (or hinted at) by sociologists, linguists, anthropologists and other academics generally include 'those who speak the same language', but thereafter go in several different directions. Some emphasize the need to consider levels of fluency, others look to geographical identities, still others foreground levels of education, economic standing and occupation. Almost all of them miss out on what seems absolutely vital in any consideration of MLMs: the *interactional* aspect of community building.

Some of the possible research questions that we might consider asking are: who is represented through a given MLM's output and who isn't? That could involve representation of gender, various age groups, economic standing, level of fluency and probably still other categories. But equally important would be questions regarding how representation is determined, in what specific ways the sense of community is reinforced and what specific actions media staff take to further encourage interaction (see Uribe-Jongbloed debate on convergence vis-à-vis participation in this volume). Reports prepared by some of the umbrella organizations that deal with community radio, such as the UK's Community Media Association (www.commedia.org.uk) and the Bangladesh NGOs Networks for Radio and Television (www.bnnrc.net) indicate ways to encourage such interaction.

That same sense of community has particular relevance where the 'social media' are concerned. Expansion of those media is breathtaking in its speed and reach, at least where industrially developed nations are concerned, but increasingly in developing nations, as vividly illustrated by the key roles played by such media in the 2011 'Arab Spring'. What we know about the use of the internet as a minority language medium certainly indicates that such usage is increasing rapidly and in many forms that range from sites featuring performance videos to online newspapers. Several of the chapters in this book deal with such usage. Also, the search engines – Google, Copernic and others – are wonderful places to look for material such as blogs and other discussion sites featuring Kabyle students in France, Kurdish opposition groups and countless others. However, as evidenced by her contribution to this book, Jones also shows how some of those search results might give an incomplete image of the vitality of some minority languages.

One 'community' issue that is already under study where 'mainstream' media are concerned is *how* are the newer media being used by linguistic minorities particularly in terms of what those media provide that the traditional MLMs do *not*? Many blogs exist for the discussion of specific broadcast programmes, and there certainly appears to be a community spirit among their participants. Also, given the widespread tendency for many bloggers and twitterers to abbreviate words, create acronyms, etc., we see communities engaged in the act of reshaping language for their own purposes – a subject that should be of particular interest where minority languages are concerned (see Johnson's contribution to this volume). The social media appear to provide a playground of sorts in which users can invent terms and acronyms, write more colloquially and, in short, enjoy themselves in the company of others who are like-minded. Such a mindset has interesting implications for any traditional MLM service that might be considering how best to attract more young people, including the sensitive question of its own role in encouraging such linguistic reshaping (see, for example, the emotionally charged nature of the discussion about Luxembourgish on Facebook, as presented by Wagner in this volume). Again, if we were to study that subject on a comparative basis, the results would be valuable to scholars and MLM services alike.

What Might Academics Do to Broaden and Improve MLM Research?

While there are many ways in which academics might broaden and improve the study of MLMs, two of them – direct comparisons and cultural sensitivity – strike us as being particularly important in terms of their relevance to our field.

Direct comparisons

What might direct comparisons *between* MLM services in various nations reveal? Thanks to the greater abundance of academic studies on linguistic minority media, all of us are able to know a great deal more about MLMs than we could have 20 or even 10 years ago. What that literature often does not cover is direct, specific *comparisons* between MLMs, and especially those outside Europe and North America. Some recent books – Wilson and Stewart's *Global Indigenous Media*, Cottle's *Ethnic Minorities and the Media*, Alia and Bull's *Media and Ethnic Minorities* – are more global, but often (with Cormack and Hourigan's *Minority Language Media* as at least one exception) don't 'pull the threads together' where the various MLM experiences are concerned.

It is axiomatic that, in order to make direct comparisons, we need comparable dimensions. Too often, it seems, that's what we *don't* have in most of the 'comparative media' literature. We have sets of different nations, to be sure. We may have different sets of language groups. Beyond that, the dimensions run in different directions. Some are political, some economic, some cultural and so on – the Ethnolinguistic Gratification Theory described in this book in Moring and Vincze's contribution seems to offer a potential avenue to provide a more holistic picture of these dimensions, as does the comparison of music, song and performance between Māori and Irish language television, in Lysaght's chapter. But if the individual studies that make up a given comparative consideration don't cover at least some of the same dimensions, then it would be difficult to come to general conclusions. For example, Hourigan (2007: 252–253) makes a case for the need to study the *media reception practices* of recent (émigré) minority language media, with particular consideration of *intergenerational* similarities and differences. If that were to be the focus of a comparative study that included not only European, North American, Australian and New Zealand experiences but also those of Asia, Africa, Latin America and North Africa/the Middle East (Israel has a number of interesting MLM services, Lebanon a few), we'd have a much better understanding of a vital topic: why and how do those populations listen to, view and read MLM output? Furthermore, the similarities and differences that we would discover would help us as scholars, but also the MLM services themselves, to better understand the appropriateness and the effectiveness of that output.

Cultural sensitivity

How can we help to ensure that the research approaches we take are sensitive to the cultural characteristics – generational, gender, occupational, etc. – of the linguistic minorities themselves, so that we can be reasonably confident that the conclusions we reach rest on the soundest possible footings? Here, a comparison of research methods as they're utilized in specific settings should yield a wealth of material that will have a direct effect on the quality of our research. For example, Browne once discussed a YLE (Finnish Broadcasting Corporation) 1994 study of listening to Sami Radio with the coordinator of that study. When asked about the composition of the interview team, the coordinator indicated that they were young people from urban areas. When asked whether the team members were instructed in generational, locational (urban–rural) and gender differences and their possible effect on subject responses, the coordinator replied that there had not been such training and that, in retrospect, it would have been valuable: those differences *were* important in Sami culture, and failure to adapt the interview event itself to recognize them certainly could affect the quality of the data (Tuhiwai-Smith, 1999, is a useful source on cultural sensitivity in research; see also Uribe-Jongbloed's contribution to this volume on participatory research).

Conclusions

There is no doubt that 'minority media,' once absent or barely visible in the media landscape of most nations, now are a world wide phenomenon. Few nations lack at least one or two examples, and some nations have thousands of them. For instance, Brazil now has over 3000 community radio stations alone, many of them carrying minority-produced programmes. Furthermore, the variety of expressive formats has expanded, both through the appropriation of 'mainstream' media formats and through the time-honoured minority formats such as storytelling. Scholarly attention to such media activity is growing, as well.

At the same time, as we suggest in this chapter, there is much relatively untilled ground to be explored. As the following chapters reveal, the generally neglected sub-field of linguistic minority media and multilingualism is receiving greater attention, and from many different perspectives. The increase in internet-based and audience-led participation in the media also expands the idea that media have ceased to be separate institutions and have become spaces of everyday life that can no longer be seen as a separate category. However, we still lack sufficient understanding of how minority languages – or languages in general for that matter – affect and are affected by the media through which they find expression. Perhaps, this decade will find that gap being addressed. The studies presented here are a most promising sign of greater willingness on the part of young scholars in particular to explore this field with fresh eyes.

Notes

1. We employ terms such as émigré and minority throughout this chapter. Readers who are already familiar with scholarship in this subject area are quite aware that such terminology is contested. We've attempted to be sensitive in our choices of terminology.
2. The 1978 Constitution of the Spanish State defines Spanish (Castilian) as the official language of the whole country, and the remaining languages as official in the respective Autonomous Communities. Although the 2006 Catalonian Statute defined Catalan as the preferential language and a requirement of knowledge of Catalan for the inhabitants of Catalunya, in 2010 the Constitutional Tribunal of Spain (Sentence 31/2010 of 28 June) challenged those two premises arguing that Spanish (Castilian) should be the only language demanded of the citizens, and derogating the preferential status of Catalan.

References

Agosta, D. (2009) *Naming the future*. Saarbrücken: VDM Verlag.
Alia, V. (1999) *Un/Covering the north*. Vancouver, BC: University fo British Columbia Press.
Alia, V. (2010) *The New Media Nation: Indigenous Peoples and Global Communications*. New York & Oxford: Berghahn Books.
Ariel (1986, 10 September), *Ariel: BBC Staff Newspaper*, p. 3.
Bosch, T. (2003) Radio, community and identity in South Africa. PhD, Ohio University.
Browne, D.R. (1996) *Electronic Media and Indigenous Peoples: A Voice of Our Own?* Ames, Iowa: Iowa State University Press.
Browne, D.R. (2005) *Ethnic Minorities, Electronic Media and the Public Sphere: A Comparative Approach*. Cresskill, NJ: Hampton Press.
Browne, D.R. (2008) Speaking in our tongues. In M. Keith (ed.) *Radio Cultures* (pp. 23–46). New York: Peter Lang.
Caracol TV (2009) Guerrilla obliga a Indígenas Awas a hablar Español, accessed 10 March 2011. http://www.caracoltv.com/node/124768.
Cormack, M. (2004) Developing minority language media studies. *Mercator Media Forum* 7 (1), 3–12.

Cormack, M. (2007) Introduction: Studying minority language media. In M. Cormack and N. Hourigan (eds) *Minority Language Media: Concepts, Critiques, and Case Studies* (pp. 1–16). Clevedon: Multilingual Matters.

Davies, J. (1994) *Broadcasting and the BBC in Wales*. Cardiff: University of Wales Press.

Fox, D. (1993) [Director of Mana Maori Media].

Frachon, C. and Vargaftig, M. (1995) *European Television: Immigrants and Ethnic Minorities*. London: John Libby.

Goodwillie, C. (2007) [Manager of Tahu FM].

Gorter, D. (1990) *Fourth International Conference on Minority Languages*. Clevedon: Multilingual Matters.

Grame, T.C. and American Folklife Center (1980) *Ethnic Broadcasting in the United States*. Washington, D.C.: American Folklife Center, Library of Congress.

Grin, F. (2003) On the costs of cultural diversity. In P. Van Parijs (ed.) *Cultural Diversity versus Economic Solidarity* (pp. 189–202). Bruxelles: de Boeck.

Grin, F. and Vaillancourt, F. (1999) *The Cost-Effectiveness Evaluation of Minority Language Policies: Case Studies on Wales, Ireland and the Basque Country*. Flensburg: ECMI.

Hippolyte, K. (1996) [Manager of Te Reo Iriraki ki Otautahi].

Hourigan, N. (2004) *Escaping the Global Village: Media, Language and Protest*. Lanham, MD: Lexington Books.

Hourigan, N. (2007) Minority language media studies: Key themes for future scholarship. In M. Cormack and N. Hourigan (eds) *Minority Language Media: Concepts, Critiques, and Case Studies* (pp. 248–265). Clevedon: Multilingual Matters.

Jones, A.G. (1993) *Press, Politics and Society*. Cardiff: University of Wales Press.

Konecky, E. (1948) *The American Communications Conspiracy*. New York: Peoples Radio Foundation.

Leguy, C. (2007) Revitalizing the oral tradition: Stories broadcast by Radio Parana (San, Mali). *Research in African Literatures* 38 (3), 136–147.

Lemke, C. (1996) Maori involvement in sound recording and broadcasting, 1919 to 1958. M.A., University of Auckland, Auckland.

Littlefield, D.F. and Parins, J.W. (1984) *American Indian and Alaska Native Newspapers and Periodicals*. Westport, CN: Greenwood Press.

Luykx, A. (2001) Across the Andean airwaves: Satellite radio broadcasting in Quechua. In C. Moseley, N. Ostler and H. Ouzzate (eds) *Endangered Languages and the Media* (pp. 115–119). Agadir, Morocco.

MacNeil, M. and MacDonald, B. (1999) *Digitalisation and Gaelic Broadcasting*. Inverness: Lèirsinn Research Centre for the Gaelic Broadcasting Committee.

Moriarty, M. (2007) *Minority Language Television as an Effective Mechanism of Language Policy: A Comparative Study of the Irish and Basque Sociolinguistic Contexts*. PhD, University of Limerick, Limerick.

Murillo, M. (2008) Weaving a communication quilt in Colombia: Civil conflict, indigenous resistance and community radio in northern Cauca. In P. Wilson and M. Stewart (eds) *Global Indigenous Media: Cultures, Poetics, and Politics* (pp. 145–159). Durham & London: Duke University Press.

National Association of Hispanic Journalists (2006, 23 October 2006) NAHJ board's statement of NBC's plans for Telemundo, accessed 17 May 2010. http://www.nahj.org/nahjnews/articles/2006/october/telemundo.shtml.

Programme Director BBC (1931) *Gaelic Programmes*. BBC Written Archives Centre Caversham, Reading.

Rodriguez, C. and El Gazi, J. (2007) The poetics of indigenous radio in Colombia. *Media, Culture and Society* 29 (3), 449–468.

Roth, L. (2006) *Something New in the Air*. Montreal: Queens University/McGill Press.

Salawu, A. (ed.) (2006) *Indigenous Language Media in Africa*. Lagos: CBAAC.

Salazar, F. and Cordova, A. (2008) Imperfect media and the politics of indulgence video in Latin America. In P. Wilson and M. Stewart (eds) *Global Indigenous Media: Culture, Poetics and Politics* (pp. 39–57). Durham & London: Duke University Press.

Tuhiwai-Smith, L. (1999) *Decolonizing Methodologies: Research and Indigenous Peoples*. London: Zed Books.

Uribe-Jongbloed, E. and Peña Sarmiento, M.F. (2008) Medios en idiomas autóctonos minoritarios en Colombia: El caso de la radio. *Palabra Clave* 11 (2), 355–366.

van de Fliert, E. and Hien, D.T.M. (2009) Communication for development: Targetting the untargetted. *Media Development* 1 (1), 29–34.

Watkins, A. (1981, 17 May) Community service for nosey parkers. *The Observer*, p. 11.

Wilson, P. and Stewart, M. (eds) (2008) *Global Indigenous Media: Cultures, Poetics and Politics*. Durham & London: Duke University Press.

Wirth, S. and Adair, J. (1972) *Through Navajo Eyes*. Bloomington: Indiana University Press.

Part 1

Theoretical Debates on Convergence and Minority Languages

1 Minority Language Media Studies and Communication for Social Change: Dialogue between Europe and Latin America

Enrique Uribe-Jongbloed

Introduction

This chapter stems from my personal interest in expanding minority language media research into the Latin American context. It also arises from a desire to present some of the achievements of Communication for Social Change in Latin America to a European media studies community not acquainted with them.

In order to do this, the chapter begins by presenting the common ground between the two areas of studies. It draws attention to the fact that language is but one of the many cultural aspects under which indigenous and ethnic communities are marginalized from and by the main media outlets in Latin America.

Because of this, research into Latin American minority language media needs to have a contextual approach that studies the processes of identity negotiation and participatory agency defined under the concepts of *hybridity* and *convergence*. It also demands research to increase participation of its subjects of inquiry, as consistently requested by practitioners of Communication for Social Change.

Finally, both of these aspects, a contextual approach to *hybridity* and *convergence* and the call for more participatory research, are presented as the fundamental dialogue both to expand minority language media studies to Latin America and to provide feedback for its advancement in Europe.

Developing Minority Language Media Studies in Latin America

Studies on minority language media (MLM) have gathered momentum in Europe recently (Cormack, 2004; Guyot, 2006). Although they do not limit themselves to recognized traditional languages, they usually refer to them, rather than to immigrant languages (Extra & Gorter, 2008; Hourigan, 2007). Cormack and Hourigan's (2007) work presented the state of the art of debates on this topic. The western European focus through which Cormack (Cormack, 1998, 2004, 2007a) has framed the specific area of studies in MLM reduces the global vision originally proposed by Riggins (1992b) and expanded by Browne (1996, 2005, 2007 see also the introductory essay to this book). Cormack (2000, 2004, see also his chapter in this book) has privileged linguistic – over cultural or ethnic – diversity to define the extent of the area of studies.

This seems almost self-evident in the case of Europe, but it is not as clear the world over. In Europe, ethnic distinctions seem to have been erased from collective memory, and nation is taken as a community based on other non-ethnic cultural parameters (Castells, 1997, presents this to be the case for Catalunya, for instance). This makes language the most salient feature of difference that justifies separate media provisions. However, in other ends of the world, issues of ethnicity are still relevant in contemporary debates.

Just like Aboriginal people in Australia (Ginsburg, 1991; Meadows & Molnar, 2002), ethnic and indigenous people in Latin America have demanded media spaces to express their own perspective, not only to the members of their groups but also to the national society at large. This demand arises because not only their language but also their whole culture and world view remain absent from the nation-state hegemonic discourse. These identities, originally marginalized from, and by, the media, aim to become *oppositional identities* which 'present themselves contesting the label of marginalisation that has been set upon them, pushing the margins of legal normalcy and social esteem' (Sampedro Blanco, 2004: 140).

The issues of marginalized groups have been fundamental to Communication for Social Change (CfSC) in Latin America. CfSC is a proposal developed by academics and activists interested in promoting social change through empowerment, granting agency to individuals to become key actors in their own development, providing them with communication tools to achieve self-representation and encouraging them to promote development from a grassroots perspective (Gumucio-Dagron, 2007; Gumucio-Dagron & Tufte, 2006; Servaes, 1996a). Among the communication tools promoted, CfSC supports the design and establishment of media outlets to modify negative collective images and one-sided representations, which is fundamental if we are convinced that 'power in the network society is communication power' (Castells, 2009: 53).

However, the interest to change negative portrayals, and provide a more ample media space, is accepted only reluctantly by the already established media structures. They allow for these alternative media spaces as long as they have a narrow area of effect, because 'when [Indigenous broadcasting] grows large enough to require valuable resources, however, hegemonic pressures kick in more fully' (Evans, 2002: 324) and hamper change to the prevalent media power status quo.

Concurrently, although the use of their own minority language within their social institutions grants them a space free from the hegemonic influence of the majority (Nichols, 2006), it also restricts their possibility to present their struggle to other population groups which, being also minorities, may be under the same hegemonic vision that oppresses indigenous peoples and ties them to poverty by excluding them from public debate, amongst other things.

Conflicting Identities

According to the model presented by Riggins (1992a), cultural assimilation towards the majority culture increases when ethnic minority media seek to reach out to larger audiences to become inclusive and use the majority language for this end. However, taking the opposite strategy and trying to avoid the use of the majority language in order to preserve linguistic cohesion leads, in turn, to the loss of an audience whose ethnic or indigenous identity may still be strong, despite having already switched to the majority language.

This dichotomy portrays the contrast between Browne's (1996) observation about language as a fundamental aspect for the establishment of ethnic minority media, and O'Reilly's (2001: 15) statement that 'there are non-linguistic aspects of ethnic identity, such as a sense of kinship and territory, which are often considered more salient than language'. The same is to be found in various indigenous groups in Latin America (Favre, 2006), because some users of 'indigenous languages identify themselves not as members of an ethnic group but as campesinos [peasants] or as people from particular communities or regions' (Smith, 2008: 187). Hence, Browne (1996: 223) concedes that 'while language revival or revitalization has been a major reason for establishing indigenous broadcasting stations, very few of them broadcast exclusively in indigenous languages and most of them broadcast in the majority culture language' despite the centrality of language to their identity.

Moreover, indigenous people are wrongly classified under one single heading, because each one of the indigenous people espouse different cultural structures and rationales, including their relationship with media (see Rodriguez & El Gazi, 2007, for the Colombian experience). Notwithstanding, there is no question that media produced, defined and established by the indigenous groups serve as spaces for their own voices and their own vision of the world (Communication for Sustainable Development Initiative, 2010; Wilson & Stewart, 2008).

Despite modernizing technology being different from a modernizing political discourse, 'in reality the two are almost always intertwined' (Sparks, 2007: 195) and, thus, the appropriation and re-signification of technologies, such as the ones required for the media, demand a process of negotiation between the cultural elements embedded in the technology and the cultural interests of the communities (Ginsburg, 1991, 2008). These negotiations can be described as falling under two categories difficult to disentangle from one another: *hybridity* and *convergence*.

Hybridization or Convergence: Two Faces of the Same Coin?

The two concepts have arisen to describe aspects of transnationalization and globalization of media products, but they can also be applied in local contexts.

Hybridization

Hybridity, as a theory, is grounded on post-colonial discourse (Kraidy, 2010) and refers to the process of appropriation, modification and re-adaptation – or deculturalization, acculturalization and reculturalization (Wang & Yeh, 2005) – of cultural products (e.g. TV shows). It is a space where external media pressures are not only adapted but also reconstructed, and their meanings are re-elaborated in an active engagement between modernization and traditional views (García Canclini, 2000; Martínez *et al.*, 2008), and it 'entails a cultural (re)creation that may or may not be (re)inscribed into hegemonic constellations' (Escobar, 1995: 220).

This process involves a negotiation that is rarely carried out on even grounds and may lead to 'rough adaptations of the local cultures to the hegemonic and transnational cultural paradigms' (Roveda Hoyos, 2008: 62). They are uneven spaces, because imported cultural goods, or those elaborated by a majority culture, have the quality standards and supposed superiority granted to them by the hegemonic economic and structural advantage of the cultural industries where they were originally produced.

But despite this hegemonic influence upon the process of hybridization, new proposals and ways of engaging with the media develop, from mere adaptation to blatant resistance and re-appropriation of media spaces as places to redefine cultural boundaries. Adaptations of audiovisual products from one market to another exemplify the different types of negotiations that may ensue: (1) *hegemonic, or centre-to-periphery*, in the case of ubiquitous Hollywood films and their canon of cinema quality (Fu & Govindaraju, 2010), and mass television products of the global north; (2) *counter-hegemonic or periphery-to-centre*, as in the case of the Colombian telenovela *Yo soy Betty, la Fea* and its American remake *Ugly Betty* (Miller, 2010; Rivera-Betancur & Uribe-Jongbloed, 2011; Rivero, 2003); and (3) *alternative or periphery-to-periphery*, in the case of amateur indigenous video, with its own outlets, distribution channels and own aesthetic proposals outside the hegemonic markets (Salazar & Cordova, 2008).

Convergence

Another term used recently to describe a similar process is *convergence* (Deuze, 2006, 2010; Jenkins, 2006; Roth, 2006) which can be summarized as 'contemporary emergent norms, values and patterns of activities that blur the boundaries between media production and media consumption' (Deuze, 2006: 268). Though participation of the public in the media is not a new trait, the amount of input, and the direct omnipresence it has on the internet, makes it more clearly visible at present (Deuze, 2010). This has occurred because consumers are at the same time producers – *prosumers* – defining the extent and shape of the society of ubiquity through manipulation of available communication technology (Islas-Carmona, 2008). Technology infrastructure and availability, and the corresponding competences they demand, are the main hurdles for active convergence (Jenkins, 2006), because disparities in access to the same channels of participation separate social groups and evidence the gap that renders the 'digital age' as nothing of the sort (Ginsburg, 2008).

Convergence means appropriating different media to provide new avenues of participation which complement, rather than replace, the role of specific outlets. It is seen as a way to expand the remit of existent media, as stated on this call to development practitioners:

While the benefits offered by the Internet are many, its dependence on a telecommunications infrastructure means that they are only available to a few. Radio, on the other hand, is a much more pervasive, accessible, and affordable medium for most people. Blending the two could be an ideal way of ensuring that the benefits accruing from the Internet have wider reach. (Communication Initiative (Organization) *et al.*, 2007: 217)

There is a caveat: technology that enables participation does not always lead to its use to modify communication imbalances and media misrepresentation. The increasing use of social networking sites and all kinds of blogging and personal internet-based media seem to expand '"phatic media" in which communication without content has taken precedence' (Miller, 2008: 398), and keeping up the internet persona for its own sake, rather than encouraging communication and fostering cultural dialogue, becomes an end in itself. Therefore, *convergence* as active participation has to be more than just the use of technological tools. It depends on how the given technologies available to a community are put to use by people at the receiving end of media messages to modify, adapt, negotiate and produce their own media output.

Hybridity and *convergence* seem to pinpoint similar debates, yet seen from opposite angles. On the one hand, *hybridity* is concerned with the negotiation spaces of cultural significance in media products from the perspective of existing institutions of cultural production and their top-down agendas. It engages with how the whole *culture* conceives the prevailing forms of cultural representation and identity construction through media. It also engages with how they negotiate their identities against a hegemonic cultural imperialistic paradigm and a growing exchange of cultural products. On the other hand, *convergence* focuses on the increased participation of *individual* consumers and grassroots action. It focuses on the bottom-up processes usually by the means of collaborative strategies incorporated in the media, although not necessarily only through them, and it poses questions about how this increased participation challenges the previous hierarchical construction of media products and information channels.

Cultural negotiations are macro, top-down developments counter-balanced by micro, bottom-up participation. *Hybridity* and *convergence* are the same processes with inverted directions of flow and constitute two fundamental aspects of the current media developments by framing the relationships between media and their users.

Hybridity and convergence as 'negotiation' and 'participation'

The interest in *hybridity* in Latin America has also been linked to an increased interest in participation. Since the early 1980s, a participatory paradigm in development communication was formulated, postulating that every given community should be the one defining its own needs, articulating their media to satisfy them and becoming the main promoter of the media use, because 'participation is the effective exercise of the right to emit messages' (Beltrán Salmón, 2006: 168). This participatory process was to be seen as a 'horizontal' model of communication, where dialogue, access and participation were fundamental elements to enable the democratization of communication (Beltrán Salmón, 2005, 2006). Part of this participatory perspective opposed imposition of external cultural conceptions of development because 'when power dynamics within societies make one culture dominant over others, true dialogue between cultures is limited' (Gumucio-Dagron & Tufte, 2006).

This participatory paradigm became a main element in development programmes, including a radical variant that implied the social modification of power structures, something that promoted empowerment for those oppressed and encouraged action through social movements (Sparks, 2007; see also the situation that took place in Europe with the campaigns for the establishment of media in minority languages in Cormack, 1998; Hourigan, 2004). Furthermore, development projects were increasingly expected to provide more tools for their target communities to achieve self-expression, by granting them more control upon their own communication strategies. This became one of the main objectives of CfSC, as one of its key tenets, since it 'strives to strengthen cultural identity, trust, commitment, voice, community engagement and ownership' (Gumucio-Dagron & Tufte, 2006).

This approach brings media producers closer to their audiences, or at least it tries to do so. It embraces simultaneously the idea of *hybridity* and *convergence*, in that it promotes participation and negotiation of cultural conceptualizations in the use of media. A recent research on indigenous and ethnic media audiences in Australia highlights this point when it claims that 'the intimate relationship between Indigenous media producers and their audiences is clear from the commentary offered by listeners and viewers across a wide variety of geographical and cultural settings' (Forde *et al.*, 2009: 97), mentioning it as one of the key elements to the indigenous broadcasting success.

However, both in terms of *hybridity* and *convergence*, dialogue does not necessarily imply agreement, and conflict is a constant part of the negotiation practice. Different contexts may lead both to different outcomes in terms of cultural incorporations and borrowings (i.e. adaptations, impositions, deconstructions, copies, rejections, etc.) and to different avenues of participation and sharing of information (i.e. copyright legislation, multi-platform production, open or closed communication channels, exclusions, collaborations, etc). Often these two aspects are simultaneous and they influence each other because cultural negotiations include ways and patterns of acceptable participation, and participatory input brings with it cultural baggage based on exposure to other creative paradigms.

For MLM this binary interrelation is made evident when the interests of linguistic maintenance and encouragement encounter opposition to creative interests, regional identifications and other professional and individual identities and goals. In ethnic minority media, ethnicity is evident and latent, even necessarily active, and may have a bearing upon the concept of professional practice, because practitioners have allegiances to professional codes of conduct, at the same time as they have commitments to the ethnic group(s) they represent (Husband, 2005).

Some minorities opt to privilege linguistic content over ethnic ascription or professional interests for purposes of language maintenance. In television production, for instance, impositions in favour of the fictional linguistic normalization of Catalan audiovisual dramas directly undermine the desired bilingual realism which creative scriptwriters want to portray (Castelló, 2007).

The opposite is also common: some minorities are willing to sacrifice linguistic spaces to achieve more influence upon the national public sphere and find a larger audience.

The trade-off between linguistic maintenance and political support is present consistently as an area of negotiation in MLM outlets all over the world. Nasa radio stations in Colombia privilege the use of the majority language, Spanish, instead of their own language, Nasa Yuwe, in order to reach out to larger audiences for political support to their territorial claims (Uribe-Jongbloed & Peña Sarmiento, 2008), whereas journalists in Sami radio in northern Scandinavia avoid the use of any non-Sami language despite its detrimental effect upon their listener base, because of their strong commitment to language revitalization (Pietikäinen, 2008a, 2008b). These two seemingly opposite perspectives evidence the breadth of *hybridity* in indigenous, ethnic and minority language media when it comes to defining the purposes and extent of their media use.

At the same time, community interest in local media projects is no guarantee of more ample *convergence*. The situation of the radio show *Kawsaypura Yachanakushun* in the Saraguro region of Ecuador is a case in point. As Martínez *et al.* (2008) highlight, community interest in the bilingual programme ensured balanced participation of indigenous and non-indigenous actors, but neither did it prevent excessive participation by government officials nor did it tackle the lack of women participants in the radio broadcast.

Another example is the network of radio stations Red Kiechwa Satelital (RKS). RKS broadcast of the Quechua/Kichwa languages in the Andes has increased participation in the shows and enlarged its audience by rotating the production between the networked radio stations in the three countries it reaches (Luykx, 2001). However, this increased participation contrasts with the reduced space of the language in the schedules of the participating stations, consisting of small windows under a couple of hours a week. Nonetheless, the recent inclusion of one live broadcast, and the availability of some of their programmes on the internet, may help expand their audience base (see http://www.aler.org/rks/ for the network information).

It is necessary to consider the intercontextual aspects that show how, in each specific case, cultural and identity concepts have been negotiated and how their outcomes reflect power struggles and cultural positions of the different communities. In this way, *hybridity* is conceptualized in an instrumental way that goes beyond description of contemporary globalization and transnationalization of cultural products (Kraidy, 2010).

Conversely, *convergence* needs to be separated from its perception as technologically biased towards the latest developments of the internet. It can be explored as the participatory input of individuals, within the technological constraints of the media they use and the extent of influence or distance that they take from the production process. *Convergence* is equally present in the recording of audio tapes to register, compile and revitalize oral tradition for radio broadcast (Leguy, 2007); in videos about indigenous manifestations recorded through the use of inexpensive camcorders, copied and distributed locally by person-to-person physical networks or through alternative distribution channels; and, also, in the use of portable mobile phones to record and upload images of human rights violations or videos of demonstrations against governments and their distribution via internet social networking sites.

Research on MLM

MLM studies and CfSC have both addressed similar aspects of the relationship between media, culture and language. Despite their epistemological differences, and their geographical focus, they agree on the importance they give to understanding the processes of *hybridity* and *convergence* as fundamental aspects of those relationships. Also, for both of them, research needs to focus on the specific contextual situation of every given community and its relationship to media. This is an aspect which has been paramount to MLM studies (Cormack, 1998, 2000, 2004, 2007a) and CfSC (Gumucio-Dagron, 2007; Gumucio-Dagron & Tufte, 2006; Servaes, 1996b).

Research focus

Because context is fundamental to *hybridity*, research on MLM has to focus, first, on understanding cultural negotiation in media practice. This means concentrating on existing provisions and the way in which media producers define their roles as cultural producers and gatekeepers (as presented by O'Connell in her contribution to this book). To this end, Husband (2005) has recommended looking at the various media production groups as communities of practice (Wenger, 1998) as a useful framework to analyse ethnic identity negotiations in the media workplace. In her chapter in this book, O'Connell also presents a series of questions whose answers might give us an insight into the linguistic negotiations within media institutions – providing evidence of *hybridity* as it occurs.

Second, there is need for research on MLM audiences, to gather their interests and requirements (Vincze and Moring's chapter makes a contribution to this topic) and assess their participatory input. This is an area of ethnic minority media that has been consistently presented as requiring further empirical research (Browne, 2005; Meadows, 2009). More research needs to focus on improving *convergence* in the media, in general, and in radio in particular. Radio has been chosen as the best community medium all over the world, because it has a relatively low cost of production and it allows ample distribution and access, which makes it an ideal tool for local communication (Browne, 2005; Fairchild, 2001; Girard *et al.*, 2003; Peissl & Tremetzberger, 2008; Unidad de Radio, 2002). Furthermore, due to the large number of languages with considerable small numbers of users in Latin America, a situation common to most Third World countries, independent national provision for any major media technology in minority languages tends economically to be an impossibility. However, the incorporation of radio shows and other media programmes, and encouraging participation through the internet, might help expand their area of influence, without sacrificing their content (see Law's chapter in this book).

Through these research processes the relations of *hybridity* and *convergence* can be mapped. They can help us understand the appearance or absence of language, or its specific usage and systems of control, and they would also evidence the trade-offs of each specific medium. They could help highlight the best practices for each medium to satisfy the specific needs of a given community while at the same time encouraging participatory processes.

Research on the two aspects seems to satisfy the requirements mentioned by Cormack (2007b) to understand how media use may affect language maintenance. It engages with the conceptual structure that defines the media and its purpose from the producers' perspective, and the effect and responses it elicits from audiences.

Participatory research

Needless to say, research that combines MLM with CfSC concepts has to be participatory in its conception and development, and needs to allow for dialogue to take place between the researcher and those researched, to ensure that the researcher's assumptions and own cultural biases do not overrule the interest of those being researched (Arnst, 1996; Communication Initiative (Organization) *et al.*, 2007; Meadows, 2009, 2010; Servaes, 1996a). This may prove difficult, especially in cases where there is less cultural proximity between the researcher and those researched, but it is necessary, ensuring that participation is seen as a way to permeate both knowledge construction and social influence.

Accepting a participatory approach may also entail admitting that any given assumptions about media and the role of language within them can be totally different from what researchers may expect or even desire, and it 'necessarily involves reflection on our own assumed – either inadvertently or deliberately – positions of power as representatives of academic institutions structured largely on Western epistemologies' (Meadows, 2010: 317). This approach implies looking at research as a process with open results, because 'to prescribe how that unfolding [of the process] should occur is not only counterproductive, it is often the antithesis of genuine participation' (Servaes, 1996a: 23). In the same way that *convergence* implies allowing for the consumers to assume a different role as producers – something not all media have been able to articulate – research needs to open itself to input and allow for participation within research processes (Arnst, 1996). This is especially relevant, since the communities' construction of knowledge might not be systematically translatable to the structures commonly used by the state and development agencies (Wallack & Srinivasan, 2009), or even academia (Meadows, 2010).

Conclusions

MLM studies have grown out of the increased prominence of debates about language in current European cultural politics (Cormack, 2004; Guyot, 2006). These recent debates, and those stemming from international resolutions or programmes for the protection of endangered cultures and languages (UNESCO, 2003, 2005, 2011a, 2011b; United Nations, 2008), as well as the political change in Latin America, in favour of indigenous and minority populations and their languages, underscore why MLM studies has risen as an important area of inquiry for contemporary European and Latin American communication research.

The indigenous and ethnic minorities which have become more visible in recent political constitutions in Latin American countries (e.g. Bolivia,

2008; Colombia, 1991; Venezuela, 1999) claim for spaces for their own views and wider access to media. Communication for Social Change has been historically connected to all those processes of media empowerment, and their lessons prove useful for research in the appearance of Latin American minority language media.

Answering the questions about *hybridity* and *convergence* in ethnic and indigenous media can provide a first assessment of MLM in Latin America. Thorough research, focused on the inner negotiations of identity within these media, would certainly be a good starting point, since only when the structures of identity of every specific group are understood would there be an opportunity to proceed to audience studies that will help understand how open to participation those media truly are.

On the other hand, MLM studies in Europe might also profit from including more participatory approaches to their research like the ones common to CfSC. They not only question the epistemological grounds of research but also address the issues of academic impact and feedback, two aspects that are now *en vogue* in higher education institutions across Europe under one question: Who *really* benefits from academic research?

Undeniably, CfSC and MLM studies can learn from each other's experience and establish a dialogue between Europe and Latin America. By doing so, they would not only expand the remit of their own areas of research but also promote a fruitful exchange between the two geographically bound communication research traditions they represent.

As highlighted above, Latin American research in communication has plenty to offer under CfSC. Its experiences and theoretical advances need to be made more widely available in European academic circles, in order to overcome Eurocentric biases still in place, because

> if the project of de-Westernizing communication science is left to the goodwill and righteousness of the oligopolistic centre, the pace of change would be very slow. (Gunaratne, 2010: 487).

References

Arnst, R. (1996) Participation approaches to the research process. In J. Servaes, T.L. Jacobson and S.A. White (eds) *Participatory Communication for Social Change* (pp. 109–126). New Delhi, Thousand Oaks & London: Sage Publications.

Beltrán Salmón, L.R. (2005) *La comunicación para el desarrollo en Latinoamérica: Un recuento de medio siglo*. Paper presented at the III Congreso Panamericano de la Comunicación, Buenos Aires. http://www.portalcomunicacion.com/both/temas/lramiro.pdf

Beltrán Salmón, L.R. (2006) A farewell to Aristotle: 'Horizontal' communication. In A. Gumucio Dagron and T. Tufte (eds) *Communication for Social Change Anthology: Historical and Contemporary Readings* (pp. 157–173). South Orange, NJ: Communication for Social Change Consortium.

Bolivia (2008) *Nueva Constitución Política del Estado*. La Paz: Asamblea Nacional Constituyente. Accessed 15 May 2011. http://www.presidencia.gob.bo/download/constitucion.pdf.

Browne, D.R. (1996) *Electronic Media and Indigenous Peoples: A Voice of Our Own?* Ames, Iowa: Iowa State University Press.

Browne, D.R. (2005) *Ethnic Minorities, Electronic Media and the Public Sphere: A Comparative Approach*. Cresskill, NJ: Hampton Press.

Browne, D.R. (2007) Speaking up: A brief history of minority languages and the electronic media worldwide. In M. Cormack and N. Hourigan (eds) *Minority Language Media: Concepts, Critiques, and Case Studies* (pp. 107–132). Clevedon: Multilingual Matters.

Castelló, E. (2007) The production of television fiction and nation building. *European Journal of Communication* 22 (1), 49–68. doi: 10.1177/0267323107073747.

Castells, M. (1997) *The Power of Identity*. Malden: Blackwell.

Castells, M. (2009) *Communication Power*. Oxford & New York: Oxford University Press.

Colombia (1991) *Constitución Política de Colombia*. Bogotá. Accessed 16 May 2011. http://www.banrep.gov.co/regimen/resoluciones/cp91.pdf.

Communication for Sustainable Development Initiative (2010) Indigenous peoples' communication for development. Rome: Food and Agriculture Organization of the United Nations. Accessed 16 May 2011. http://www.fao.org/docrep/012/i1552e/i1552e00.pdf.

Communication Initiative (Organization), FAO-UN and World Bank (2007) *World Congress on Communication for Development: Lessons, Challenges, and the Way Forward*. Washington, DC: World Bank.

Cormack, M. (1998) Minority language media in Western Europe. *European Journal of Communication* 13 (1), 33–52.

Cormack, M. (2000) Minority language media in a global age. *Mercator Media Forum* 4 (1), 3–15.

Cormack, M. (2004) Developing minority language media studies. *Mercator Media Forum* 7 (1), 3–12.

Cormack, M. (2007a) Introduction: Studying minority language media. In M. Cormack and N. Hourigan (eds) *Minority Language Media: Concepts, Critiques, and Case Studies* (pp. 1–16). Clevedon: Multilingual Matters.

Cormack, M. (2007b) The media and language maintenance. In M. Cormack and N. Hourigan (eds) *Minority Language Media: Concepts, Critiques, and Case Studies* (pp. 52–68). Clevedon: Multilingual Matters.

Cormack, M. and Hourigan, N. (eds) (2007) *Minority Language Media: Concepts, Critiques and Case Studies*. Clevedon: Multilingual Matters.

Deuze, M. (2006) Ethnic media, community media and participatory culture. *Journalism* 7 (3), 262–280. doi: 10.1177/1464884906065512.

Deuze, M. (2010) Convergence culture in the creative industries. In D.K. Thussu (ed.) *International Communication: A Reader* (pp. 452–467). London & New York: Routledge.

Escobar, A. (1995) *Encountering Development: The Making and Unmaking of the Third World*. Chichester & Princeton, NJ: Princeton University Press.

Evans, M.R. (2002) Hegemony and discourse: Negotiating cultural relationships through media production. *Journalism* 3 (3), 309–329.

Extra, G. and Gorter, D. (2008) The constellation of languages in Europe: An inclusive approach. In G. Extra and D. Gorter (eds) *Multilingual Europe: Facts and Policies* (pp. 3–60). Berlin & New York: Mouton de Gruyter.

Fairchild, C. (2001) *Community Radio and Public Culture: Being an Examination of Media Access and Equity in the Nations of North America*. Cresskill, NJ: Hampton Press.

Favre, H. (2006) La emergencia de identidades étnicas y la multiculturización de la sociedad en América Latina. *istor* 6 (24), 95–101.

Forde, S., Foxwell, K. and Meadows, M. (2009) *Developing Dialogues: Indigenous and Ethnic Community Broadcasting in Australia*. Bristol & Chicago: Intellect.

Fu, W.W. and Govindaraju, A. (2010) Explaining global box-office tastes in Hollywood films: Homogenization of national audiences' movie selection. *Communication Research* 37 (2), 215–238. doi: 10.1177/0093650209356396.

García Canclini, N. (2000) *Culturas híbridas: Estrategias para entrar y salir de la modernidad*. Bogotá: Grijalbo.

Ginsburg, F. (1991) Indigenous media: Faustian contract or global village? *Cultural Anthropology* 6 (1), 92–112.

Ginsburg, F. (2008) Rethinking the digital age. In P. Wilson and M. Stewart (eds) *Global Indigenous Media: Cultures, Poetics, and Politics* (pp. 287–305). Durham & London: Duke University Press.

Girard, B., Friedrich-Ebert-Stiftung and Food and Agriculture Organization of the United Nations. Communication for Development Branch (2003) *The One to Watch: Radio, New ICTs and Interactivity*. Rome: Food and Agriculture Organization of the United Nations.

Gumucio-Dagron, A. (2007) Vertical minds versus horizontal cultures: An overview of participatory process and experiences. In J. Servaes (ed.) *Communication for Development and Social Change* (pp. 68–81). Los Angeles: Sage.

Gumucio-Dagron, A. and Tufte, T. (2006) Roots and relevance: Introduction to the CfSC anthology. In A. Gumucio Dagron and T. Tufte (eds) *Communication for Social Change Anthology: Historical and Contemporary Readings* (pp. xiv–xxxvi). South Orange, NJ: Communication for Social Change Consortium.

Gunaratne, S.A. (2010) De-westernizing communication/social science research: Opportunities and limitations. *Media, Culture and Society* 32 (3), 473–500. doi: 10.1177/0163443709361159.

Guyot, J. (2006) Diversidad lingüística, comunicación y espacio público. *Comunicación y Sociedad* 5, 115–136.

Hourigan, N. (2004) *Escaping the Global Village: Media, Language and Protest*. Lanham, MD: Lexington Books.

Hourigan, N. (2007) Minority language media studies: Key themes for future scholarship. In M. Cormack and N. Hourigan (eds) *Minority Language Media: Concepts, Critiques, and Case Studies* (pp. 248–265). Clevedon: Multilingual Matters.

Husband, C. (2005) Minority ethnic media as communities of practice: Professionalism and identity politics in interaction. *Ethnic and Migration Studies* 31 (3), 461–479. doi: 10.1080/13691830500058802.

Islas-Carmona, O. (2008) El prosumidor: El actor comunicativo de la sociedad de la ubicuidad. *Palabra Clave* 11(1), 29–39.

Jenkins, H. (2006) *Convergence Culture: Where Old and New Media Collide*. New York & London: New York University Press.

Kraidy, M.M. (2010) Hybridity in cultural globalization. In D.K. Thussu (ed.) *International Communication: A Reader* (pp. 434–451). London & New York: Routledge.

Leguy, C. (2007) Revitalizing the oral tradition: Stories broadcast by Radio Parana (San, Mali). *Research in African Literatures* 38(3), 136–147.

Luykx, A. (2001) Across the Andean airwaves: Satellite radio broadcasting in Quechua. In C. Moseley, N. Ostler and H. Ouzzate (eds) *Endangered Languages and the Media* (pp. 115–119). Agadir, Morocco.

Martínez, M.J., Paladines G.F.Y. and Yaguache Q.J.J. (2008) Relación medio-comunidad a través del estudio del programa Kawsaypura Yachanakushun en el cantón Saraguro. *Palabra Clave* 11 (1), 41–52.

Meadows, M.H. (2009) Walking the talk: Reflections of indigenous audience research methods. *Participations: Journal of Audience & Reception Studies* 6 (1), 118–136.

Meadows, M.H. (2010) Conducting conversations: Exploring the audience–producer relationship in indigenous media research. *Observatorio (OBS*)* 4 (4), 307–324.

Meadows, M.H. and Molnar, H. (2002) Bridging the gaps: Towards a history of indigenous media in Australia. *Media History* 8 (1), 9–20.

Miller, J.L. (2010) Ugly Betty goes global. *Global Media and Communication* 6 (2), 198–217. doi: 10.1177/1742766510373717.

Miller, V. (2008) New media, networking and phatic culture. *Convergence: The International Journal of Research into New Media Technologies* 14 (4), 387–400. doi: 10.1177/1354856508094659.

Nichols, R.L. (2006) 'Struggling with language': Indigenous movements for linguistic security and the politics of local community. *Ethnicities* 6 (1), 27–51.

O'Reilly, C.C. (2001) Introduction: Minority languages, ethnicity and the State in the European Union. In C.C. O'Reilly (ed.) *Language, Ethnicity and the State: Vol. 1: Minority Languages in the European Union* (pp. 1–20). Hampshire & New York: Palgrave.

Peissl, H. and Tremetzberger, O. (2008) Community medien in Europa: Rechtliche und wirtschaftliche Rahmenbedingungen des dritten Rundfunksektors in 5 Länder. In RTR (ed.) *Nichtkommerzieller Rundfunk in Österreich und Europa* (Vol. 3). Wien: RTR-GmbH.

Pietikäinen, S. (2008a) Broadcasting indigenous voices. *European Journal of Communication* 23 (2), 173–191. doi: 10.1177/0267323108089221.

Pietikäinen, S. (2008b) 'To breathe two airs': Empowering indigenous Sámi media. In P. Wilson and M. Stewart (eds) *Global Indigenous Media: Cultures, Poetics and Politics* (pp. 214–231). Durham & London: Duke University Press.

Riggins, S.H. (1992a) The media imperative: Ethnic minority survival in the age of mass communication. In S.H. Riggins (ed.) *Ethnic Minority Media: An International Perspective* (pp. 1–20). Newbury Park, London & New Delhi: Sage Publications.

Riggins, S.H. (ed.) (1992b) *Ethnic Minority Media: An International Perspective.* Newbury Park, London & New Delhi: Sage Publications.

Rivera-Betancur, J.L. and Uribe-Jongbloed, E. (2011) La suerte de la fea, muchas la desean: De 'Yo soy Betty, la Fea' a 'Ugly Betty'. In M.Á. Pérez-Gómez (ed.) *Previously On: Estudios multidisciplinares sobre las series de la tercera edad dorada de la televisión.* Sevilla: Biblioteca de la Facultad de Comunicación de la Universidad de Sevilla.

Rivero, Y.M. (2003) The performance and reception of televisual "Ugliness" in Yo soy Betty, la fea. *Feminist Media Studies* 3 (1), 65–81. doi: 10.1080/1468077032000080130.

Rodriguez, C. and El Gazi, J. (2007) The poetics of indigenous radio in Colombia. *Media, Culture and Society* 29 (3), 449–468.

Roth, L. (2006) *Something New in the Air.* Montreal: Queens University/McGill Press.

Roveda Hoyos, A. (2008) Identidades locales, lenguajes y medios de comunicación: Entre búsquedas, lógicas y tensiones. *Signo y Pensamiento* 53 (1), 61–69.

Salazar, F. and Cordova, A. (2008) Imperfect media and the politics of indulgence video in Latin America. In P. Wilson and M. Stewart (eds) *Global Indigenous Media: Culture, Poetics and Politics* (pp. 39–57). Durham & London: Duke University Press.

Sampedro Blanco, V.F. (2004) Identidades mediáticas e identificaciones mediatizadas: Visibilidad y reconocimiento identitario en los medios de comunicación. *Revista CIDOB d'Afers Internacionals (66–67)*, 135–149.

Servaes, J. (1996a) Introduction: Participatory communication and research in development settings. In J. Servaes, T.L. Jacobson and S.A. White (eds) *Participatory Communication for Social Change* (pp. 13–25). New Delhi, Thousand Oaks & London: Sage Publications.

Servaes, J. (1996b) Participatory communication research with new social movements: A realistic utopia. In J. Servaes, T.L. Jacobson and S.A. White (eds) *Participatory Communication and Social Change* (pp. 82–108). New Delhi, Thousand Oaks & London: Sage Publications.

Smith, L. (2008) The search for well-being: Placing development with indigenous identity. In P. Wilson and M. Stewart (eds) *Global Indigenous Media: Cultures, Poetics, and Politics* (pp. 183–196). Durham & London: Duke University Press.

Sparks, C. (2007) *Globalization, Development and the Mass Media*. Los Angeles & London: Sage.

UNESCO (2003) Convention for the Safeguarding of Intangible Cultural Heritage. Paris: UNESCO. Accessed 17 May 2011. http://unesdoc.unesco.org/images/0013/001325/132540e.pdf

UNESCO (2005) Convention on the Protection and Promotion of the Diversity of Cultural Expressions, accessed 18 May 2011. http://unesdoc.unesco.org/images/0014/001429/142919e.pdf.

UNESCO (2011a) Endangered languages, accessed 16 May 2011. http://www.unesco.org/new/en/culture/themes/cultural-diversity/languages-and-multilingualism/endangered-languages/.

UNESCO (2011b, 11 May 2011) UNESCO Atlas of the world's languages in danger, accessed 16 May 2011. http://www.unesco.org/culture/languages-atlas/en/atlasmap.html.

Unidad de Radio (2002) *Memorias del encuentro internacional de radios indígenas de América*. Bogotá: Ministerio de Cultura.

United Nations (2008) United Nations Declaration on the Rights of Indigenous Peoples. UN. Accessed 21/11/2009. http://www.un.org/esa/socdev/unpfii/documents/DRIPS_en.pdf.

Uribe-Jongbloed, E. and Peña Sarmiento, M.F. (2008) Medios en idiomas autóctonos minoritarios en Colombia: El caso de la radio. *Palabra Clave* 11 (2), 355–366.

Venezuela (1999) *Constitución de la República Bolivariana de Venezuela*. Caracas: Gaceta Oficial. Accessed 17 May 2011. http://www.ucv.ve/fileadmin/user_upload/auditoria_interna/Archivos/Material_de_Descarga/Constitucion_de_la_Republica_Bolivariana_de_Venezuela_-_36.860.pdf.

Wallack, J.S. and Srinivasan, R. (2009) Local–global: Reconciling mismatched ontologies in development information systems. *HICSS*. Accessed 16 May 2011. http://rameshsrinivasan.org/wordpress/wp-content/uploads/2010/03/FinalDocWallackSrinivasan1.pdf.

Wang, G. and Yeh, E.Y-y. (2005) Globalization and hybridization in cultural products. *International Journal of Cultural Studies* 8 (2), 175–193. doi: 10.1177/1367877905052416.

Wenger, E. (1998) *Communities of Practice: Learning, Meaning, and Identity*. Cambridge: Cambridge University Press.

Wilson, P. and Stewart, M. (eds) (2008) *Global Indigenous Media: Cultures, Poetics and Politics*. Durham & London: Duke University Press.

2 Towards Ethnolinguistic Identity Gratifications

László Vincze and Tom Moring

Introduction

This chapter presents a theoretical approach to study the relation between media and language in bilingual settings. Taking Social Identity Gratifications (Harwood, 1997, 1999) as a starting point, we propose that ethnolinguistic identity can be a motivational factor worth considering when studying the impact of media on language minorities. Media, in turn, can strengthen or weaken ethnolinguistic identity. To examine the relevance of this approach, we deliver an empirical investigation of the patterns and contexts of bilingual media use in Finland among both the Finnish-speaking and the Swedish-speaking population. This study, unique in its way, indicates that ethnolinguistic identity indeed is a determining component of media use. However, the language character of media use is considerably affected by other circumstances as well, that is the availability of a rich and varied media supply targeted at the minority.

Ethnolinguistic Identity Gratifications

The Social Identity Gratifications Theory was developed based on the Social Identity Theory (Tajfel & Turner, 1979) and the Uses and Gratifications Theory (Katz et al., 1973, 1974). This theory suggests that social categories like age, gender, social class and others can be motivational variables for searching specific media uses, while media in this way can support positive social comparisons with other groups (Harwood, 1997, 1999). Harwood (1999: 123) argued that individuals may seek media depictions that 'strengthen their identification with a particular social group and/or make that identification more positive'.

In a similar vein, we propose that ethnolinguistic identity can also be a motivational variable for using specific media, while media in this way can support a positive ethnolinguistic identity. According to Ethnolinguistic

Identity Theory (ELIT; see Giles & Johnson, 1981, 1987), in cases where language is a valued component of identification, individuals 'will wish to assume a positive differentiation along ethnolinguistic dimensions in search of a positive ethnolinguistic identity' (Giles & Byrne, 1982: 19). ELIT claims that the degree to which individuals are motivated to maintain a positive social identity that is derived from membership of a particular ethnolinguistic group depends mainly on perceived ethnolinguistic vitality. Ethnolinguistic vitality is composed of several components: the status, the demography and the institutional support of the ethnolinguistic group (see Bourhis *et al.*, 1981); perceived group boundaries (Giles, 1979; Ross, 1979); and the features of their multiple group memberships, that is how determining is language in the whole identity construction.

Ethnolinguistic Identity Gratifications can be considered as an integration of two separate theories, Ethnolinguistic Identity Theory (developed within social psychology) and Uses and Gratifications Theory (developed within media and communication research). However, in contrast to much of the research based on Uses and Gratifications Theory, in Ethnolinguistic Identity Gratifications research the focus is not only on the message but also on the mode of transmission, that is the language of the media use. Furthermore, this approach implies that ethnolinguistic identity is not the only, exclusive variable in the process of media use. Rather, it can be seen as a co-function, whereas other functions considered by Uses and Gratifications research, such as surveillance or entertainment, work simultaneously. Taken all these assumptions together, Ethnolinguistic Identity Gratifications brings the reflection that language is seen not only as a tool but also as an aim of media use.

Nonetheless, the gratification of specific ethnolinguistic needs through media is influenced also, to a great extent, by the linguistic composition of the media system (in other words, the quantity and quality of media provided in the different languages). The supply of minority language media is of key importance to language minorities, and it determines the habits of media use (see Moring, 2007). Language minorities often do not have the possibility to access certain media contents in their native language, and in such cases they have no other option but to rely on the majority language. Consequently, offering sufficient media in the minority language is an objective condition for Ethnolinguistic Identity Gratifications.

Therefore, turning back to Uses and Gratifications traditions (Palmgreen *et al.*, 1980), we regard it necessary to make a distinction between gratifications sought (GS) and gratifications obtained (GO). This differentiation refers to gratifications a person wants to reach/gain via media use and gratifications she or he has reached/gained only after the use of the media. In an ethnolinguistic context, to put it simply, we distinguish between the language in which somebody seeks different media contents and the language in which the given media content is obtained.

Swedish in Finland

Regarding ethnolinguistic vitality (Bourhis *et al.*, 1981), the Swedish language group in Finland can be considered as being strong in status and institutional support, but weaker when it comes to demography. Being one of Finland's two national languages, Swedish has high status. The rights of the languages are ensured by the language act, according to which Finnish or Swedish can be used in municipalities where the speakers of the language make up 8% or more of the local population or more than 3000 persons. The high status of Swedish is accompanied by a strong institutional support at both formal and informal level, including educational institutions at all levels, political parties, a Swedish Lutheran diocese and a navy marine infantry where the training is provided in Swedish. Today, Swedish speakers make up 5.4% of the population of Finland (about 285,000 people). However, it is important to note that the Swedish-speaking population has continuously decreased from the 1940s, both in absolute and relative terms (Tandefelt & Finnäs, 2007).

In comparison to its modest size in Finland, the media landscape at the service of this small population is quite rich; there are eight daily newspapers, one has a national role, whereas the other are local or regional, although in two cases with a full-fledged agenda; there are two radio stations, one targeted mainly at a younger audience; and there is also a Swedish language television channel. It has to be noted that this media supply is produced in Finland and distributed by Finnish media companies, of which the Finnish Broadcasting Company (Yle) is one.

In addition to this domestically produced media, there is access to online services produced in Finland and Sweden.

Furthermore, in the region of Ostrobothnia, on the Finnish west coast where one-third of the Swedish speakers live, a good supply of television from Sweden (including also commercial channels) has traditionally been available either as transborder broadcast overspill or retransmitted at a small additional cost for the audience. This supply has, however, not been available in southern Finland, where the transborder supply has been limited to an edited channel including domestic production from the two Swedish public service television channels.

With regard to mainstream media supply, the landscape available in Swedish is thus almost *institutionally complete* (see Moring, 2007 for a definition of this term). The main shortcomings are a lack of heavily commercially driven media (e.g. commercial television outside Ostrobothnia, a yellow press and commercial weeklies) that are available only in Finnish, or as imports from Sweden. The relative completeness of the Swedish media landscape in Finland may also explain why community media, such as radio stations or local cable television, plays only a minuscule role in media provision and consumption among Swedish-speaking Finns. This generally rich media landscape provides an ideal case study on how media supply in a minority language may enhance linguistic vitality.

Material and Methods

- Participants: The empirical data was collected in 2009 amongst persons with Finnish ($N = 1122$) and Swedish ($N = 703$) as their registered mother tongue. The data was collected by TNS-Gallup Finland through pre-recruited and demographically representative panels, responding over internet.
- Measures: Ethnolinguistic Identity Gratifications sought (GS) and obtained (GO) were assessed in two ways. In the case of traditional media types, the respondents scored, on a five-grade scale, the language which they want to use and in which they actually use the different media (1 = only in Finnish; 5 = only in Swedish). In the case of new media, gratifications were measured by a nominal variable with the categories 'mostly in Finnish', 'mostly in Swedish' and 'mostly in English'. In other words, as the use of new media is usually very complex, these categories do not refer to monolingual activities but activities which are dominated by one language, not excluding the use of other languages.

    The independent variables can be grouped into two. Five grade scales were used to gauge in-group identification (1 = Finnish speaker; 2 = Finnish-dominated bilingual; 3 = balanced bilingual; 4= Swedish-dominated bilingual; 5 = Swedish speaker). Perceived inter-group boundary (1 = very soft; 5 = very hard) was composed from two variables, one measuring the strength of the border between the two language groups and the other assessing the quality of relationship between the two language groups (from 'very negative' to 'very positive'). Family language was measured by a nominal variable including three categories (1 = Swedish; 2 = Finnish; 3 = bilingual) based on the mother tongue of the respondent's spouse.

    The concept of local ethnolinguistic vitality is based on the idea that language competence, ethnolinguistic behaviour and ethnolinguistic identity can be affected by the local variation in the objective ethnolinguistic vitality (Henning-Lindblom & Liebkind, 2007; Landry & Allard, 1994). Because of this, municipalities were grouped into four categories according to the proportion of the Swedish speakers as part of the local population. The four categories were (1) monolingual Finnish municipality, and municipalities where Swedish speakers accounted for (2) up to a third (1%–33%), (3) between one-third and two-thirds (33%–67%) or (4) more than two-thirds (67%–100%) of the total population.

- Procedures: We examined the relationship between Ethnolinguistic Identity Gratifications obtained and the independent variables with different logit models. Regarding the traditional media types as dependent variables, we performed ordinal regressions with logit link-function. When investigating new media use, participants who use new media mostly in English were excluded from the analysis since English is not a local language. In the case of Swedish speakers, this resulted in a dichotomous dependent variable with categories 'mostly Swedish' and 'mostly Finnish'. Thus, nominal logistic regression was an appropriate tool for the analysis. In the case of the Finnish speakers, however, a regression could not be carried out since all respondents reported using Finnish or English as their major language when online. Descriptions of both the overall models and the effects of the individual predictors were summarized in tables.

Results

In the media use of the Swedish speakers, the Swedish language has its strongest position in newspaper reading. It is weaker in radio listening and weakest in TV viewing (see Figure 2.1). In parallel to this, it can also be stated that sought and obtained gratifications seems to be met in newspaper reading. They are farther from each other in radio listening, and the distance between them is largest when it comes to TV viewing.

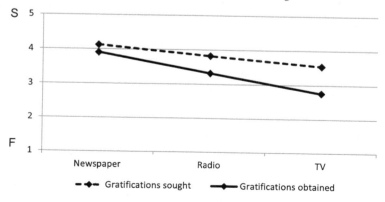

Figure 2.1 Ethnolinguistic Identity Gratifications sought and obtained

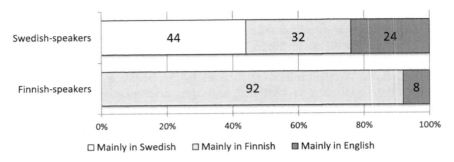

Figure 2.2 Use of new media

The Finnish language plays a decisive role particularly in new media use among Swedish speakers. As the chart in Figure 2.2 indicates, almost one-third of the participants use new media mostly in Finnish, while nearly a quarter use it in English. These outcomes could be difficult to be compared with the gratifications sought as the latter was measured on a bipolar scale from 'only in Swedish' to 'only in Finnish'; nevertheless, it is worth mentioning that roughly four times more respondents reported to prefer Swedish to Finnish in new media.

The results of the regression analyses (see Table 2.1) indicate that in-group identification, local vitality and family language are good predictors, while perceived intergroup boundary is not as good for media use in a given language. Participants who identify themselves stronger with the Swedish language group use the media more in Swedish than those whose identification with Swedish is weaker; people having a Swedish-speaking spouse use the media more in Swedish than those whose partner is a Finnish speaker; and respondents who live in municipalities where the local vitality of Swedish is stronger use the media more than people who live in locations where the share of Swedish speakers is smaller.

Divergence from the mother tongue in media use is considerably smaller among Finnish speakers than among Swedish speakers. Finnish speakers tend to use the traditional media almost only in Finnish regardless of the type of media (see Figure 2.3). Besides, it also seems to be apparent that gratifications sought and gratifications obtained fit well among the Finnish language group. Yet, it can be noticed that similar to Swedish speakers the linguistic flexibility is greater in the case of the electronic media.

The results of the regression analyses (see Table 2.2) highlight that people with a Swedish-speaking spouse use the media more regularly in Swedish than those whose partner speaks Finnish. It must be noted,

Table 2.1 Model fitting and estimates of logistic regressions of Ethnolinguistic Identity Gratifications obtained among Swedish speakers

	Newspaper	Radio	TV	New media
Overall model				
χ^2	203.422	218.606	215.276	199.136
p	<0.001	<0.001	<0.001	<0.001
Cox and Snell	0.288	0.296	0.292	0.351
Nagelkerke	0.340	0.313	0.320	0.472
McFadden	0.182	0.120	0.141	0.317
Individual predictors				
Family language				
Swedish	1.425***	0.721**	0.700***	1.427***
(bilingual)	–	–	–	–
Local vitality of Swedish				
High	1.004***	0.579**	1.745***	2.268***
Medium	0.437*	0.160	0.101	−0.419
(Low)	–	–	–	–
In-group identification	1.008***	1.168***	0.941***	1.192***
Inter-group boundary	−0.173*	−0.076	0.087	−0.224

Note: $^*p<0.05$, $^{**}p<0.01$, $^{***}p<0.005$

however, that the number of Finnish speakers with Swedish spouses in our sample is very small (only 20 persons) and can be assigned only indicative value. Similarly, respondents who identify themselves (at least to some extent) with Swedish tend to use media more regularly in Swedish than those who identify themselves only with the Finnish language. Interestingly, the local vitality of the Swedish language affects only the language use in radio listening. People who often have contact with the Swedish language in their environment are also more likely to use radio in Swedish. In contrast, local vitality of Swedish, that is the linguistic composition of the municipalities, plays no role when it comes to newspaper reading and TV-watching. Moreover, *inter-group boundary* seems to be associated with the use of radio and TV. In other words, Finnish speakers who perceive the *inter-group boundary* to be less marked use the two media types more commonly in Swedish than those who perceive the boundary to be harder.

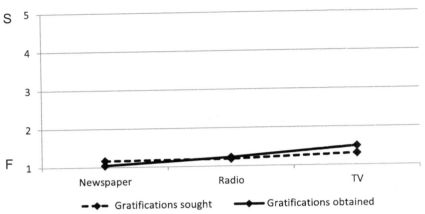

Figure 2.3 Ethnolinguistic Identity Gratifications sought and obtained among Finnish speakers ($N = 1122$)

Table 2.2 Model fitting and estimates of logistic regressions of Ethnolinguistic Identity Gratifications obtained among Finnish speakers

	Newspaper	Radio	TV
Overall model			
X^2	35.009	95.387	62.208
p	<0.001	<0.001	<0.001
Cox and Snell	0.045	0.104	0.069
Nagelkerke	0.244	0.162	0.092
McFadden	0.226	0.107	0.052
Individual predictors			
Family language			
Finnish	3.363***	1.929**	1.604**
(bilingual)	–	–	–
Local vitality of Swedish			
medium	-1.251	0.208	0.144
low	-0.692	-0.622**	0.249
(Finnish municipality)	–	–	–
In-group identification	-1.488**	-2.673***	-2.606***
Inter-group boundary	-0.402	0.157*	0.193**

Note: *$p<0.05$, **$p<0.01$, ***$p<0.005$

Conclusions and Discussion

This chapter has provided a theoretical model to study the language aspects of media use among ethnolinguistic minorities. Ethnolinguistic Identity Gratifications theory was tested in Finland among the two main language groups, the Finnish speakers (more than 90% of the population) and the Swedish speakers (less than 6% of the population). Our comparison of media use in the two groups showed a pattern that is clearly asymmetric in regards to media language, irrespective of a relatively institutionally complete media landscape in the minority language.

Among Finnish speakers, we saw small divergence from Finnish, and among Swedish speakers relatively large divergence from Swedish. Gratifications sought and obtained seemed to be met among Finnish speakers, but not amongst Swedish speakers. While the gratification gap showed similar variations between different media types, newspapers and radio being more related to language than television, the differences were clearly larger for the minority group.

Some variables did not prove to be good predictors of minority language media use. Family language and in-group identification as background variables work likewise for both groups. Perception of inter-group boundary does not seem to be crucial among Swedish speakers (it is significant only in the use of one out of the four media types). Nonetheless, in-group boundary seems to be more important among Finnish speakers, as it was significant regarding the use of two out of the three examined media types. This may be explained by the fact that, in Finland, *inter-group boundary* is quite soft, as indicated by the great number of linguistically mixed marriages. The proportion of bilingual people and inter-group partnerships is, however, much larger among Swedish speakers than among Finnish speakers.

Interestingly, local vitality of Swedish is a very important predictor in media use among Swedish speakers, whereas it is a rather weak predictor of media use among Finnish speakers. This outcome is yet another indicator of the asymmetries that prevail between majority and minority; the linguistic composition of the surrounding environment affects linguistic affiliation and behaviour much more among Swedish speakers than among Finnish speakers. Most probably, Swedish speakers use more Finnish if it is more present in their environment *but* Finnish speakers do not use much more Swedish even when it is more present in their environment.

Finally, we must point out the importance of the supply factor. Considerable *institutional completeness* is a prerequisite to the application of the Ethnolinguistic Identity Gratification Theory, since it affects not only gratifications obtained but also gratifications sought: nobody seeks media content that does not exist. This finding highlights the importance of a rich and varied media landscape in the minority language. These results have been further qualified by within-group comparisons between media use among Swedish speakers in the more bilingual southern Finland and the more linguistically divided region of Ostrobothnia (Moring & Nordqvist, 2002).

In conclusion, we consider that this empirical test of Ethnolinguistic Identity Gratifications Theory proves the usefulness of the approach as a tool in examining bilingual media use. However, further refinement and more empirical support are still required in order to furnish more general results about the appropriateness of the variables included in this work.

Acknowledgements

The authors would like to acknowledge that this chapter has been written as part of the project 'Bilingualism, Identity and the Media in Inter- and Intra-cultural Comparisons (BIM)'. This project has received financing from the Academy of Finland (Project 1123686). We also want to show our gratitude to Andrea Nordqvist who collected the data used here.

References

Bourhis, R.Y., Giles, H. and Rosenthal, D. (1981) Notes on the construction of a 'subjective vitality questionnaire' for ethnolinguistic groups. *Journal of Multilingual and Multicultural Development* 2 (2), 145–155.

Giles, H. (1979) Ethnicity markers in speech. In K.R. Scherer and H. Giles (eds) *Social Markers in Speech* (pp. 251–289). Cambridge: Cambridge University Press.

Giles, H. and Byrne, J.L. (1982) An intergroup approach to second language acquisition. *Journal of Multilingual and Multicultural Development* 3 (1), 17–40.

Giles, H. and Johnson, P. (1981) The role of language in ethnic group relations. In J.C. Turner and H. Giles (eds) *Intergroup Behaviour* (pp. 199–243). Oxford: Blackwell.

Giles, H. and Johnson, P. (1987) Ethnolinguistic identity theory: A social psychological approach to language maintenance. *International Journal of the Sociology of Language* 63, 69–99.

Harwood, J. (1997) Viewing age: Lifespan identity and television viewing choices. *Journal of Broadcasting & Electronic Media* 41 (2), 203–213.

Harwood, J. (1999) Age identification, social identity gratifications, and television viewing. *Journal of Broadcasting & Electronic Media* 43 (1), 123–136.

Henning-Lindblom, A. and Liebkind, K. (2007) Objective ethnolinguistic vitality and identity among Swedish-speaking youth. *International Journal of the Sociology of Language* 187/188, 161–184.

Katz, E., Blumler, J.G. and Gurevitch, M. (1974) Utilization of mass communication by the individual. In J.G. Blumler and E. Katz (eds) *The Uses of Mass Communications: Current Perspectives on Gratifications Research* (pp. 19–32). Beverly Hills: Sage Publications.

Katz, E., Haas, H. and Gurevitch, M. (1973) On the use of the mass media for important things. *American Sociological Review* 38 (2), 164–181.

Landry, R. and Allard, R. (1994) Diglossia, ethnolinguistic vitality, and language behavior. *International Journal of the Sociology of Language* 108, 15–42.

Moring, T. (2007) Functional completeness in minority language media. In M. Cormack and N. Hourigan (eds) *Minority Language Media: Concepts, Critiques and Case Studies* (pp. 17–33). Clevedon: Multilingual Matters.

Moring, T. and Nordqvist, A. (2002) *Svenska medier i Finland [Swedish media in Finland]*. Forskningsinstitutet, Svenska social- och kommunalhögskolan vid Helsingfors universitet.

Palmgreen, P., Wenner, L. A. and Rayburn, J.D. (1980) Relations between gratifications sought and obtained. *Communication Research* 7 (2), 161–192. doi: 10.1177/009365028000700202.

Ross, J.A. (1979) Language and the mobilisation of ethnic identity. In H. Giles and B. Saint-Jacques (eds) *Language and Ethnic Relations* (pp. 1–14). New York: Pergamon.

Tajfel, H. and Turner, J. (1979) An integrative theory of intergroup conflict. In W.G. Austin and S. Worchel (eds) *The Social Psychology of Intergroup Relations* (pp. 94–109). Monterey, CA: Brooks-Cole.

Tandefelt, M. and Finnäs, F. (2007) Language and demography: Historical development. *International Journal of the Sociology of Language* 187/188, 35–54.

3 Minority Language Media, Convergence Culture and the Indices of Linguistic Vitality

Elin Haf Gruffydd Jones

Introduction

This chapter first emerged as a conference paper with the somewhat mischievous pre-title 'Brezhoneg [Breton] overtakes Cymraeg [Welsh] in the 21st century', the purpose of which was to draw attention to three particular aspects of the discourse of linguistic vitality, before focusing more specifically on its relationship with minority language media and convergence culture. First of all, the pre-title was used to tease out the relationship between any singular index (or combination of indices) of linguistic vitality and the tacit knowledge of the strengths and weaknesses of language communities based on a 'common sense' judgement; second, to emphasize the temporality of linguistic vitality and recall the rapidity with which transformational shifts can occur in linguistic communities; and third, to consider the pervasiveness of the comparative approach – both across language communities and over time – that seems to be fundamental in the debate concerning linguistic vitality.

In the case of the first aspect, anyone with a basic understanding of the sociolinguistic positions of both Welsh and Breton would be expected to respond that if a vitality indicator leads to the result that Breton is overtaking Welsh in the 21st century, then it must be the case that the selected index is quite insignificant (such as 'the number of bombard players' who speak either language) or that the methodology (or its application) is seriously flawed. For this pre-title goes against the grain of our 'common sense' judgement regarding the positions of Welsh and Breton and thus raises the question of the significance and meaning of individual indices. Which indices are best used to fully comprehend the linguistic vitality of a language community?

As far as the second aspect is concerned, that of the temporality of linguistic vitality, the statistical evidence that we have access to indicates that Breton did, in fact, exceed Welsh at the turn of the 20th century, in numbers of speakers at least. This is hardly an insignificant or a controversial vitality indicator; on the contrary, in terms of language endangerment and language death, it is ultimately the only real, absolute, single indicator that counts. In the absence of any data from the official French state census, Ofis (Publik) ar Brezhoneg/Office (public) de la langue bretonne affirms that 'at the beginning of the twentieth century, it is estimated that the number of Breton speakers was more than one million, almost the whole of the population of Lower Brittany'. The Diwan Schools Movement cites 1.3 million Breton speakers in 1900 and other sources suggest 1.5 and 1.8 million in the last decades of the 19th century. In the case of Welsh, the UK Census of 1891 shows some 900,000 Welsh speakers (monolingual and bilingual) in Wales and 928,000 in 1901. By the turn of the 21st century, however, Ofis Publik ar Brezhoneg estimated that the number of Breton speakers was at 206,000 (according to Broudic's study) with 61% of them over 60 years old, resulting in some 80,000 Breton speakers under the age of 60. The UK Census 2001 showed 582,368 Welsh speakers with some 20% over 65 years old, therefore some 485,000 under the age of 65, six-fold the Breton equivalent. Therefore, in the course of a century, we have witnessed two quite different trajectories in the cases of Breton and Welsh, though both are, nevertheless, in a state of decline. A closer look at the Welsh figures reveals that it is only in the oldest age group of the adult population (75 years or older) that the percentage of Welsh speakers is over 20%, whereas the overall average of whole population including children over 3 years old is 21.7%. During the course of this 21st century, what is the likely prognosis for the two languages? How likely are we to see a language shift that leads to the number of Breton speakers 'overtaking' that of Welsh, possibly through a rapidity of decline over two or three generations in the Welsh case? Will there be a major revival in either of the two language groups? Shall we a see a levelling out? The underlying question here is whether the indices that we select can be applied in such a way that damaging and rapid shifts in linguistic vitality can be foreseen, so that there may be attempts to counteract them, in part at least.

Third, to what extent is it useful to retain a comparative aspect to questions of linguistic vitality across language communities? How can comparative analysis assist positive language planning, promote meaningful interventions and induce successful community action? How can comparative analysis lead to a better understanding of the singular or specific case studies, again with a view towards positive planning? Can comparison help us tease out factors that may have remained hidden otherwise? To what extent do minority language communities need to engage in comparative analysis with other such groups? After all, the condition of being a 'minority' or 'minoritised' implies a comparative status, even if this is viewed only in relation to the majority group. Instead of using the latent comparative context of the majority language group, would the minority language group gain a different view of itself by comparison with other minority groups? Can taking a closer look at comparative cases (even if their circumstances are quite different in our 'common sense' approach) alert us to potentially harmful situations?

The specific index used in the playful pre-title that produced the outcome of Breton overtaking Welsh in the 21st century was the 'number of Wikipedia articles in each language'. This was certainly not the most conventional of indices, and quite provocatively yielded the result that in May 2010 there were 33,362 articles in Breton and 27,320 in Welsh, with 37,667 and 32,463, respectively, a year later. It is by no means the only index that could be taken from the Wikipedia context (other examples might be the number of users, number of accessed pages, edits, administrators, contributors or 'depth' of articles, etc.), but is it an entirely insignificant index? It certainly reveals that the sections of the Breton language community that are engaged in creating the Breton Wikipedia are having more success than those in the Welsh language community in terms of producing numbers of articles. There may well be a myriad of reasons for this. It may simply be the case of volunteer-dependent Breton organizations taking an opportunistic approach to Wikipedia in the face of scarce public funding and the more institutionalized, affluent Welsh sector presenting a sense of reluctance or snobbery towards it. Has the Breton language culture 'got' what it is to create online resources using their established sense of volunteerism or what Shirky has termed as 'cognitive surplus' (Shirky, 2010) and what Jenkins refers to as 'collective intelligence' (Jenkins, 2006)? Are Breton language activists, in fact, behaving in ways that are comparable to those of fan cultures?

Whatever the significance of the 'number of Wikipedia articles' as a meaningful index of linguistic vitality, similar performance indicators are increasingly being used both in serious research and in our 'common sense' repertoires of such indices, such as the presence of minority languages on Facebook (see chapters in this volume) and Twitter, which according to http://indigenoustweets.com, shows that up to May 2011, there were almost as many Welsh Twitterers as there were Breton tweets. Some 305,296 tweets in Welsh compared to 2791 in Breton (including 1705 or 60% from a single source) and 2738 Twitter users of Welsh compared to 45 of Breton. Social media indicators are increasingly being used in order to measure the linguistic vitality of language communities.

The underlying question that this chapter aims to address is what kind of changes should be made to the existing sets of indices of linguistic vitality as we establish ourselves in the age of convergence culture? Which new indicators should be included and which are no longer useful? How should we adapt the indices pertaining to 'minority language media' in the context of the emergence of social media? In the first instance, however, it is useful to review the position of 'media' as a significant indicator of linguistic vitality in existing indices.

'Media' as a Significant Indicator

While few people would seriously question the validity of including 'education in the language' in the repertoire of significant indices of linguistic vitality, the same cannot always be said of 'media in the language'. Several commentators working in the field of minority language media studies (for instance, Cormack, 2004; Jones, 2007; Kelly-Holmes, 2001; O'Connell in this volume) have highlighted the reluctance on the part of highly reputed sociolinguists and firm advocates of language planning to seriously consider the importance of the media in minority language communities by citing Joshua Fishman's somewhat cavalier footnote that refers to the 'mass-media "fetish" of some minority language activists appears in its true unrealistic light' (Fishman, 2001: 482). This is not a singular throw-away comment at the margins of his writings; he confirms this view further in the main body of the text, and states that 'the Xish media (Fishman's term for "minority language") are really a weak reed for RLS (Reversing Language Shift) to lean upon substantially' (Fishman, 1991: 107).

Fishman is not alone in his view that an eagerness to establish media in one's own language cannot always be substantiated with real progress in minority language use and lead to an increase in linguistic vitality. As Donald Browne has observed, 'There is virtually no "hard" (scientific) evidence to indicate that the initiation of an indigenous language media service helps to restore or revive its usage, but all stations broadcasting substantial amounts of such languages certainly have that hope and expectation' (Browne, 1996: 169). In the same vein, Guyot (2004: 19) also commented that '(m)edia use is not a sufficient condition in itself to change the situation' for minoritised languages.

Of course, many of these comments echo the arguments found in conventional media studies with regard to the 'media effects' debate. The prevailing 'common sense' view in the general population is that excessive exposure to some types of media products (usually violent films or games are cited) can induce some 'copy cat' behaviour, especially in children and the vulnerable. Yet this view is considered to be too simplistic in academic debate and has long been rejected. The 'hypodermic needle effect' theory has for several decades been superseded by a succession of theories and contemporary debates focuses on a multifaceted, contextualized approach to the relationship between text and user (for a concise, comprehensive review of the 'media effects' debate see, for example, Williams, 2003), drawing on the polysemy of texts, the processes of multiple readings, genre analysis, audience reception and other extra-textual factors. Claims to direct, causal, immediate and universal relationships between media content and human behaviour are highly contentious and are not substantiated by reputable empirical evidence. The 'media violence' debate illuminates this point quite effectively, where high-profile claims of direct influence continue to have currency in public debate yet are not substantiated with empirical, independent evidence (see Barker & Petley, 1997). Within such an environment, why should we expect to find empirical evidence to support a causal relationship between 'exposure' to minority languages through the media and ensuing linguistic 'behaviour' of the speakers of the languages concerned?

However, researchers of minority language media, including those who point to lack of direct, causal empirical evidence, have continued to draw attention to the indirect benefits of having media operating in one's own language. Guyot (2004: 22) refers to media's role as 'part of the range of means that help a language to conquer a wider audience and escape marginalization'. Examining the specific case of television, I have outlined the 'five primary functions of television – communicative, cultural, economic, status and linguistic' that 'form the basis of the arguments why this medium is essential for the well-being of any (minority) language community' indicating that '[t]hey also point to the limitations that a language community might experience if it does not have its own television service' (Jones, 2007: 190). Discussing the media more widely, Moring and Husband (2007: 78) present seven aspects of media impact, drawing on Cormack (2004) for the first five, namely the symbolic, the economic, the public sphere, the representational and the cultural aspects, and incorporating another two, which may be summarized as 'routine exposure to the language' and 'linguistic reconstruction'. Such views reinforce the contextualized and holistic approach that recognizes an inter-dependence between a variety of factors at play and an acknowledgement of the difficulties in attributing a simple, direct, causal, immediate and universal relationship between the media and the linguistic behaviour and hence language vitality.

Reviewing the Position of 'Media' in Indices of Linguistic Vitality

An overview of the dominant existing indices of linguistic vitality shows that 'media' are generally identified as separate and significant indicators. Gorter (2008) has produced a very useful synthesis of four of the most well-known and most widely applied frameworks of assessing linguistic vitality: Joshua Fishman's Graded Intergenerational Disruption Scale or GIDS (1991; see Table 3.1), Euromosaic's Cluster Analysis of Production and Reproduction of the Minority Language Groups (1996; see Table 3.2), the Specific Articles of the Council of Europe's (1992) European Charter for Regional or Minority Languages (see Tables 3.3 and 3.4) and the UNESCO Vitality Factors (2003; see Table 3.5).

Table 3.1 Adaptation of Fishman's GIDS

Stage 1	Some use of the language in higher education, occupational, government and **media*** efforts (without political independence)
Stage 2	Use of language in lower government services and **mass media** but not in the higher spheres of either
Stage 3	Use of language in lower work sphere
Stage 4	Language in compulsory primary/lower education sector
Stage 5	Attain 'guided literacy' through informal routes (family, neighbourhood, etc.) without extra-communal (or official) reinforcement
Stage 6	Attain intergenerational informal oralcy, demographic concentration and institutional reinforcement
Stage 7	Used in socially integrated and ethnolinguistic adult population beyond childbearing age
Stage 8	Language is being reassembled and taught to demographically dispersed adults

*My adaptation (in bold) from Fishman's Graded Intergenerational Disruption Scale.

Table 3.2 Euromosaic Study 1996

General description on the language group
1. Geographical and language background 2. General history of the region and the language group 3. Legal status and official policies *Presence and use of the language in various fields* 1. Education 2. Judicial authorities 3. Public authorities and services **4. Mass media and information technology** 5. The arts 6. The business world 7. Family and social use of the language ▪

Source: From Nelde *et al.* (1996)

Table 3.3 European Charter for Regional or Minority Languages (Council of Europe, 1992)

Specific Articles of the European Charter for Regional or Minority Languages (1992)	
Article 8	Education
Article 9	Judicial authorities
Article 10	Administrative authorities and public services
Article 11	**Media**
Article 12	Cultural activities and facilities
Article 13	Economic and social life
Article 14	Transfrontier exchanges

Table 3.4 Focus on 'media' in European Charter for Regional or Minority Languages (1998)

Article 11: Media
1(a). Radio station and television channel and/or broadcasters offer programmes 1(b). Radio station and/or the broadcasting of radio programmes 1(c). Television channel and/or the broadcasting of television programmes 1(d). Production and distribution of audio and audiovisual works 1(e). Newspaper and the publication of newspaper articles 1(f). Media and audiovisual productions 1(g). Training of journalists and other staff 2.   Freedom of direct reception of radio and television broadcasts from neighbouring countries; re-transmission of radio and television broadcasts 3.   Guarantee the freedom and pluralism of the media

Table 3.5 UNESCO vitality factors

Factor 1	Intergenerational language transmission
Factor 2	Absolute number of speakers
Factor 3	Proportion of speakers within the total population
Factor 4	Trends in existing language domains
Factor 5	**Response to New Domains and Media**
Factor 6	Materials for language education and literacy
Factor 7	Government and institutional language attitudes and policies
Factor 8	Community members' attitudes toward their own language
Factor 9	Amount and quality of documentation

Source: UNESCO Language Vitality and Endangerment

Gorter's comparative table draws attention to the commonalities and differences between these four frameworks, noting that the GIDS and Euromosaic are more 'research orientated' and that the Charter and the UNESCO vitality factors have more of a 'directly applied purpose'. Although his specific focus in this publication is the context of language learning (Gorter, 2008: 174), his comments are useful in the context of the media in relation to the four frameworks, and concludes that '[h]ow and how much language learning takes place through the media is difficult to establish because as a separate factor it is hard to isolate' (Gorter, 2008: 175).

In terms of other impacts on linguistic vitality through the media, all four frameworks recognize the role of the media, even if there are variations as to the significance and effectiveness of such intervention.

Changes in the Media Landscape

The four frameworks noted above refer to the media in the pre-convergence age. Proposals have been made recently to extend Fishman's GIDS (see Lewis & Simons, 2010). However, these suggestions have not been inspired by the changes in the media and communication environment. Instead, they are largely motivated by a concern that the upper and lower ends of Fishman's scale do not encompass the necessary distinctions to incorporate all the world's languages into the framework. Two additional categories (Stages 9 and 10) are proposed at the bottom end of the scale and one at the top, so that a distinction can be made between 'national' languages (Fishman's Stage 1) and 'international' languages' (Lewis and Simons' proposed Stage 0). The authors also add that it is assumed that 'few if any minority languages will even aspire to this level of safety and use' (Lewis & Simons, 2010: 111). Given the context of increased human mobility and the internationalization of communication through the internet, it seems quite likely that even minority languages will experience a greater sense of 'international' or transnational presence, even if this kind of international presence will by no means guarantee 'safety'.

The UNESCO vitality factors were under review at the time of writing this chapter, but in any case 'new domains' are included in the same vitality factor as 'media'. The details of UNESCO's approach to new communications through social media will be worth further studying. The text of the European Charter for Regional or Minority Languages specifies the channel of distribution, as well as the form of media (using pre-convergence genres, radio station, television channel and programmes, newspapers, see Table 3.4), is unlikely to be changed in its wording in response to the new context. However, it has already been pointed out (Moring & Dunbar, 2008: 13) that 'the provisions of the charter do not clearly define exactly how these matters [e.g. the internet] should be assessed'. Difficulty in 'isolating the media as a separate factor' is likely to continue if not intensify in the age of convergence as we see fundamental changes to the structures within which media operate. Indeed, the extent of the changes in media production, consumption and distribution alongside significant transformations in social communication may mean that radically new approaches may be necessary in order to apply 'media' as an indicator of linguistic vitality. Sonia Livingstone (2009) has referred to the 'traditional dualism of mass and interpersonal forms of communication' now encompassing 'new, interactive, networked forms of communication whose influence may be traced across multiple spheres of modern life'. It seems that the distinction between 'interpersonal communication' and the 'mass media' is being diminished quite substantially. She notes that 'it is commonly claimed that "everything is mediated"' representing 'a historically significant change' (Livingstone, 2009: 1).

In fact, a re-reading of Fishman's view on media and their place in the GIDS framework suggests that under the conditions of 'new', converged media, Fishman would possibly be more inclined to advocate the potential of mediated communication as a useful tool for reversing language shift. His unwillingness to recognize a positive role for the media was largely rooted in the organizational power structures that control the media, which he (rightly) states are usually located beyond the minority language community and outside its influence and control.

According to Fishman, the media are less under minority language community control than are 'local nurseries, kindergartens, neighbourhood health services, scouting groups, sports clubs, choruses, dramatic groups, job training services, libraries, homework assistance groups, test-review groups, hobby clubs, charitable outreach organisations, summer camps, etc.' (Fishman, 2001: 474). These community activities 'serve as the sinews of growing up' in the minority language- speaking community and 'can more evenly compete' with their majority language counterparts 'and at lesser expense when doing so' than can minority language media with majority language media (and international media under the auspices of the majority language). In Fishman's view, 'Neighbourhood and community events and activities are real neighbourhood life and they feed back to one's family immediately. Media, at best, creates only a 'virtual' community (Fishman, 2001: 474). The last sentence, however, is evidence of the pre-convergence dichotomy between 'real' and 'virtual' with 'virtual' very much the poor relation. Today, however, the 'virtual' is considered part of the real. 'Real neighbourhood life' takes place in and alongside mediated communication.

Terry Flew (2007: 24) has summarized the changes from 'old' (or pre-convergence) media environment to the 'new' (or converged) media environment placing the 'virtual' very much at the forefront of the new environment (see Table 3.6).

Jenkins (2006: 3) has argued that media convergence should not be understood 'primarily as a technological process' and that it does not 'occur through media appliances'. He maintains that 'media convergence has less to do with devices and technological advances and more to do with cultural practices and heightened levels of participation and interactivity'. The significant changes in the internet that occurred simultaneously have been summarized by Tim O'Reilly, juxtaposing the characteristics of the 'post-hoc' labelled Web 1.0 against the more familiarly named Web 2.0 (see Table 3.7).

Table 3.6 Old and new media environments

'Old' media environments	'New' media environments
Analogue media	Digital media
Discrete media	Converged media
Corporations	Networks
'Lived' culture	Virtual culture
Nation states	Globalization
Journalism as a profession	Blogging and DIY media

Source: Terry Flew (2007: 24).

Table 3.7 What is Web 2.0

Web 1.0	Web 2.0
DoubleClick ->	Google AdSense
Ofoto ->	Flickr
Akamai ->	BitTorrent
mp3.com ->	Napster
Britannica Online ->	Wikipedia
Personal websites ->	Blogging
evite ->	upcoming.org and EVDB
Domain name speculation ->	Search engine optimization
Page views ->	Cost per click
Screen scraping ->	Web services
Publishing ->	Participation
Content management systems ->	Wikis
Directories (taxonomy) ->	Tagging ("folksonomy")
Stickiness ->	Syndication

Source: O'Reilly (2005), 'What is Web 2.0'.

Commenting upon this change, Androutsopoulos (2010) notes that 'in that early era, the web was predominantly a medium of information retrieval' (Androutsopoulos, 2010: 207). He elaborates that 'content was professionally produced for consumption by users who could not do much more than surf, read, and print out' noting that 'interpersonal communication was carried out on applications that predated the web and operated separately from it, such as e-mail, newsgroups and Internet Relay Chat (IRC)' (Androutsopoulos, 2010: 207). As noted in O'Reilly's table (Table 3.7), the web has evolved from being a platform for 'publishing' to become one that supports 'participation' (O'Reilly, 2005). Hinchcliffe (2006, cited in Androutsopoulos, 2010) comments that Web 2.0 environments are indeed shaped by an 'architecture of participation that encourages user contribution' (Androutsopoulos, 2010: 207).

This emphasis both on the 'participation' in convergence culture and on the inclusion of the 'virtual' into the 'lived' and the 'real' appear to lower some of the 'barriers to entry' into mediated communication, bringing such media closer to community level than in analogue times. Indeed, it could be argued that 'social' and 'participatory media' should be features that relate to Stage 5 of Fishman's GIDS, that is at the stage of the development of literacy outside formal and official contexts, rather than Stage 3 or above. Including social media as a tool at Stage 5 of GIDS should mean that a higher number of language communities are utilizing these means of communication, and what will be the impact on linguistic vitality? However, it should be noted

Table 3.8 Crystal's progress factors for endangered language

An endangered language will progress if its speakers
increase their prestige within the dominant community
increase their wealth relative to the dominant community
increase their legitimate power in the eyes of the dominant community
have a strong presence in the educational system
can write their language down
can make use of electronic technology

Source: Adapted from David Crystal (2000: 130–143).

that the association of social media with new technologies might result in 'digital diglossia', whereby speakers are reluctant to use the minority language in an unfamiliar mode of communication, or one that is too closely linked to literacy.

David Crystal (2000: 130–143) has identified a number of factors that can contribute to positive outcomes for endangered languages (see Table 3.8).

Crystal's views on the importance of social media and internet communication is well-known and his passion echoes much of Negroponte's (1995) thoughts. Negroponte, of course, was no linguist, yet he placed linguistic diversity very much at the forefront of thought about the internet with comments such as '$2,000 of capital equipment and $10 per month of recurring costs, you can publish on the Net, say, in Romansch ... and it is probably unimportant that only 70,000 people in the southeast corner of Switzerland speak this language' (Negroponte, 1996). However, on occasion Crystal's enthusiasm for the internet as a means of communication to 'replace' the traditional media paradigm may provoke a response such as Carpentier's that warns that participation can become 'trapped in a reductionist discourse of novelty, detached from the reception of its audiences and decontextualized from its political-ideological, communicative-cultural and communicative-structural contexts' (Carpentier, 2009: 407). Crystal's view is as follows:

> Traditionally, it [media] is an expensive business: newspaper space, or radio and television time, does not come cheaply. Only the 'better off' languages could afford to make routine use of these media. But with the internet, everyone is equal. The cost of a Web page is the same, whether the contributor is writing in English, Spanish, Welsh or Navajo. (Crystal, 2000: 142)

Carpentier, on the other hand, argues that 'the popularization of "new" Internet-based media has generated much optimism about the social and participatory-democratic potentialities of these media, leading to predictions about the demise of the mass communication paradigm, and its replacement by a many-to-many communicative paradigm' (Carpentier, 2009: 407). He adds that 'the basic concepts of the mass communication paradigm are still very much alive' (Carpentier, 2009: 407). While the existence of the internet cannot obliterate past inequalities between people and communities and it cannot in and of itself lead to the destruction of linguistic diversity, it is a means of communication – rather like the invention of print or broadcasting that will contribute to and be affected by other overarching factors in the political order and the global economy. Wider discourses on the importance of sustaining linguistic diversity, on the autonomy of peoples and communities and on the role of democracy in relation to global capitalism will ultimately decide the future of the internet and its relationship with the survival of minority languages.

Conclusions

In conclusion, it appears that attempts to integrate the existence of online communication into the existing frameworks of assessing linguistic vitality will require a substantial overview of the present indices and the concepts from which they are derived. A simple assimilation of online communication within the indices associated with the old media paradigm of 'one-to-many' distribution is not sufficient in itself for this restricts our understanding of online communication as a mere shift in technology and the invention of new appliances without recognizing that convergence culture has, according to Jenkins and others, more to do with changes in cultural practices and heightened levels of participation and interactivity. At the same time, we cannot ignore the fact that our 'old' media paradigms are being strongly influenced by convergence, yet simultaneously the vast majority of them still remain powerful players as they are joined by additional corporate gatekeepers who between them retain significant control over the whole media landscape.

This 'vertical' approach of grouping together various indices associated with online communication under the auspices of a 'media' index can easily distort the representation of minority languages in the media, leading to a situation (not dissimilar from that at the beginning of this chapter) whereby the number of Wikipedia articles in a language is viewed on with the existence of a publicly funded television broadcaster. Equally, a more 'horizontal' approach of integrating online communication into all other indices, such as education, governance and community life, could also lead to an eclipsing of the role of the media and mediated communication – both negative and positive – on the linguistic vitality of different language communities.

The indices of linguistic vitality are useful tools in the wider debate on linguistic diversity and focus the mind on comparative analyses over time or across language communities. We are at a significant point in time where predictions of language loss coincide with an amplification of communication age. At this stage, it is important to elaborate adequate and useful indices, especially if we want to do more than merely record and document the demise of linguistic diversity.

References

Androutsopoulos, J. (2010) Localizing the blobal on the participatory web. In N. Coupland (ed.) *The Handbook of Language and Globalisation* (pp. 203–231). Oxford: Wiley-Blackwell.

Barker, M. and Petley, J. (1997) *Ill Effects: The Media/Violence Debate*. London: Routledge.

Browne, D.R. (1996) *Electronic Media and Indigenous Peoples: A Voice of Our Own?* Ames, Iowa: Iowa State University Press.

Carpentier, N. (2009) Participation is not enough. *European Journal of Communication* 24 (4), 407–420. doi: 10.1177/0267323109345682.

Cormack, M. (2004) Developing minority language media studies. *Mercator Media Forum* 7, 3–12.

Council of Europe (1992) European Charter for Regional and Minority Languages. Strasbourg: Council of Europe. Accessed.

Crystal, D. (2000) *Language Death*. Cambridge: Cambridge University Press.

Fishman, J.A. (1991) *Reversing Language Shift: Theoretical and Empirical Foundations of Assistance to Threatened Languages*. Clevedon: Multilingual Matters.

Fishman, J.A. (2001) From theory to practice (and vice versa): Review, reconsideration, and reiteration. In J.A. Fishman (ed.) *Can Threatened Languages be Saved? Reversing Language Shift Revisited: A 21st Century Perspective* (pp. 451–482). Clevedon: Multilingual Matters.

Flew, T. (2007) *Understanding Global Media*. Basingstoke: Palgrave Macmillan.

Gorter, D. (2008) European minority languages: Endangered or revived? In T.D. Graaf, N. Ostler and R. Salverda (eds) *Endangered Languages and Language Learning: Proceedings of the Conference FEL XII, 24–27 September 2008 Fryske Akademy, It Aljemint, Ljouwert/Leeuwarden, The Netherlands* (1st ed., pp. 169–175). Bath: Foundation for Endangered Languages & Ljouwert/Leeurwarden: Fryske Academy.

Guyot, J. (2004) Languages of minorities and the media. *Mercator Media Forum* 7, 13–28.

Jenkins, H. (2006) *Convergence Culture : Where Old and New Media Collide*. New York & London: New York University Press.

Jones, E.H.G. (2007) The territory of television: S4C and the representation of the 'whole of Wales'. In M. Cormack and N. Hourigan (eds) *Minority Language Media: Concepts, Critiques and Case Studies* (pp. 188–211). Clevedon: Multilingual Matters.

Kelly-Holmes, H. (2001) *Minority Language Broadcasting: Breton and Irish*. Clevedon: Multilingual Matters.

Lewis, P. and Simons, G.F. (2010) Assessing endangerment: Expanding Fishman's GIDS. *Revue roumaine de linguistique* 2010 (2), 1–18.

Livingstone, S. (2009) On the mediation of everything: ICA presidential address 2008. *Journal of Communication* 59 (1), 1–18. doi: 10.1111/j.1460-2466.2008.01401.

Moring, T. and Dunbar, R. (2008) *The European Charter for Regional or Minority Languages and the Media*. Strasbourg [France]: Council of Europe Publishing.

Moring, T. and Husband, C. (2007) The contribution of Swedish-language media in Finland to linguistic vitality. *International Journal of the Sociology of Language* 187/88, 75–101.

Negroponte, N. (1995) *Being Digital*. London: Hodder & Stoughton.

Negroponte, N. (1996) Pluralistic, not imerialistic. *Wired,* 2.03. Accessed 24 May 2011. http://yoz.com/wired/2.03/negroponte.html.

Nelde, P., Strubell i Trueta, M. and Williams, G. (1996) *Euromosaic: The Production and Reproduction of the Minority Language Groups in the European Union*. Luxembourg: European Commission.

Shirky, C. (2010) *Cognitive Surplus: Creativity and Generosity in a Connected Age*. New York & London: Penguin Press.

Williams, K. (2003) *Understanding Media Theory*. London: Arnold.

Part 2

Web 2.0, Social Networking Sites and Minority Languages

4 Investigating the Differential Use of Welsh in Young Speakers' Social Networks: A Comparison of Communication in Face-to-Face Settings, in Electronic Texts and on Social Networking Sites

Daniel Cunliffe, Delyth Morris and Cynog Prys

Introduction

The advent of the internet and social networking sites can be seen by those interested in minority languages as both a threat and an opportunity to language maintenance. Krauss (1992) famously described electronic media, and especially television, as *cultural nerve gas*, due to its deadly effect on language mortality. However, others (e.g. Crystal, 2000; Cunliffe, 2007, 2009) see the possibility of using the internet and electronic technology as a tool to strengthen linguistic communities and revive weakened languages by producing easily accessible content in minority languages, and providing networks of support for fluent speakers and learners alike.

One important aspect of internet usage is the prevalence of social networking sites (SNS) such as Facebook, Bebo and MySpace which have become increasingly popular amongst the public, and especially with the younger generation (Ofcom, 2008). Considering that language use among young people is seen as an area of particular importance (Morris, 2010) for minority language maintenance, the prevalence of these social networking sites as a means of communication becomes significant. As a result, the use of minority languages on the internet by young people is an important area of research.

This chapter will concentrate on recent research conducted into the online use of Welsh and English on social networking sites by pupils of four Welsh medium secondary schools in Wales: two in the north-west and two in the south-east. The research concludes that the use of SNS is extremely widespread amongst secondary school age pupils in both areas. However, the differing linguistic profiles of the areas mean that the language use on SNS varies significantly between the north-west and south-east.

Young People and Minority Language Usage

It is generally accepted that the teenage years are a crucial period for the development of attitudes towards a minority language (Ó Riagáin et al., 2008), and the use young people make of their minority language skills during this period can affect their continued use in later stages of their life cycle, such as starting a family. In Wales this group is seen to be of particular importance as regards language planning policies. The National Assembly for Wales, which was established in 1999 and is a devolved assembly of the UK government with some powers to make legislation in Wales, has placed considerable stress upon maintaining the Welsh language and promoting bilingualism throughout Wales. The Welsh Assembly Government is aware of the importance of promoting the Welsh language amongst young people. In *Iaith Pawb,* the Assembly's Action Plan for a Bilingual Wales, it is stated that:

> The Assembly Government is acutely aware that if Welsh is to flourish young people in particular need to develop a sense of ownership for the language and to see it as their language and not simply the language of school and culture. (Welsh Assembly Government, 2003: 4.38)

Although we are aware from consecutive Census data that there has been an increase within the last generation in the percentage and numbers of young people who are able to speak Welsh, especially in south-east Wales, it has also been noted by several researchers and in the work of the Welsh

Language Board itself that the actual use of Welsh among these young people is fairly low (Welsh Language Board, 2006). It is generally acknowledged that the growth in the number of young Welsh speakers in recent years is due, in large part, to the huge increase in Welsh medium education. Welsh is now the main teaching medium in 448 primary schools across Wales, and 54 secondary schools in Wales are defined as Welsh medium (Morris, 2010: 81). Many pupils in Welsh-medium education came from non-Welsh speaking homes, particularly in the south-east, where the percentage of Welsh language speakers is low. As a result, the large increase in speakers has come in areas where Welsh has not been widely spoken as a family or community language.

Wales is a country of approximately 3 million people, located on the western periphery of the United Kingdom, where English is the dominant language and where around 20% of the population can speak Welsh. In some parts of Wales, particularly in the north and west, the concentrations of Welsh speakers is much higher with 70% of the population in the north and 50% of the population in west Wales being Welsh speaking (Welsh Language Board, 2003). However, in the south and east of Wales, the percentage of the Welsh-speaking population is low, ranging between 9.3% in Monmouthshire and 11% in Cardiff (Welsh Language Board, 2003). The communities of the so-called *Fro Gymraeg* (Welsh heartlands) in the north and west of Wales have been under increasing pressure over the past 30 years because of a steady in-migration of non-Welsh speakers, mainly from England.

In Wales we find that while young people's social networks have traditionally been maintained largely by face-to-face contact and the telephone, new technology is increasingly playing a role. Studies show that 71% of people aged 16–24 in Wales personally access the internet, 58% have home internet connections and 88% have a mobile phone (WCC, 2007). In the general population of fluent and non-fluent Welsh-speaking internet users, 76.6% use the internet for emailing/keeping in touch and 37.34% use it for social networking/sharing information (e.g. MySpace, chat forums) – this figure is likely to be significantly higher among young people (Cunliffe *et al.*, 2010). Previous research work (Ellison *et al.*, 2007) has shown that online social networks tend to replicate real-world social networks, rather than creating new social networks. Social networking sites (such as MySpace, Bebo and Facebook) have enjoyed a rapid increase in popularity in the United Kingdom, particularly among young people, as almost half (49%) of children aged 8–17 years who use the internet have set up their own profile on a social networking site. The likelihood of setting up a profile is highest among 16–24 year olds (54%) (Ofcom, 2008).

To date there has been little research on the use of Welsh in social networking sites. The work that has been conducted by Honeycutt and

Cunliffe (2010) shows that the Welsh language is being used on Facebook, both on Facebook Groups and on peoples' personal profiles. From the limited sample studied, it appears that some 45% of the personal profiles which featured the Welsh language used it exclusively (compare with similar results in Twitter, as presented by Johnson in this book). On the other hand, 29% of Welsh speakers were not using Welsh on their profiles at all. The study did not focus in particular on young people; ages ranged between 18 and 53 years with an arithmetic mean of 26.36 and a median of 23. Research by Ofcom (2008) suggests that Facebook may be more popular with older users, and that Bebo may be more popular with children. Owing to the widespread use of SNS, it is likely that these sites form an important element in the maintenance of social relationships between young (and old) Welsh speakers.

Research Focus

The research project aimed to study the language patterns of young Welsh speakers when interacting within their social networks. Their differential use of Welsh in different modalities (i.e. speech, texting, email and social networking sites) and the reasons behind this were investigated, in order to identify the modalities that support Welsh language use and those which do not. The research has also led to a clearer understanding of people's motivations, and the perceived barriers to language use associated with each modality.

Given the observation that language patterns vary between different parts of Wales, it was decided to conduct a multisite study, in order to identify differences in the language choices in different modalities, as well as differences in the motivation, and perception of barriers. It was hoped that as a result of this investigation, it would be possible to identify specific types of intervention that might encourage the use of Welsh in modalities where English dominated, whether this was due to attitudinal factors or due to technical constraints. It was presumed that this would lead to the increased use of Welsh in the social networks and increased benefits from those networks in resisting language shift, and feed into the Welsh Assembly Government's declared aims and objectives regarding the Welsh language.

Methodology

The study of young people was conducted in four Welsh medium secondary schools, two in south-east Wales and two in north-west Wales. The work was carried out in two stages: (i) establishing a baseline of information about minority language use in both areas through a questionnaire survey of young people and (ii) an in-depth study of language attitudes and behaviour through the use of focus groups with a sample of the young people surveyed. This chapter focuses on the qualitative data collected in the focus groups.

A sample of 200 young Welsh speakers aged 13–18 years was selected, 100 in south-east Wales and 100 in north-west Wales, and an online questionnaire was administered to collect information about their demographic and educational background, the language of their home, their self-perceived language ability, their use of Welsh and English in different social contexts and their use of Welsh and English in emails, texting and social networking sites. The focus groups discussed these issues in more depth.

The quantitative data was analysed by using SPSS. From these 200 respondents, we selected 8 groups, 4 groups of 8 participants aged 13–15 years (school years 9–11) and 4 groups of 8 participants aged 16–18 years (school years 12–13), with an even geographical spread, to take part in a further focus group discussion on the issues raised in the quantitative exercise. Each focus group lasted between 40 and 50 minutes – the length of a lesson in the school timetable – and usually included six participants chosen at random. These interviews were recorded using a digital voice recorder. The qualitative data thus obtained produced a more rounded and in-depth view of the participants' attitudes and behaviour.

To protect the anonymity of the schools, the schools in the north-west of Wales are called NW1 and NW2, while the schools in the south-east are called SE1 and SE2. Years 9–11 are denoted as (1), while years 12–13 are denoted as (2).

Preliminary Research Findings

Offline language use

Before considering the language used by the participants on the internet and social networking sites, we will consider their use of both English and Welsh in offline activities. There were significant differences in daily language use between the north-west and the south-east schools. In both north-west schools, Welsh was used as a community language and as an integral part of daily life for many in the area – used in school, on the school yard, in family and community activities. The south-east schools were in areas where Welsh was not spoken widely as a community language. For these pupils, the use of Welsh was confined to the classroom. Nonetheless, the oral Welsh language competence of the participants in the south-east was high as they received education through the medium of Welsh.

The use of Welsh at home also differed between the areas. Pupils from both north-west schools tended to come from Welsh-speaking families. All the focus group participants from SE1 came from families where Welsh was not spoken at home, either by parents or by grandparents. Pupils from SE2 came mainly from English-speaking homes; however, some of them came from homes where one parent could speak Welsh, although English was used as the main language of the household.

The pupils from SE1 and SE2 would always or mostly use English to socialize with their friends outside of the classroom. For these participants, Welsh was seen as the language of school and authority, while English was seen as the language of socializing and relaxation. Some participants in SE noted that there was a certain stigma attached to the use of Welsh and that pupils who would speak Welsh outside of the classroom were considered 'sad' and mocked at by other pupils. Also, some of the participants noted that they spoke Welsh in primary school, and in the first year of secondary school, but switched over to English to conform to the older pupils. This also suggests that the use of the Welsh language is stigmatized.

Welsh was used more widely as a social language in the north-west schools, especially in NW2. Participants in the north-west noted that they have different individuals and groups of friends with whom they use Welsh and English. Some of the participants from the NW schools noted that it would 'feel weird' if they spoke English with their Welsh-speaking friends. As a result, it could be argued that language use between individuals is static to a large extent.

Our research findings suggest that language use in the offline world by the focus group participants was largely determined by the language used in the home (cf. Vincze and Moring arrive to a similar conclusion in their chapter in this collection). Even in the face of the success of Welsh medium education, particularly in areas where fewer Welsh speakers live, the language of the home and family continues to be the language of choice for informal interaction. Similar findings have also been previously reported in separate research by Morris (2010).

The use of the internet

One of the main research findings is that the use of the internet was central to the life of the vast majority of the focus group participants, both in north-west Wales and south-east Wales. All participants had broadband internet access at home (observe, however, that this result may have been slightly overstated by the participants in an attempt to maintain status amongst their peers) and several had internet access on their mobile phones or on their personal media players (e.g. iPod Touch). The internet was also used in both areas for watching videos on the BBC iPlayer and YouTube, online shopping and online gaming. For many of the participants, the internet was the main source of entertainment in the home, as it was used for social networking, gaming and homework, shopping and viewing television programmes.

The use of social networking sites was widespread. All participants in the year 12–13 focus groups held a current Facebook account, while two of the participants in year 9 did not have account because of the lack of their parents' consent. The majority of users had used Bebo before transferring to use Facebook, as Bebo became unfashionable, with the perception that it was an SNS for children, while Facebook was for adults. The instant messaging services of MSN and Facebook Chat were also used by many of the participants as a free method of communication with school friends after school hours. Twitter was used only by a few participants and was perceived by most as something for older people and public figures.

Social networks on SNS

The vast majority of the focus group participants' friends on Facebook and other SNS were their school friends with whom they came in contact on a daily basis. This finding supports the work of Ellison *et al.* (2007). However, most participants had at least some friends from outside of their school, from the local community and from other schools, and family members on their Facebook accounts. As a result, their Facebook community was a close reflection of their real-world community. However, their SNS offered easier access to a wider community, and the focus group participants used the SNS (mainly Facebook) to keep in touch with friends from different towns and villages, and their extended family that lived outside of their local community.

Language use on SNS

As it was the most widely used, SNS, used by all but three of the focus group participants, the discussion will concentrate on language use on Facebook. Facebook, like other SNS, has various methods of communicating with individuals in their network of contacts or 'Friends'. These methods include wall posts, personal messages, status updates and Facebook Chat. The various means of communication can have implications for language use as some are one-on-one private communications, while others are semi-public group communications. Here, we will look at these various means of communicating within Facebook and its implications (if any) for language choice.

Private messages and wall posts

A private message in Facebook is a message similar to an email (notice, however, that emails were not commonly used by participants) that is usually sent to an individual, although it is possible to send them to more than one person at once. On the other hand, wall posts are messages sent to an individual's 'wall' and can be seen by all of their Facebook friends. As a result, they can be described as directed to a specific individual, but are open to other friends to see. According to the respondents, the language used when writing a private messages or wall posts to an individual on Facebook, and other SNS, reflected the language used for face-to-face communication.

In the north-west, Welsh was often spoken in school, socially with friends and with family members, and Welsh was used to send Facebook messages to their Welsh-speaking friends. English was also used, depending on the preferred language of the message recipient. As a result, it can be seen that both languages are commonly used in the north-west. However, in schools in the south-east, where Welsh is not spoken widely outside the classroom, the language used on Facebook tended to be English.

Conversely, the focus groups suggest that individuals tend to speak only one language with another individual and do not change according to the form of communication, as doing so would, in the words of one respondent from NW2, 'feel weird'. Here, embedded language practice seems to be the norm in both areas, as the language use reflected the language norms of those areas. As a result, it is possible to describe language use on SNS as an extension of their language use in their daily lives. This is a key research finding, and was seen in all the focus groups.

Nonetheless, many of the participants in the north-west noted the tendency to use English words and sentences, in a message that was otherwise mainly in Welsh. This tendency to code-switch was reported in all four interviews in the north-west. The participants in the south-east also noted a tendency to code-switch, but this time to a lesser extent, and of using a few Welsh words in a mainly English sentence. For example, some of the participants would wish some of their friends a *Penblwydd Hapus* (Happy Birthday) or sign off with *cariad* (love) or *nos da* (good night) at the end of a message. This symbolic use of Welsh could be described as symbolic markers of their Welsh identity. Similar findings have been reported by Coupland *et al.* (2005: 16) and interpreted as 'iconic value of Welsh'.

Status update

Status updates are messages that can be read by all friends on their Facebook account. These messages are not usually directed at a specific user and often include an update on the activities or thoughts of the Facebook user. These messages can be considered as mass communication, rather than one-on-one. As a result, the linguistic practices behind status updates were more complicated than one-on-one messaging of a 'wall post' or 'private message'. The focus groups suggested that there was more of a tendency to use English to write status updates, even for some of the participants belonging to a mostly Welsh-speaking social network, and who used Welsh for their personal messages.

The dominance of English as the language of status update was prevalent in both the north-west and the south-east. However, the participants in the north-west were more likely to use Welsh for their status updates than the south-east.

The reason given for using English was that everybody in their social network would understand English status updates. Some participants, both in the north-west and in the south-east noted that using Welsh on status updates could be seen as 'rude' since it excludes some people from understanding the post. Similar results as regards 'language politeness' were reported in Wales by Jones and Morris (2005) who studied Welsh language socialization within the family and found a tendency among Welsh speakers to use English in the presence of non-Welsh speakers, 'out of politeness and in order to include the non-Welsh speaker in the conversation'(Jones & Morris, 2005: 9). This same practice also seems to be present in the online world of SNS.

In the south-west schools, English was used by almost all the participants to update their Facebook status. Two main reasons were given for this trend. First, these pupils had a much higher percentage of friends and family who could not speak Welsh in their social network. It can be argued therefore that the real-world social network of the pupils plays an important part in their language use on SNS (as previously noted by Wei, 2000; Milroy, 2001). Second, English was the language spoken at home by these pupils, and as a result many were more comfortable and accustomed to using English as their first language, and it was the language used for socializing. However, there were some examples of when the participants in the south-east school would use Welsh, although these were comparatively rare: Welsh was used on occasion as a 'secret language' in the SE as a language that only their school friends would understand; moreover, it was used to quote humorous comments that were made by their fellow pupils during the school day. Questions about school homework were sometimes posted in Welsh as a status update. However, the use of Welsh was rare, with English being the main language, with the occasional Welsh word used within a broader English sentence.

The fact that many first-language Welsh speakers in the north-west use English for status updates suggests that the use of English has more to do with institutionalized language behaviour than the language of social networks and language competence alone. Due to the localized nature of their Facebook friends, the percentage of the individuals who would have the ability to understand a Welsh language status update would be very high in the north-west. The majority of the participants from the north-west schools had Welsh-speaking friends who also spoke Welsh at home, with the vast majority being pupils at the same school. Nonetheless, English was commonly used by the participants to update their status.

Even with English being the widely used language for status updates in the NW, Welsh was also used regularly. One focus group in NW1 noted that they use mainly Welsh for their status updates. The purpose of the message was often cited as a factor in deciding in which language to write the update, with messages directed to school friends more likely to be in Welsh. Once again, school-related topics were more likely to be posted in Welsh due to the fact that they were targeted to a Welsh-speaking audience. However, it is worth noting that some of the participants in the NW would use only Welsh to post status updates as everybody in their social network at least understood Welsh.

Conclusions

The preliminary results from these findings lead us to some tentative conclusions. One important finding is that young Welsh speakers, like young non-Welsh speakers across the United Kingdom, are avid users of the internet and social networking sites (Ofcom, 2010). Many hours are spent by these young people on SNS, and our findings conclude that the Welsh language is used (to different degrees) on these social networking sites, such as Facebook. These results are in line with recent research by Honeycutt and Cunliffe (2010).

However, the amount of Welsh used on SNS does depend on a number of factors, one of which is their home language and the language of their communities. It could be argued, as does Ellison *et al.* (2007), that online social networks tend to replicate real-world social networks, rather than create new ones. As a result, this research suggests that language use on these SNS largely reflects the language of their real-world communities. This is reflected by the fact that Welsh was used much more commonly on SNS by Welsh speakers in the north-west than by Welsh speakers in the south-east. Even with the success of Welsh medium education outside of the Welsh-speaking heartlands, the use of Welsh outside of the classroom, and on social networking sites, continues to be low. Changing the linguistic habits could be a difficult task, as this research suggests that the participants tend to use only one language with their friends – regardless of the means of communication.

Nonetheless, the results are not so clear-cut as to suggest that their language use on SNS was an exact replication of the linguistic communities they inhabit. While our findings suggest that modalities did not play a substantial part in the language choice of SNS, the type of communication, and the intended audience, was a factor. A prime example was the language use by Facebook users for 'status updates' and the use of English as an inclusive language. First-language Welsh speakers who did use Welsh to communicate one-on-one (in the real-world and on Facebook 'personal messages') were found to use less Welsh when it came to status updates. According to the focus group participants, the reasoning behind this lay in their desire to include their whole social network in their communication. However, for some of these young Facebook users who spoke Welsh as first language, it seemed that very few, if any, of their Facebook friends did not understand Welsh. This suggests that there is more to their choice of English rather than Welsh than inclusion alone. While language competence and preference may well play a part, it could also be argued that some of these pupils feel pressure to conform to the use of English as the language of the internet.

English was by far the most widely used language in both areas for surfing the internet. For the participants in the north-west, Facebook was the only place online they used Welsh regularly. As one focus group participant in NW1 noted, 'Our Facebook is a Welsh section of the Internet, where our friends speak Welsh'. As a result, it could be argued that SNS such as Facebook could play an important role in maintaining Welsh language social networks, by providing Welsh speakers with space to use their language. Also, SNS provide individuals from areas where there are fewer Welsh speakers with access to Welsh language social networks and provide extra opportunities to use the language socially. With the increasing concern over the future of some of the traditional Welsh-speaking heartlands, SNS could play a vital role in keeping connections between Welsh speakers alive even when they are not living in a Welsh-speaking area.

References

Coupland, N., Bishop, H., Williams, A., Evans, B. and Garrett, P. (2005) Affiliation, engagement, language use and vitality: Secondary school students' subjective orientations to Welsh and Welshness. *International Journal of Bilingual Education and Bilingualism* 8 (1), 1–24. doi: jBEB.v8.i1.pg1.

Crystal, D. (2000) *Language Death*. Cambridge: Cambridge University Press.

Cunliffe, D. (2007) Minority languages in the Internet: New threats, new opportunities. In M. Cormack and N. Hourigan (eds) *Minority Language Media: Concepts, Critiques, and Case Studies* (pp. 133–150). Clevedon: Multilingual Matters.

Cunliffe, D. (2009) The Welsh language on the Internet: Linguistic resistance in the age of the network society. In G. Goggin and M. McLelland (eds) *Internationalizing Internet Studies: Beyond Anglophone Paradigms* (pp. 96–111). New York: Routledge.

Cunliffe, D., Pearson, N. and Richards, S. (2010) E-commerce and minority languages: A Welsh perspective. In H. Kelly-Holmes and G. Mautner (eds) *Language and the Market* (pp. 135–147). Basingstoke: Palgrave Macmillan.

Ellison, N.B., Steinfield, C. and Lampe, C. (2007) The benefits of Facebook 'friends': Social capital and college students' use of online Social Network Sites. *Journal of Computer-Mediated Communication* 12 (4), 1143–1168. doi: 10.1111/j.1083-6101.2007.00367.x.

Honeycutt, C. and Cunliffe, D. (2010) The use of the Welsh language on Facebook: An initial investigation. *Information, Communication & Society* 13 (2), 226–248.

Jones, K. and Morris, D. (2005) Welsh language socialization within the family. Network to Promote Linguistic Diversity. http://www.npld.eu/Documents/Welsh%20Language%20Socialisation%20in%20the%20Family.pdf.

Krauss, M. (1992) The world's languages in crisis. *Language* 68 (1), 4–10.

Milroy, L. (2001) Bridging the micro–macro gap: Social change, social networks and bilingual repertoires. In J. Klatter-Folmer and P. Van Avermaet (eds) *Theories on Maintenance and Loss of Minority Languages: Towards a More Integrated Explanatory Framework* (pp. 39–64). Munster: Waxman.

Morris, D. (2010) *Welsh in the Twenty-First Century*. Cardiff: University of Wales Press.

Ó Riagáin, P., Williams, G. and Moreno, X. (2008) *Young People and Minority Languages: Language Use Outside the Classroom*. Dublin: Trinity College.

Ofcom (2008) Social networking: A quantitative and qualitative research report into attitudes, behaviours and use, accessed 17 May 2011. http://stakeholders.ofcom.org.uk/binaries/research/media-literacy/report1.pdf.

Ofcom (2010) Communications market report, accessed 21 April 2011. http://stakeholders.ofcom.org.uk/binaries/research/cmr/753567/CMR_2010_FINAL.pdf.

WCC (2007) *Consumers and ICT in Wales*. Welsh Consumer Council.

Wei, L. (2000) Towards a critical evaluation of language maintenance and language shift. *Sociolinguistica* 14, 142–147.

Welsh Assembly Government (2003) *Iaith Pawb: A National Plan for a Bilingual Wales*. Cardiff: WAG.

Welsh Language Board (2003) *2001 Census: Main Statistics about Welsh*. Cardiff: WLB.

Welsh Language Board (2006) *Young People's Social Networks and Language Use: Final Report*. Cardiff: WLB.

5 Luxembourgish on Facebook: Language Ideologies and Writing Strategies

Melanie Wagner

Introduction

This chapter discusses the preliminary findings of a research project on the presence of Luxembourgish on Facebook. Before introducing the larger project, let me provide a brief introduction to the current language situation in Luxembourg. With a geographical size of 2586 square kilometres and a population of 493,500 (STATEC, 2009), the Grand Duchy of Luxembourg is the second smallest member-state of the European Union (EU).

The language situation in Luxembourg is frequently referred to as triglossic in reference to the three languages recognized by the 1984 language law: Luxembourgish, French and German. The spoken/written distinction is pivotal to understanding long-standing norms and patterns of language use in Luxembourg, with most spoken communication taking place in Luxembourgish and written functions carried out primarily in standard French and/or German. Luxembourgish language varieties are Germanic and bear similarities to Moselle/Franconian varieties spoken in parts of Germany, Belgium and France (for details on Luxembourgish history and policy, see Berg, 1993).

This relationship provides the rationale underpinning the decision for basic literacy skills to be taught via standard German in state schools. French is introduced as a subject in the second year of primary school, it becomes a full subject in the third year and gradually replaces German as the main medium of instruction, particularly in the framework of the *lycée classique* or college preparatory secondary school. Based on the Education Act of 1843, state schooling institutions and practices have perpetuated elite bilingualism, or the valorisation of standard written German plus French (Davis, 1994).

The Luxembourgish language law dating back to 1984 defines Luxembourgish as the national and German and French as administrative and legal languages (cf. Berg, 1993). Joseph (2004) has stated that the existence and acceptance of a national language is crucial to the development of a national identity. At present, although it is difficult to establish whether Luxembourgish was regarded as national language in 19th century, it can be assumed that Luxembourgish has taken on this symbolic national status since the first half of 20th century (Gilles & Moulin, 2003; Moulin, 2006). The height of this development may have been the passage of the language law in 1984 as mentioned earlier.

One central aspect in the recognition and the establishment of Luxembourgish as the national language is the development of a written language. For Luxembourgish, the transition from solely spoken to a written language is marked by the emergence of Luxembourgish literature, starting with Antoine Meyer (1801–1857) in 19th century. Another important factor is that of language learning and teaching. The teaching of Luxembourgish at primary school was introduced in 1912 (Mémorial du Grand-Duché de Luxembourg, 1912: 769), but the curriculum was very vague with regard to the content:

Art. 23: the compulsory subjects to be taught at primary school are [...] an introduction to the country's history and Luxembourgish [...].
Art. 23: Die obligatorischen Lehrgegenstände des Primärunterrichts sind: [...] die Anfangsgründe der Landesgeschichte und Luxemburgisch [...].

Hence, it is difficult to know if Luxembourgish was actually taught and if taught to what extent. The textbook used for the teaching of Luxembourgish *Das Luxemburgische und sein Schrifttum* (Luxembourgish and its Literature) was written by Engelmann and Welter. It contained a description of Luxembourgish, which in the introduction to the 1914 edition is referred to as *Luxemburger Mundart* (Luxembourgish dialect), a history of Luxembourgish literature, extracts from Luxembourgish poetry and literature and, on the last four pages, a short description of the orthography.

Ab initio reading and writing is, and was, taught through the medium of German. The teaching of Luxembourgish then was limited to the first year of secondary school and to 1 hour a week in primary school, as it remains today. The present curriculum for Luxembourgish both at primary and at secondary school level is not very explicit with regard to what should be taught. At primary school level, it puts an emphasis on children acquiring speaking and reading competence in Luxembourgish and reduces the teaching of writing Luxembourgish to a minimum 'in order not to worry the pupils'

(Plan d'études, 1989: 3). In years 5 and 6 of primary school, the child should be introduced to the main rules of Luxembourgish orthography, but writing is not compulsory at this level either (Plan d'études, 1989: 8), and no marks are awarded for writing. The curriculum for the first year of secondary school, after which Luxembourgish is no longer taught, talks of pupils 'being introduced to our orthography' but emphasizes that in tests 'only one sixth of the marks is to be taken off for orthographic mistakes' (MENFP, n.d.). This means that many of those people who write Luxembourgish apply their own strategies of writing, sometimes supported by published orthographies, such as Josy Braun's *Eis Sprooch richteg schreiwen* (Writing our language correctly), or by teachers who try to impart the writing system. Unfortunately, no research has been conducted on teaching and learning of Luxembourgish at school, and it is therefore not at all clear what is being covered and taught during these lessons.

Until quite recently, Luxembourgish was rarely written and this could be explained by the fact that its teaching is so unstructured and irregular. Many people have felt insecure when writing Luxembourgish and have been worried about making mistakes (Wagner, 2010). The rise of written Luxembourgish came with the development of the new media. Within these media, Luxembourgish became a popular written form of language for text messages, blogs, emails and so on. In an interview with the daily newspaper *Luxemburger Wort*, Professor Peter Gilles states (cf. Gilles, 2009):

> The biggest chance is offered by the new media and the internet. When writing text messages or emails, when posting on Facebook, Luxembourgers use Luxembourgish almost exclusively – here reigns monolingualism.
>
> *Die ganze große Chance bieten aber die neuen Medien und das Internet: Beim Verfassen von SMS, beim Schreiben von Emails, bei Einträgen im Facebook benutzen Luxemburger sozusagen nur noch das Luxemburgische - hier herrscht die Einsprachigkeit.* (Morbach, 2009)

This statement is confirmed when one looks at examples of Luxembourgish websites, like the online forums in www.sokrates.lu, where all posts are written in Luxembourgish, or the site of the only newspaper, written mostly in Luxembourgish, which can be found on the website www.rtl.lu. Here, one finds links to a daily and a Sunday paper, with articles written in Luxembourgish, and links to different columns within each section such as politics, sports and culture. This site also features a section with letters to the editor, where the majority of posts and responses to them are in Luxembourgish.

Luxembourgish on Facebook

The use of Luxembourgish on the networking site Facebook, which is very popular in Luxembourg, will be our main focus now. Facebook went online in 2004 and according to the market researcher *checkfacebook* (http://www.checkfacebook.com/) it has 663 million users. Many Luxembourgers have registered, created their own profile and posted group pages. According to *socialbakers* (2011), Facebook had around 191,000 users (38.38% of the population of Luxembourg) in April 2011. When looking at the languages most frequently used by Luxembourgish users on Facebook, one comes to realize that most Luxembourgish Facebook users post their status updates in Luxembourgish and write messages to each other in this language. So far, there is no version for the popular networking site in Luxembourgish and while users in Luxembourg use Facebook mainly in French, German or English, some users will prefer other languages. The fact that there is no Luxembourgish version has led to the creation of a group calling for a Luxembourgish version of the site. On this particular group page, it reads as follows:

Of course Facebook exists in every crappy language … but in Luxembourgish? No why?! =.=
So if anyone here knows how and where one translates … then do it; or let me know ;-)
We want to stay what we are!
Natierlech ass Facebook op all fuerzsprooch … mee op letzebuergesch? Nee wisou?! =.=
Also wann een wees wei an wou een iwersetzt … dann maacht et, oder soot mär bescheed ;-)
Mir wölle bleiwen waat mär sin! (Ridgi, 2011)

What one comes to realize when looking at written Luxembourgish in the new media is a high degree of variation. This can be attributed to two factors: first, the fact that written language in the new media is highly variable in any language; second – and this I think is the more salient point in the case of Luxembourgish – the fact that writing Luxembourgish is not explicitly taught at school and hence many people are not aware of its orthography or grammar, and apply their own writing strategies.

Letzebuerg[esch], Lëtzebuerg[esch] or Letzeboiesch

Other research projects, such as the one looking into the language values and attitudes of Luxembourgish writers during World War II, have shown that the Luxembourgish language had and still has a great deal of emotional value for the Luxembourgish people; for them, it was the language of the home, the language used for oral communication and, for some people, for private written communication (Wagner & Davies, 2009). When one looks at groups formed on Facebook, one finds that a great number of groups focus on the topic of language in Luxembourg, often very emotionally loaded. A search for 'Lëtzebuerg' in early August, 2009, resulted in 352 groups with a reference to the country or the language in their title. When one tries other variants for the spelling of Lëtzebuerg or looks for variants of the language's name itself, one comes up with even more hits.

Lëtzebuerg – 352 results
Letzebuerg – 500 results
Lëtzebuergesch – 69 results
Letzebuergesch – 35 results
Letzeboiesch – 6 results

The corpus

In the following pages, I will look at the names and descriptions of the groups and study the meta-linguistic comments made about language. When building the corpus for this study, I looked at the different groups that existed in the earlier mentioned searches and categorized them into four different types of groups. The criteria for the categorization were the topic of the group, the message delivered by the group title and the description:

Category A

The groups that refer to clubs based in Luxembourg (e.g. Hondsclub Lëtzebuerg, Motorradclub Lëtzebuerg) or petitioning for specific shops, bars or clubs to be opened in Luxembourg (e.g. Burger King fir Lëtzebuerg, Starbucks fir Lëtzebuerg).

Categories B and C

These groups refer directly to the Luxembourgish language or the people in Luxembourg, but one can differentiate between two different types of groups. Category B is made of those groups whose title or group description has a nationalistic ring to it, with often a racist and xenophobic aftertaste, whereas those groups fighting against these nationalistic overtones and attacks and make specific reference to their antipathy towards these groups are classified under category C.

Category D

This category brings together the groups for which the issue of languages spoken in Luxembourg is of great importance but who, in contrast to category B, make sure to point out that they are neither racist nor xenophobic.

Those groups classified under category A will not be explored further because they do not focus on language in Luxembourg. A corpus of 22 groups was compiled to study the names and descriptions of the groups and these groups were put in Categories B, C and D. A list of the different groups studied, including names of the groups (in English with the original name in *italics*), number of members and categorization, is given in Table 5.1.

Before embarking on the analysis, the groups were categorized. Out of the 22 groups, 10 groups were placed in category B, 4 in category C, 5 in category D and 3 in categories B and D. The analysis of the meta-linguistic comments will provide an insight into language ideologies and attitudes towards the different languages.

When talking about language ideologies, the following definition by Wolfram and Schilling-Estes (2005: 9) is most appropriate: 'ingrained, unquestioned beliefs about the way the world is, the way it should be, and the way it has to be with respect to language'. The data presented here will show that in many cases, the groups are concerned with what languages they think should and should not be spoken.

5.3.2 Analysis of group titles and descriptions

An analysis of the group names has shown that in most cases the names reflect the purpose of the group and sum up its description. The titles often give an inkling of the tendency and the general tone of the group. The group National Party Luxembourg – Luxembourg to the Luxembourgers (*NPL: Lëtzebuerg, den Lëtzebuerger*), In French!!!! – No, Mr/Mrs … in Luxembourgish please!!!! (*EN FRANCAIS!!!! Nee, Monsieur/Madame … op LËTZEBUERGESCH w.e.g.!!!!*) or the group Foreigners and cross-border workers should adapt themselves!! (*Fir dass d'Auslänner an Frontalieren sech un Letzebuerg unpassen sollen!!*) all, for example, reflect the content of the group description and by their tone make quite clear from the beginning the general feeling towards language use and foreigners. This is often achieved by using a particular font or writing style. For instance, in the mentioned example, the author uses capital letters to emphasize the message that he wants to get across. In the new media, the capital letters are also frequently used to symbolize shouting.

Table 5.1 Categorization of Luxembourgish Facebook groups

Number	Group name	Members	Category
1	NPL: Luxembourg, to the Luxembourgers *NPL: Lëtzebuerg, den Lëtzebuerger*	150	B
2	Stop Racism in Luxembourg! *STOP Rassismus zu Lëtzebuerg! HALTE au racisme au Luxembourg!*	511	C
3	In French, No Mr/Mrs ... in Luxembourgish please *EN FRANCAIS!!!! Nee, Monsieur/Madame ... op LËTZEBUERGESCH w.e.g.!!!!*	3855	B
4	We want to remain what we are *Mir Wëlle Bleiwen Wat Mir Sin*	1259	D
5	I speak only Luxembourgish in shops *Ech schwätzen just nach lëtzebuergesch an de Geschäfter*	3571	B
6	Luxembourgish is not French *Letzebuergesch as keen Franséisch!*	3977	B
7	We are proud to be Luxembourgers, but are no racists *mir sinn houfreg, Lëtzebuerger ze sinn, mä mir si keng Rassisten!!*	614	D
8	Luxembourgers are also not Germans *Lëtzebuerger sinn och keng Preisen*	3	B
Number	Group name	Members	Category
9	Yes!!!... Luxembourgish is a language!!!!	5040	D
10	Foreigners and cross-border workers should adapt themselves *Fir dass d'Auslänner an Frontalieren sech un Letzebuerg unpassen sollen!!*	888	B
11	Luxembourgish should be spoken in Luxembourg *Et soll Letzeboiech an Letzebuerg geschwaat ginn*	3458	B
12	I speak only Swahili in shops! *Ech schwätze just na Swahili an de Geschäfter!*	511	C
13	I speak French only with rightwing Luxembourgers! *Ech schwätzen just nach Franséich mat rietspopulistegen Letzebuerger!*	274	C

Number	Group name	Members	Category
14	No to rightwing groups! *Nee zu rietspopulisteschen Gruppen!*	1477	C
15	Luxembourg is Luxembourgish, show that you are not careless about your identity *Lëtzebuerg ass lëtzebuergesch, weist datt Ierch eis Identitéit net eegal as*	360	B
16	Luxembourgish should become a main subject at school!!! *Lëtzebuergesch soll een haaptfach an der Schoul gin !!!*	2110	B and D
17	Luxembourgish: A MUST for every doctor and nurse at the children's hospital!! *Lëtzebuergesch: Een MUSS fir all Doc an Infirmière an der Kannerklinik!!*	329	B and D
18	Not wanting French, but not being able to write Luxembourgish *Keen franséisch schwätzen wëllen, awer keen lëtzebuergesch schraiwen kënnen*	15	D
19	Luxembourgish should be spoken in Luxembourg *Et soll Letzeboiech an Letzebuerg geschwaat ginn*	3438	B
20	Studies and school in Luxembourgish *Studien an Schoul op Letzebuergesch*	52	B
Number	Group name	Members	Category
21	Luxembourgish must be spoken in Luxembourg!!!! *Et muss Letzebuergesch an Letzebuerg geschwaat gin!!!*	3890	B and D
22	I want to speak Luxembourgish with my green bean soup! *Ech well mat menger Bouneschlupp letzebuergesch Schwätzen!*	168	D

Other groups position themselves clearly in their title. The group '*mir sinn houfreg, Lëtzebuerger ze sinn, mä mir si keng Rassisten !!*' (We are proud to be Luxembourgers, but are no racists) states that even though they are proud to be Luxembourgers, they are not racist, and groups such as '*Et soll Letzeboiech an Letzebuerg geschwaat gin*' (Luxembourgish should be spoken in Luxembourg) present their request in their title.

Another interesting fact that can be easily observed through a closer look at the different group titles is the use of modal verbs. In 5 of the 22 groups, the titles use either the modal verb *sollen*/shall or *mussen*/must when referring to behaviour of foreigners in Luxembourg or to the use of Luxembourgish and the idea that Luxembourgish is the language that should be spoken in Luxembourg:

- Foreigners and cross-border workers should adapt themselves.
- *Fir dass d'Auslänner an Frontalieren sech un Letzebuerg unpassen sollen!!*
- Luxembourgish should be spoken in Luxembourg.
- *Et soll Letzeboiech an Letzebuerg geschwaat ginn.*
- Luxembourgish should become a main subject at school.
- *Letzebuergesch soll en Haptfach an der Schou ginn.*
- Luxembourgish: A MUST for every doctor and nurse at the children's hospital!!
- *Lëtzebuergesch: Een MUSS fir all Doc an Infirmière an der Kannerklinik!!*
- Luxembourgish must be spoken in Luxembourg!!!!
- *Et muss Letzebuergesch an Letzebuerg geschwaat gin!!!*

The different types of discourses that can be observed from the group descriptions analysed here show that the language ideologies linked to Luxembourgish are very positive and quite nationalist. What emerges is that Luxembourgish is part of the Luxembourgish identity and that to a large extent, for foreigners and cross-border workers, not speaking Luxembourgish is not acceptable.

In a number of group descriptions, there is the *us* versus *them* and the *ours* versus *yours* distinction that Kristine Horner also found in her analysis of texts published in Luxembourg's printed press. One example for this type of discourse can be found in an excerpt of the following group description:

NPL: Luxembourg, to the Luxembourgers:
I am fed up to see how this nation worries about the fact that *we* may upset some individuals or their culture. As Luxembourgers *we* have *our* own culture, *our* own language, *our* own rules of society and *our* own way of life. This culture has developed over centuries. *We* speak Luxembourgish and not Portuguese, French, Arabic, Yugoslav, Cap Verdean or any other language, so if *you* would like to become part of *our* society, then go and learn the language! '*We* want to remain what *we* are' is *our* national slogan. That is not just a political slogan. *We* took to this slogan because Christian women and men gave their lives for it, it is absolutely normal to carry that slogan to the outside, if *you* feel upset by God then I recommend,

that *you* find another place on this earth to live, because God is part of *our* culture and if that bothers *you* then *you* should really think about moving to another part of this planet. *We* here are happy with *our* culture and do not have any wish to change and *we* do not care about how things *were* done where *you* come from, this is *our* state, *our* country, *our* way of living, and *we* are happy to share that with *you*. (…)

NPL: *Lëtzebuerg, den Lëtzebuerger:*

Ech hunn ës genuch z'erliewen, wéi sech dëss natioun gedanken doriwwer mëscht, op mer iergendéen individuum oder seng kultur beleidëge kéinten. als lëtzebuerger hu mer eis éege kultur, eis éege sprooch, eis éege gesellschaftsuerdnung an eisen éegene liewensstil. dëss kultur huet sech während jorhonnerten entwëckelt. mir schwätze lëtzebuergësch a nët portugiesësch, franséisch, arabësch, yugoslawësch, capverdianësch oder soss iergend eng aner sprooch. wann dir also déel vun eiser gesellschaft wëllt gin, da léiert gefällecht d'sprooch ! "mir wëlle bleiwe waat mer sin" as eise nationale motto. daat as nët irgendée politësche slogan. mir hunn dëse slogan ugeholl, wëll chrëschtlëch männer a fraen dofir hiert liewe geloos hunn. ët as also absolutt normal dé slogan no baussen ze droen. wann der iech vu gott beleidëgt fillt, da schloen ech vir, dir sicht iech eng aner plaz op dëser welt fir äre wunnsëtz, well gott as nun émol déel vun eiser kultur a wann iech daat stéiert misst der iech éechthaft gedanken doriwwer maan, an én aneren déel op dësem planéit ze plënneren. mir sin hei zefridde mat eiser kultur an hu nët de gerëngste wonsch eis grouss z'änneren an ët as eis och ganz égal wéi d'saachen do ofgelaaf sin, wou dir hierkommt. dëst as eise staat, eist land, eis liewensart. mir gönnen iech gär d'méiglechkéet, daat alles mat eis ze déelen.(…). (Pascal, 2011)

Another discourse that emerged in the analysis of the descriptions was the one around the languages Luxembourgish and French. There are 12 groups that refer to the fact that Luxembourgish should be spoken in Luxembourg and point out that foreigners and cross-border workers should learn to speak Luxembourgish. This is, however, not the only point made about language use. The dislike for French and the unhappiness with the use of French in shops and other public places or service sectors is made clear by six groups. For instance, in its description group 11 says, 'It can't be true that when one goes to a shop one always has to speak French or when one asks someone something on the road' (*Ed kann dach net sinn, dass wann een an een geschäft gehd, dass een do emmer franseich schwetzen muss. oder wann een op der stross iergenteen eppes freet*).

The third type of discourse is that of language purism. In the group 'Luxembourgish is not French', of which 3977 people are members, the use of French borrowings is criticized and reprimanded.

When looking at the groups belonging to category C or D, the re-emerging discourse is that of reacting against those groups categorized as B or of concern and justification. In those groups categorized as D, the worry and concern about the Luxembourgish language situation is voiced and described on the one hand, but on the other hand, justification for this is sought and it is pointed out that the concerns are not linked to either racism or xenophobia (e.g. group 7: 'We are proud to be Luxembourgers, but are no racists!!').

What is interesting in these groups is the fact that they always make sure to point out that their wish for Luxembourgish to be used more frequently and in more places does not mean that they are racist.

The groups classified under category C are either sarcastic spin-offs of other groups (i.e. group 12: 'I speak only Swahili in shops!' or group 22: 'I want to speak Luxembourgish with my green bean soup!') or criticism of the rightwing groups and comments (i.e. group 13: 'I speak French only with rightwing Luxembourgers!' and group 14: 'No to rightwing groups!'). In their group descriptions, these group creators state the fact that these groups were founded as a reaction to the 'Racist and xenophobic groups' and that they voice their concern about and disagreement with the more nationalistic groups and the racist remarks in their posts.

Conclusions

The chapter has tried to provide you with an insight into the different types of group pages posted by Luxembourgish users on Facebook. What emerged when looking at these pages was the fact that discussions about language use and language value are very prominent and important on an SNS like Facebook. The group titles and descriptions reveal the general message and the tone of the group early on, and one comes to realize that the topic of language in Luxembourg is very emotionally charged. The language attitudes towards Luxembourgish are very positive and the link between the language and the identity emerges to be strong in people's minds. The discourse of 'us' versus 'them' shows clearly how there is considerable difference between those who speak Luxembourgish and those who do not, and people appear upset by the fact that so many people working and living in Luxembourg do not speak Luxembourgish. On the other hand, there are also reactions to these posts by other people who are embarrassed by these discussions and who point out that speaking Luxembourgish is not that important and that it is ok for other languages to be spoken in Luxembourg. Overall, one can say that Facebook is being used as a platform to discuss these issues, to voice concern and frustration – a platform for written Luxembourgish that did not exist before and which has brought attention to discussions never before available to the public eye.

References

Berg, G. (1993) 'Mir wëlle bleiwe, wat mir sin': Soziolinguistische und sprachtypologische Betrachtungen zur luxemburgischen Mehrsprachigkeit. Tübingen: M. Niemeyer.

Davis, K.A. (1994) Language Planning in Multilingual Contexts: Policies, Communities, and Schools in Luxembourg. Amsterdam: John Benjamins.

Gilles, P. (2009) Jugendsprachliche Schriftlichkeit auf Luxemburgisch in den Neuen Medien. In C. Berg, L. Kerger, N. Meisch and M. Milmeister (eds) Savoirs et engagements: Hommage à Georges Wirtgen. (pp. 166–175). Differdange: Éditions Phi.

Gilles, P. and Moulin, C. (2003) Luxembourgish. In A. Deumert and W. Vandenbusche (eds) Germanic Standardizations: Past to Present (pp. 303–329). Amsterdam: de Gruyter.

Joseph, J.E. (2004) Language and Identity: National, Ethnic, Religious. Basingstoke: Palgrave Macmillan.

Mémorial du Grand-Duché de Luxembourg (1912) Law from 10 August 1912 regarding the organisation of elementary schooling (Gesetz vom 10. August 1912, die Organisation des Primärunterrichtes betreffend), accessed 6 May 2011. http://www.legilux.public.lu/leg/a/archives/1912/0061/a061.pdf.

MENFP (n.d.) Curriculum for Luxembourgish at secondary school (Enseignement Secondaire, Classe de VIIe: Luxembourgeois). LUXEM 7e. Accessed 5 May 2011. http://content.myschool.lu/sites/horaires/2007-2008/pdf/7e/LUXEM/LUXEM_7e_1_0.pdf.

Morbach, F. (2009, 20 February 2009) Professor Peter Gilles: 'Luxemburgisch ist eine Success-Story'. Luxemburger Wort. Accessed 3 May 2011. http://www.wort.lu/wort/web/letzebuerg/artikel/07502/unesco-sprachenbericht-vieles-stimmt-einfach-nicht.php.

Moulin, C. (2006) Grammatisierung und Standardisierung des Luxemburgischen: Eine grammatikographisch-sprachhistorische Annäherung. In D. Nübling and C. Moulin (eds) Perspektiven einer linguistischen Luxemburgistik (pp. 277–311). Heidelberg: Winter Verlag.

Pascal, J. (2011) NPL: Lëtzebuerg, den Lëtzebuerger!!! Facebook Group. Accessed 5 May 2011. https://www.facebook.com/group.php?gid=36860484076.

Plan d'études (1989) Arrêté Ministériel du 1er septembre 1989 portant révision du plan d'études pour les écoles primaires du Grand-Duché de Luxembourg.

Ridgi (2011) Facebook op Letzebuerg. Facebook Group. Accessed 5 May 2011. http://www.facebook.com/group.php?gid=64181135107.

Socialbakers (2011) Luxembourg Facebook Statistics. Accessed 5 May 2011. http://www.socialbakers.com/facebook-statistics/luxembourg.

STATEC (2009, 5 April 2011) Le portal des statistiques. Accessed 12 April 2011. http://www.statistiques.public.lu/fr/acteurs/statec/index.html.

Wagner, M. (2010) Lesenlernen: die Situation in Luxembourg. In M. Lutjeharms and C. Schmidt (eds) Lesekompetenz in Erst-, Zweit-, und Fremdsprache (pp. 117–128). Tübingen: Gunter Narr.

Wagner, M. and Davies, W.V. (2009) The role of World War II in the development of Luxembourgish as a national language. Language Problems & Language Planning 33 (2), 112–131.

Wolfram, W. and Schilling-Estes, N. (2005) American English: Dialects and Variation (2nd ed.). Oxford: Blackwell.

6 Audience Design and Communication Accommodation Theory: Use of Twitter by Welsh – English Biliterates

Ian Johnson

Introduction

This chapter explores the use of social networking site (SNS) Twitter by fluent bilingual speakers of Welsh and English, assessing their use of computer-mediated communication on the site.

Twitter is an internet-based computer application that, similar to other social networking sites such as Facebook, enables users to regularly update their status, by sending messages of less than 140 characters. Users are encouraged to update their status on a regular basis to inform 'followers' (e.g. people who, by opting-in, receive updates from friends, acquaintances, organizations, news providers and others) as to their activities and opinions.

The site becomes interactive through 'following' a number of people; responding to their status updates; 're-tweeting' or repeating interesting messages from others that you are 'following' to those who are 'following' you and linking to outside websites of interest.

This chapter addresses the following questions:

1. To what extent do bilingual speakers of Welsh and English use either or both languages in their 'tweets' (i.e. messages sent via Twitter)?
2. What are the most popular uses of Twitter for bilingual Welsh and English speakers?

3.   In which language do bilingual Welsh and English speakers interact
      with one another and with non-Welsh speakers?
4.   What strategies are adopted by bilingual Welsh and English speakers
      in their use of Twitter?

These questions will be answered through a mixed quantitative and qualitative methodology.

Literature Review

The Welsh language

According to the 2001 UK national census, Welsh, a Brythonic Celtic language, is spoken by approximately 600,000 speakers inside Wales, or 21.4% of the country's population aged above 3 years at that time. Of more import to this study are writing and reading skills in Welsh. According to the same census, 18% of the population of Wales, approximately 540,000 people, claim to be able to write in Welsh (National Statistics, 2004). The overwhelming majority of Welsh speakers above the age of 3 years are presumed to be fluent in English, meaning that all speakers are bilingual in Welsh and English as part of an additive bilingualism.

The actual use of Welsh on the internet remains largely unexplored from an academic perspective (Honeycutt & Cunliffe, 2008), despite the fact that the importance of Welsh on the internet is frequently mentioned (Cunliffe & Honeycutt, 2008; Davies, 2005; Mackay & Powell, 1998; Parsons, 2000), although this is slowly coming to the fore (Cunliffe, 2009; Kemp, 2010). It appears that the symbolic use of Welsh online and a projection that Welsh is a language of the internet (e.g. that a Welsh language page is available, a typical example of Web 1.0, or that a discussion forum such as maes-e exists) is more important in debates in Wales than the use of the language, either from a quantitative perspective (i.e. how much Welsh is used online?) or from a qualitative perspective (i.e. what type of Welsh is used online?). In assessing the use of Twitter by bilingual speakers of Welsh and English, both of these questions will be addressed.

Frustratingly, much debate and discussion of Welsh on the internet was lost when the website *Metastwnsh* lost much of its content, including articles by Rhodri ap Dyfrig mapping the development of Welsh on Web 2.0 (2009a) and Welsh users on Twitter (2009b). Other projects such as *Hacio'r Iaith* (http://haciaith.com) investigate the use, and development, of Welsh language software online, while Hedyn (http://hedyn.net/wici/

Categori:Blog_Cymraeg) includes a wiki-style list of Welsh language blogs and recognized users of Twitter.

Audience design and communication accommodation theory

The growth in interactivity in Web 2.0 subsequently leads to the need for investigation into how 'classic' sociolinguistic and social-psychological theories operate in cyberspace and how they are mediated in the online world.

Audience design

Allan Bell's (1997) theory of language style and language style shift as audience design follows the suggestion that speakers style shift in reaction to the audience which they face.

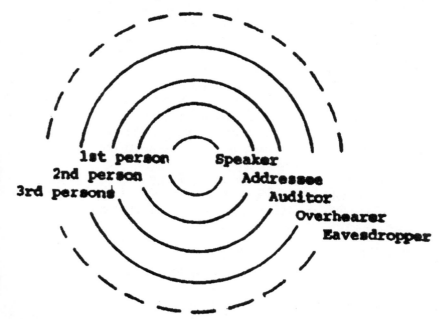

Figure 6.1 Persons and roles in the speech situation (Bell, 1984: 159).

Bell's design, shown in Figure 6.1, begins with the 'speaker' at the centre of the utterance and, a slow distancing away, with a direct 'addressee' for conversation who is known to the speaker, whose presence is accepted and

Table 6.1 Hierarchy of attributes and audience roles (Bell, 1984: 160)

	Known	Ratified	Addressed
Addressee	+	+	+
Auditor	+	+	−
Overhearer	+	−	−
Eavesdropper	+	−	−

is the intended recipient of the speech act; 'auditors', who are part of a group known to the speaker; 'overhearers', those who are present but not part of the group being addressed, and 'eavesdroppers' being people that the speaker is unaware as being present. These relationships between known, ratified and addressed speakers are shown in Table 6.1.

Bell argues that speakers are able to subtly adjust their style when a stranger joins the group and becomes an 'auditor' – present in the group but not directly addressed. They even respond to the presence of an overhearer who is within earshot but is not part of the speaker's conversational circle.

Bell's theory, originally developed in the case of New Zealand radio news broadcasting, implies the ability of the speaker to employ different styles and repertoire when talking to their audience, and has been criticized for its acceptance of this ability to define an audience, which some speakers may be unable to achieve. It has also been criticized for ignoring other facets of speech, for example that speakers may wish to insert their own sense of 'self' or 'face' into the conversation.

Through reference to the actions of bilingual Twitter users, the discussion will consider to what extent Bell's theory of audience design is relevant to the use of Twitter online and, specifically, to bilinguality online.

Communication accommodation theory

This theory is most commonly associated with work by Howard Giles (Giles & Coupland, 1991; Giles & St Clair, 1979; Giles et al., 1973) as a means of explaining style shift by speakers at a hospital in Wales. This theory represents a convergence in spoken accent or style or, in an inter-language situation, an agreement in use of language over another. However, Giles notes the presence of 'intentional disassociation', a verbal or non-verbal divergence from the other speaker. A non-convergence of this type may lead to competition between speakers or suggests that one speaker does not need the approval of the other speaker and so refuses to accommodate.

In a bi- or multilingual setting, attribution is also important and so ability to code-switch between languages is recognized by speakers, for example a presumed non-French speaker in Canada will not be judged negatively because they use English rather than French (Giles *et al.*, 1973), thereby creating a different dynamic in conversation to a situation in which it is assumed that one of the interlocutors can speak French and is refusing to accommodate the other speaker. However, accommodation is not a precise science but a reaction to conversational cues, so as Giles (2009: 283) notes, 'an important feature of communication accommodation theory is that people converge … towards the style they believe them [the other participants] to be using'. He goes on to say that satisfying communication needs requires a delicate balance between convergence – broadly to demonstrate willingness to communicate – and divergence – broadly to incur a healthy sense of group identity, in that way identifying the speaker as part of a group and displaying their own identity but also showing willingness to mediate their identity in discussion with an out-group. The theory implies a conscious or unconscious ability to style shift according to context and that this takes place in all settings.

The discussion in this chapter will examine the use of communication accommodation strategies by bilingual users of Twitter and to what extent accommodation is used in their 'tweets' in online interactivity.

Methodology

A convenience sample of 25 Welsh-speaking users of Twitter was identified by viewing their publicly available Twitter profiles, initially searching for keywords in Welsh using Twitter's search function, identifying a user and then step-by-step 'following' their followers, that is identifying a Welsh language user of Twitter among the followers of the first individual, then a Welsh language user amongst that second individual's followers and so on. This approach ensured that there were communicative links between users who, together, make up a part of the Welsh language usage community on Twitter. Although note was made of the informants' gender and approximate age, who were primarily in their 20s and 30s and approximately two-thirds male and one-third female, these did not lead to statistically significant results and are not discussed further. Only regular users of Twitter were included in the study – those who had not participated in the previous fortnight were not included.

The Welsh community is generally small and many of these informants are or have been linked through real-world interests such as location, cultural activities, social activities and employment, in addition to through the internet.

The most recent 20 tweets from each informant were coded according to the language in which the tweet was written, and whether the tweet was an original self-generated comment a 're-tweet' of someone else's update, or a response to another tweet.

The 500 tweets were analysed through a quantitative and qualitative methodology, using the coding software, PAWS 17.0.2, to discover any statistical information regarding the use of language in bilinguals' tweets with further analysis of 'outlying' tweets that suggest creative use of the languages or strategies employed by the bilingual tweeters.

Quantitative Study Results

The 500 tweets were inputted into PAWS 17.0.2, with their language use coded on a 5-point Likert scale ranging from 1 as a tweet entirely in English to 5 being a tweet entirely in Welsh. Intermediate points on the scale reflected varying levels of bilingualism within the tweet, with 3 on the scale equating to a roughly similar use of both languages or an indeterminate use of language that could be either Welsh or English in form.

Overall use of language in tweets

As can be seen in Table 6.2, there were relatively few tweets which were not written exclusively or primarily in the matrix language of either English or Welsh.

English makes up a narrow majority of the total number of tweets made, with 256 of the 500 tweets sampled (51.2%) being written solely in this language. In comparison, there were 206 tweets (41.2%) written entirely in Welsh. Together, 462 or 92.4% of the 500 tweets included in the sample were clearly written in a matrix language which was wholly one of the two languages spoken by the bilingual informants.

Table 6.2 Use of language in corpus by number of tweets

Language	No. of tweets	% of total tweets
English	256	51.2
Mostly English/some Welsh	10	2
Bilingual/indeterminate	23	4.6
Mostly Welsh/some English	5	1
Welsh	206	41.2
Total	500	100

The remaining 38 tweets include those which either have no or have non-classifiable language and those which employ a specific language strategy.

Personal language choice

The tweets per person were analysed according to the language used in each tweet and can be seen in Figure 6.2, in descending order from the user of most Welsh in their tweets to the user of least Welsh.

As can be seen, there was a great difference between informants in the number of tweets in Welsh and English that they had made in their 20 most recent updates.

At the highest end of the scale, informant 7 used Welsh in every single tweet written. In other contexts, it might be argued that this informant is not actively bilingual, but in the Welsh situation a young person is assumed to hold communicative competence in English and is therefore choosing to use only Welsh in their tweets.

He was followed by informant 17 in the use of Welsh. She tweeted just once in English, re-tweeting a generic message of support.

Informant 3 was also consistent in his use of Welsh, using the language 18 times. Informant 8, informant 20 and informant 6 all made at least three-quarters of their tweets through the medium of Welsh.

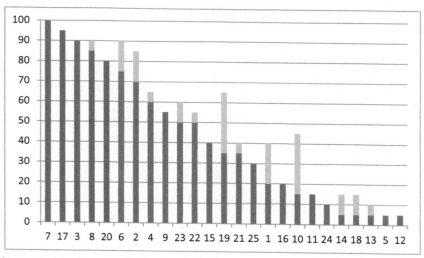

Figure 6.2 Percentage of Welsh posts by individual Twitter users in corpus, according to informant (dark shade shows Welsh, lighter shade shows indeterminate or bilingual use).

Meanwhile, at the lowest end of the scale, informants 5 and 12 used Welsh just once in 20 updates on Twitter, with the remainder of their usage being in English. They were joined in low usage of Welsh by informants 13, 18, 24 and 14. Informant 13 used Welsh just once in a tweet with a further tweet in indeterminate language, with a similar language profile for informant 18 and 14. Informant 24 used Welsh in two tweets.

A One-way ANOVA was carried out on the informants' use of Welsh in tweets in order to establish whether this reflected a statistically significant difference in their use of language in this context.

This led to the conclusion that there was a significant result of $F(24, 475) = 13.615$, $p < 0.001$, and that there was a difference of language used in general by the bilinguals when 'tweeting'.

Language in response

However, in analysing the use of language on an SNS, the interactivity of the site must be taken into consideration, and therefore factors other than the individual's own use of language must be analysed.

As noted in the methodology, tweets were coded not only according to language used but also according to the type of contribution in the interactivity of Twitter (i.e. the originality of the message or its link to other contributions).

After a preliminary analysis of the data, these were coded into five uses of style.

1. Original contributions to Twitter
2. 'Re-tweets' of a contribution made by another user (usually noted in the tweet by the use of 'RT: @username' at the start of the tweet or (via @username) at the end of the tweet)
3. Response to another user, either to a previous update of theirs or to specifically draw an issue to their attention
4. Generic re-tweet
5. Multiple tweets of the same message (often in different languages)

The result of this coding across the 500 tweets can be seen in Table 6.3.

It shows that a majority of tweets made by the 25 informants can be considered as 'original contributions' to Twitter, that is tweets that were self-generated by the user as a response to their surroundings or thoughts. These made up 292 or 58.4% of the total number of tweets.

Table 6.3 Style of tweet used in corpus

Style of tweet	No. of tweets	% of total tweets
Original contributions	292	58.4
Re-tweets	26	5.2
Response	156	31.2
Generic re-tweet	7	1.4
Multiple tweets of same message	19	3.8
Total	500	100

The second largest group were responses to other users of Twitter or messages directed at a specific user. These are deliberately public messages as a private 'direct message' function is also available. They made up another 156 or 31.2% of the 500 tweets that were analysed, nearly a third of the total in the corpus.

The remaining three categories, all performing a function of re-tweeting either content generated by others or repeated by the same user, together make up a little over 10% of the total tweets. These can generally be categorized as re-tweets of information or interesting links by other Twitter users, a forwarding of a generic link for support of a campaign or the user consciously repeating tweets in both languages.

In this section, the use of language in original contributions to Twitter will be assessed, followed by the use of language in responses. Further analysis of generic re-tweets and multiple tweets of the same message will be made in the qualitative section.

Table 6.4 shows the choice of language by informants when making an original contribution to Twitter.

It shows that, of the 292 original contributions made by the informants, 156 (53.4%) of the contributions were made in English, while 113 (38.7%) were in Welsh. The remaining 23 contributions were either in a mixture of languages, with no language, or of indeterminate language.

As might be expected, the most frequent users of Welsh in general, informants 7 and 17, wrote all of their original contributions in Welsh (or

Table 6.4 Language of original contributions to Twitter

Original contribution	No. of tweets	% of tweets
English	156	53.4
Welsh	113	38.7
Mixture (bilingual, none, indeterminate)	23	7.9
Total	292	100

predominantly Welsh), as did informants 6, 8 and 23. At the other end of the spectrum, four users, informants 11, 13, 14 and 18, made no original contributions in Welsh.

This, of course, leaves 16 informants who varied between English and Welsh when making an original contribution to Twitter. While in some cases, such as informant 12, there is only one contribution in Welsh and the opposite is true of informant 20, who made just one tweet in English, many informants show a willingness to use either language – informant 4 expresses herself in English on 6 occasions and in Welsh on 11, while informants 9 and 22 use both languages on a consistent basis (9 and 8 original tweets, respectively, in English and 7 each in Welsh). A fuller analysis of this pattern of usage will be covered in the discussion.

The different patterns of Twitter usage are clearly also of importance here, as, while some users self-generate the overwhelming majority of their content (notably informant 12 who only writes own updates without any attempt at public interactivity), the majority of tweets from eight of the bilingual Twitter users are in response to other stimuli.

The language used in response to other individual users of Twitter, which, as already noted, could be a direct response to a tweet by the other user or 'flagging up' an issue for the other user, is shown in Table 6.5, across the 156 tweets in the corpus which were identified in this manner.

This analysis shows that exactly half the responses were made entirely in Welsh (78 responses or 50%) while 69 or (44.2%) were made in English. The producers of these texts may be fluently bilingual in Welsh and English, but it is likely that many of their friends may speak only English which would in all likelihood skew linguistic behaviour in a comment directed primarily, if not solely, at a non-Welsh speaker.

Further research was therefore carried out on the use of language by the other Twitter users identified as being the recipient of tweets (established by the use of @username at the beginning of the tweet) in order to discover which of the receiving users were also bilingual. This is not a foolproof system, as lack of use of Welsh in their tweets or in their

Table 6.5 Language use in 'response' to others

Language	No. of tweets	% of tweets
English	69	44.2
Welsh	78	50
Mixture (bilingual, none, indeterminate)	9	5.8
Total	156	100

Table 6.6 Language 'response' to bi-literates

Language	No. of tweets	% of tweets
Mostly English	35	30.8
Mostly Welsh	79	69.2
Total	114	100

profiles does not necessarily reflect their passive ability to understand the language.

This showed that while all of the 78 responses made in Welsh were for the attention of other Welsh-speaking bilinguals, 31 of the responses made in English (45% of the total responses in English) were for identified bilinguals. This left another 38 responses in English (55% of the total responses in English) that were for the attention of Twitter users for whom there was no evidence of any ability in Welsh.

Taking into consideration other tweets made predominantly in one language or the other, of the 114 tweets that were aimed at a bilingual, shown in Table 6.6, 79 tweets (69.2% of the total) were made in Welsh, while 35 (the remaining 30.8%) were made predominantly in English.

On the surface, this suggests that the bilingual users of Twitter in this study are more than twice as likely to tweet in Welsh to a fellow bilingual as to use English for this purpose. It also suggests a sense of community in that 114 of the 152, exactly three-quarters of the tweets made, were as responses to other bilingual users of Twitter. However, it is also worth noting that the use of English to other bilinguals is increased significantly by two outliers.

The removal of these two specific profiles changes the picture quite dramatically. Of the remaining 91 tweets between bilinguals, only 15 (or 16.5%) are predominantly in English with 76 (or 83.4%) in Welsh.

Even this, though, does not tell the full story, as several of the remaining tweets in English are song lyrics or insults that suggest linguistic play and the participants' bilingualism, leaving only a handful of tweets between bilinguals that are written in English purely for communicative purposes.

It therefore appears that a community of practice is in place between these Welsh bi-literates with the norm of using Welsh among each other. As this was a convenience sample identified by following the tweets of linked individuals, it cannot be identified whether this is common behaviour between all Welsh–English bi-literates on Twitter or an exceptional group.

Qualitative Study Results

As previously noted, the overwhelming majority (92.4%) of the 500 tweets in the study were clearly identifiable as being either in English or in Welsh. This leaves 38 tweets whose status needs to be classified and defined.

These remaining tweets can be broken down into six categories as follows:

1.   Tweets with no independent text
2.   Tweets in an indeterminate language
3.   Bilingual Welsh and English tweets
4.   English language tweets with some Welsh
5.   Tweets with English but where Welsh speaking is an advantage
6.   Other languages used

No text

There are several tweets which contain no independent text and link directly to outside websites, usually photographs. These will not be discussed further here.

Indeterminate language

This category refers to tweets where the language in which the tweet is meant to be written is unclear. Usually, this is because the tweet is very short, as little as one word, and makes reference to a proper noun, for example a name or computer program, or a phrase used in colloquial conversation in both languages.

An example of a proper noun, from informant 8, would be

'@username Robin Williams?!'
Informant 8, Tweet 158

A phrase used in colloquial conversation in both languages could be expressed as that by informant 14:

'@username ta x'
Informant 14, Tweet 278

Another example of a proper noun is provided by informant 18, who gives a one-word response as follows:

'@username Tweetie!!'
Informant 18, Tweet 358

In each of these cases, there is too little information to determine whether the intention of the author was to tweet in Welsh, English or bilingually.

Bilingual tweets

There are several examples of bilingual tweets, in which the same information or message is relayed in both Welsh and English.

This is predominantly a feature of tweets from informant 1, but also others, including informants 19 and 23.

Informant 1, who uses this method four times in the 20 tweets analysed, produces the pattern in a variety of ways: twice in commenting a photo he links to the tweet, and once on an article he links in his tweet. There is a fourth tweet without a link which is a general behavioural comment.

Examples of his comments include

'[link] – Wel, munudau wedi'r machlud ta beth… wel, just after sunset anyway'
Informant 1, Tweet 2

The process of writing tweets bilingually appears to be primarily as a means of giving information quickly in one tweet and respecting Welsh and non-Welsh-speaking audiences. This is most effectively achieved when tweeting or highlighting information, which can be done simply through use of digits and in both languages within the 140-character words pace of Twitter.

Often, though, there are a number of 're-tweets' which are actually the same message repeated in the other language, presumably when the message itself is too long to repeat in both languages within the same tweet. The use of bilingual provision of information comes partly out of courtesy and a need to communicate information effectively and partly out of a sense that non-Welsh speakers should not be 'left out' of conversation.

The purpose of literal translation in English first and Welsh second is limited as Welsh speakers will almost all be comfortable with reading English, thereby making the Welsh translation redundant. Therefore, it is not a surprise to see bilingual Twitter users generally adopt a 'Welsh first' approach when tweeting in both languages within the same message.

Welsh language display

When English is used as the primary language of a tweet with Welsh as a secondary language, it has the effect of being symbolic – a form of language display that will not impact upon the effectiveness of communication to a non-Welsh speaker while at the same time expressing their Welsh linguistic identity.

This can be seen in the following tweet from informant 14:

'@username Diolch [username], have a good holiday x'
Informant 14, Tweet 265
('Diolch' is the Welsh for 'thank you' and therefore one of the most common words learnt or understood by non-Welsh speakers.)

The informant, whose professional connections mean a larger than average 'following' on Twitter who do not speak Welsh, is addressing a fellow bilingual but is probably aware of the interest in following both her and the friend to whom she is responding. This leads to a tweet which is primarily in English and therefore understandable to an English-speaking audience while displaying her, or indeed their, Welshness.

The same could be true of informant 18, when he tweets

'sori – bottom right...of the tweet'
Informant 18, Tweet 346

In this case, 'sori' is a borrowed form of the English 'sorry', with an orthography that is recognized as Welsh but whose meaning will also be clear to non-Welsh speakers.

Another example of this can be found in a tweet from informant 21, who writes

'just read 'At least nine killed in German school shooting' as 'At last, nine killed in German school shooting'. Wps'
Informant 21, Tweet 420

Again, 'wps' is a common Welsh spelling for English 'oops' (which usually has the meaning of a light-hearted mistake). In both this example and the previous one, the two borrowings used from English are both produced orthographically in Welsh using fewer characters than in the original language. The choice of Welsh words even in a predominantly English language phrase may be a reflection of the need to communicate on Twitter using the fewest possible number of characters due to the limitations of the programme, and, in reverse, an English phrase or concept where it involves fewer characters than the Welsh. This suggests that bilingual informants are comfortable code-switching between languages when appropriate for the limitations of the technology and understanding of the recipients, and these limitations may have other impacts upon language choice when using social networking media.

Welsh advantage

Finally, there is a group of tweets where information is available in English, but where the Welsh provides an added value for Welsh speakers, going beyond the functional bilinguality of translation.

An example of this can be seen from the following tweet by informant 1:

'[#username] Another lovely sunset in Preseli tonight. 'Un funud fach cyn elo'r haul o'r wybren, un funud fwyn cyn delo'r hwyr i'r hynt' '
Informant 1, Tweet 5

This is a quote from a Welsh language poem, Cofio ('Remember') by Waldo Williams. It's meaning and cultural references are not available to a non-Welsh speaker reading the tweet. However, an English speaker will nevertheless be able to understand the opening part of the tweet referring to the sunset. In this way, there is no loss of comprehension of the purpose of the tweet for the English speaker, who understands that a lovely sunset has taken place, but the bilingual Welsh and English literate will have a greater appreciation of the intention behind the tweet.

Other languages

There are two examples of 'other languages' being used, that is neither English nor Welsh. These are both produced by the same user, informant 20, who is learning a foreign language. He produces two tweets which include words in the foreign languages, alongside a translation into English and a semi-phonetic explanation of their pronunciation. This is considered to be an outlier rather than indicative of any particular practice by bilinguals.

Discussion

In answering the questions set out at the beginning of this chapter, the following broad conclusions can be reached:

1. The group of bilingual literates in Welsh and English use both languages in their 'tweets', but with a wide internal variation according to the speaker. In quantitative terms, they only occasionally mix both languages within a tweet, usually maintaining a distinction between the two languages.

2. Twitter is most often used by the informants to send original self-generated content to the internet, followed by addressed tweets designed for the specific attention of another user, often in response to a comment by the other person. Other uses involve re-tweeting messages sent by other users or sometimes tweeting their own message in two different languages.

3. The bilingual Welsh and English users of Twitter in this survey predominantly interact with each other in Welsh when tweeting, but a small minority use English far more often than the others. English is used exclusively with Twitter users who show no sign of proficiency in Welsh.

4. As noted above in response to 1, the vast majority of tweets are expressed in one language or another, but there are examples of bilingual tweets. These may repeat the same information in both languages within the same tweet, repeat the same information in two different tweets, illustrate a symbolic use of Welsh or give a Welsh advantage where a tweet may be understood by a non-Welsh speaker but where privileged information is provided for the bilingual.

How, then, do these responses assist in understanding the classical sociolinguistic and social-psychological concepts such as audience design and communicative accommodation theory and their application to bilingual users of Twitter.

In terms of audience design, Twitter allows the user to make a distinction between a direct addressee and a general tweet, through the use of @ username at the beginning of a tweet. As previously illustrated, the bilingual Welsh and English literate users of Twitter in the study predominantly used Welsh when addressing another bilingual directly, but used English more frequently when making a general tweet. This can therefore be seen as a form of audience design, and also as an understanding of audience design, not dis-similar to that suggested by Bell (1997).

A tweet aimed at a direct addressee is clearly comparable to an addressee in that they are known, ratified and addressed. Meanwhile, an eavesdropper who does not have an account or is not following the tweeter but can read their tweets is at the other extreme – unknown, not ratified and, broadly speaking, not addressed. The intermediary positions are more difficult to clarify. Users are informed of being followed, and so are aware of the recipient of general tweets – although these may run into hundreds or thousands of individuals. Those who follow both participants in an addressed tweet will also receive tweets. It is therefore unclear to what extent these individuals are 'known', 'ratified' and 'addressed' by the user, and a lack of clarity in Bell's original schema between being known and ratified does not help. Similarly, as a general tweet goes to all who are following the user, this is the audience, and they are therefore 'addressed', even though the user may be unclear as to exactly who makes up this audience.

As a follower, either an auditor or an overhearer, is the audience then they must be taken into consideration in the user's language choice. Therefore, the number of followers, or at least, the language choice or ability of followers, must be noted, and it is apparent that the two individual users with highest number of followers, with a large number outside Welsh-speaking circles, use a large amount of English in their tweets. While not all followers are necessarily welcome (there are examples of spamming, e.g. following as many people as possible while trying to sell products), the specific public roles of these users require the linguistic choices and abilities of others to be taken into consideration. This suggests evidence of communicative accommodation theory in action through Twitter.

By changing language according to the intended audience of the tweet, broadly speaking more Welsh for a specific audience and more English for a general audience, the Twitter users appear to be defining their audience according to a priori knowledge of the individual for whom the tweet is intended and language choice is clearly influenced. That Welsh language tweets are more likely to be used with bilinguals and that exclusively English language tweets are used with non-Welsh speakers illustrates that communicative accommodation theories of convergence are generally played out here, as are Welsh bilingual norms in terms of the community of practice – that Welsh is the normal language of communication between fluent bilinguals with communicative competence in both languages. Twitter, as an interactive online platform, is one in which Welsh and English are both engaged for communication by bilingual Welsh and English speakers.

After establishing that Bell's theories of audience design is relevant to the use of Twitter, it must be taken into consideration that the context is very different from a normal social interaction. The major form of communication of Twitter by the bilingual group studied, the self-generated tweet, is intended for the consumption of auditors or overhearers, perhaps comparable to talking loudly in a pub so that you are listened to by acquaintances walking past, rather than aimed at a more defined audience. In fact, to define your audience with an addressee is to make a marked contribution to Twitter, rather than an unmarked contribution intended for all followers. It is in this sense that Web 2.0 poses a threat to small bilingual communities as an unmarked contribution may be more likely to be expressed in the majority language of a user's followers (which will in a bilingual society include many monolinguals) so as to be inclusive of as many followers as possible.

Conclusions

A convenience sample of bilingual Welsh and English defines their audience on Twitter according to Bell's theory of audience design and choose the language of their tweets accordingly. They do not deliberately diverge when dealing with non-Welsh-speaking Twitter users, and generally conform to Welsh–English bilingual community of practice norms. It appears that the greater the number of non-Welsh-speaking followers, the more likely the user to tweet a general comment in English, but the overall pattern shows that there are significant differences in language choice between different users. There are certainly a number of Twitter users who consistently and almost exclusively use Welsh except for in communication with non-Welsh speakers. Future research might compare the use of Welsh on Twitter, with its sense of 'following' (i.e. audited or overheard in Bell's schema) with that of Welsh on Facebook, in which you become the 'friend' of another Facebook user which has arguably a different dynamic due to greater multimedia and personal interaction (specifically the use of photographs).

This study is centred on observed use of Welsh by bilingual Welsh and English speakers on Twitter, but can only guess at the intentions of the contributors themselves. Individual interviews with Twitter users or focus group studies might give a greater insight into their language choices online and their understanding of the impacts or aims of their Tweets, especially vis-a-vis the theories discussed above. Perhaps using online discussion forums, such as maes-e, or developing other online methodologies for conducting social studies research would assist in understanding these choices.

In understanding language choice and community activities online, it must be questioned whether a minority language or bilingual community's online presence can be divorced from 'real-world' personalities and issues. There are often small number of people who are 'active' in the community and these may well be those involved in online issues. This convenience sample, identified through links between individuals, acts as a 'speech' community of Welsh between members. They may be unlikely to be representative of all users and, similarly, their practices and 'face' may be more likely to reflect real-world experiences and use than online communities where anonymity can be almost guaranteed. A separate sample of Welsh–English bi-literates may produce a different community of practice and online norms.

According to the 2001 census, there is a drop between the number of those claiming to be able to speak Welsh and those claiming literacy skills in the language. However, the census measures only the self-assessed ability to use the language, not practice. The research collected for this chapter suggests a far greater difference between the use of spoken and written Welsh than that implied in the census returns. A number of Welsh–English bilingual speakers, known to the author to use Welsh in face-to-face contexts, showed no bi-literate skills in their use of Twitter. There are a number of possible explanations for this, including their ability in the language, for example a lack of literacy skills in Welsh or a lack of confidence in their Welsh literacy skills. Some users may express a preference for English or be less familiar with Welsh written norms due to the pre-dominance of English textual cues compared to Welsh, especially outside education and with relatively small circulations for Welsh books and periodicals. Relevant to some of the theories explored in this chapter, the belief that Welsh should not be used online with non-Welsh speakers present (a facet of audience design) or a divergence from Welsh online community practices and their positioning as English users online in a separate expression of 'self' from their physical self-interactions. This non-use of Welsh online is a very important topic of research for those interested in minority language revitalization.

In terms of practical application, minority language users and supporters face challenges to discover methods in which Web 2.0 can work to the benefit of minority languages when they must compete against majority language resources, which, almost by definition, includes a greater number of speakers, resources for development of web portals, etc. as well as traditional language discourse and attitudes, including, as shown by some members of the bilingual community in this study, the 'inclusion' of non-minority language speakers. While each minority language setting is contextual, similar issues apply across the spectrum.

References

ap Dyfrig, R. (2009a, 5 January 2009) Cymru a Gwe 2.0. *Metastwnsh*. Accessed 9 September 2009. http://blog.metastwnsh.com/erthygl/cymru-a-gwe-20/

ap Dyfrig, R. (2009b, 14 January 2009) Defnyddio Cymraeg ar Twitter. *Metastwnsh*. Accessed 9 September 2009. http://blog.metastwnsh.com/erthygl/defnyddio-cymraeg-ar-twitter/.

Bell, A. (1997) Language style as audience design. In N. Coupland and A. Jaworski (eds) *Sociolinguistics: A Reader and Coursebook* (pp. 240–250). New York: St Mattin's Press.

Cunliffe, D. (2009) Implications of Web2.0 for bilingualism on websites: Towards best practice, accessed 27 April 2011. http://www.byig-wlb.org.uk/english/publications/Pages/PublicationItem.aspx?puburl=/English/publications/Publications/20090812%20AD%20S%20Implications%2.0of%20web2.0%20for%20bilingual%20websites%20f1.doc

Cunliffe, D. and Honeycutt, C. (2008) The Blogiadur: A community of Welsh-language bloggers. In F. Sudweeks, H. Hrachovec and C. Ess (eds) *Proceedings of the 6th International Conference on Cultural Attitudes Towards Technology and Communication (CATaC)* (pp. 230–244). Nimes: CATaC.

Davies, G. (2005) Beginnings: New media and the Welsh language. *North American Journal of Welsh Studies* 5 (1), 11–22. Accessed 19 May 2011. http://spruce.flint.umich.edu/~ellisjs/Grahame%20Davies.pdf.

Giles, H. (2009) The process of communication accommodation. In N. Coupland and A. Jaworski (eds) *The New Reader in Sociolinguistics* (pp. 276–286). Basingstoke, UK: Macmillan.

Giles, H. and Coupland, N. (1991) *Language: Contexts and Consequences*. Milton Keynes: Open University Press.

Giles, H. and St Clair, R.N. (1979) *Language and Social Psychology*. Oxford: Blackwell.

Giles, H., Taylor, D.M. and Bourhis, R.Y. (1973) Towards a theory of interpersonal accommodation through language: Some Canadian data. *Language in Society* 2, 177–192.

Honeycutt, C. and Cunliffe, D. (2008) (Re)creating Welsh-speaking communities in Facebook: An initial investigation, Accessed 24 April 2011. http://www.slis.indiana.edu/phd/people/phd_forum/2008/Honeycutt_2008_ForumAbstract.pdf.

Kemp, L. (2010, 26 April 2010) Facebook key to Welsh language survival: Study, *South Wales Echo*. Accessed 24 April 2011. http://www.walesonline.co.uk/news/wales-news/2010/04/26/facebook-key-to-welsh-language-survival-study-91466-26316296/.

Mackay, H. and Powell, T. (1998) Connecting Wales: The internet and national identity. In B. Loader (ed.) *Cyberspace Divide* (pp. 203–216). London: Routledge.

National Statistics (2004) *Focus on Wales: Its People*. National Statistics. Accessed 26 April 2011. http://www.statistics.gov.uk/downloads/theme_compendia/fow/Wales.pdf.

Parsons, W. (2000) Becoming a diaspora: The Welsh experience from Beulah Land to cyber-Cymru. In A.J. Kershen (ed.) *Language, Labour and Migration* (pp. 92–117). Aldershot: Ashgate Publishing.

7 Kashubian and Modern Media: The Influence of New Technologies on Endangered Languages

Nicole Dołowy-Rybińska

Introduction

Changes that have been occurring in the media over the past two decades compel us to consider how they impact minority languages and the ways in which those languages are used by the young generation. Many sociolinguistic researchers have overlooked the implications of this new media environment on the development of minority languages. Such neglect is usually combined with a failure to properly understand this recent revolution and the fact that young people today live very differently from even the generation of 30–40 year olds. We could go as far as to suggest that the world is experiencing the most powerful media metamorphosis in history. In the past, the shift from oral to written language took place slowly, with those two worlds coexisting before writing became the dominant medium influencing people's way of thinking and existing in the world (Goody, 1986). In addition, the invention of the printing press, although revolutionary, took time to find its place in society, and the consequences of its growing influence (the development of novels, national languages, the Reformation, etc.) (cf. Goody, 1986; Goody & Watt 1963; Ong, 2002) stretched over many generations. Each subsequent medium which dominated in a given era (radio and television) allowed people to adapt easily to the changing conditions and did not cause as dramatic a generational change as we are seeing today. Meanwhile, the internet and practices associated with it have made it difficult for parents to imagine how children and young people think and function; they do not understand their needs, behaviours or the multifaceted way they function in the world.

Many researchers do not approach the new media and the changes they bring about analytically and with scientific openness, but instead with a kind of bitterness, full of worry and resentment over the changing and dehumanizing world, a world where they see bonds and interpersonal relationships being broken or extremely oversimplified. This is hardly surprising if we look back at the way past luminaries described a new dominant medium during the transitional period of its introduction. In *Phaedrus*, Plato attributes the following accusation of writing to Socrates: writing is not a remedy for memory, but the opposite; it is a remedy for reminding, not remembering; it gives the illusion of wisdom, but not the reality of wisdom; future generations will hear much without being properly taught, and will appear wise but not be so, making them difficult to get along with[1] (Plato & Cobb, 1993). His fears were justifiable – writing really does alter the way of remembering, influence inter-group relations and many other human actions.

However, an anthropologist should not approach a new medium with such judgement. If we engage with every medium in the spirit of relativism, assuming that there are no better or worse media but that we should simply study the entirety of a culture that exists in a given medium, we will notice that McLuhan's theory that 'the medium is the massage (message)' (McLuhan *et al.*, 1967) is justified here, and the digital world is not worse than those that preceded it but is simply different. The internet is not only a medium but also a social space that comes into being thanks to the medium. No one doubts today that anthropological studies of cultures must include the perspective of a dominant medium and those that mediate it, and focus on the person using the given media: the spoken word, handwriting, print and the internet. The researcher should focus on the practices of utilizing the medium in a broader cultural context. The internet appears to be a special case, if only because of its novelty: not only is the technology being used creatively to communicate specific messages but it also allows for the process of communication, of being together regardless of distance or time. The technological aspect of each online society influences the type and shape of communication, defining the character and language of individual types of transmission.

When things are viewed from this perspective, it seems impossible not to ask about the functioning of minority languages in the multimedia sphere. Mediated communication is especially justified in the case of such languages, as every researcher uses it anyway, whether consciously or unconsciously. Therefore, it is worth examining the consequences of the dominance of subsequent media systems that affect the language shift in autochthonous minorities.

Ethnic Languages and Writing

For a long time members of ethnic cultures existed in a spoken world. Their relationships were based on strong interpersonal contact, on direct connections and on community members identifying with a group that handed down its own constitutive stories and tales from generation to generation. Ferdinand Tönnies described the ties that bound them in terms of the *Gemeinschaft* (community). Representatives of those groups lived in their own cultures, separate from the dominant one, without having to contemplate their ethnicity or identity. Everyday lives, meetings, festivals and rites marked the passage of time, bonding the group and giving it common grounds and points of reference. Anthony David Smith, Professor of Nationalism and Ethnicity at the London School of Economics, states that the basis of ethnicity is formed by myths, recollections, values and symbols due to a given group. Therefore, in order to capture the specific character of ethnic identities

> one has to look at the nature (forms and content) of their myths and symbols, their historical memories and central values, which we can summarize as the 'myth–symbol' complex, at the mechanisms of their diffusion (or lack of it) through a given population, and their transmission to future generations. (Smith, 2007: 15)

In the era of oral communication, ethnic cultures created their reference points and ties by themselves. The language used by people within their villages and communities was well-adapted to the world in which they existed – it was used to express the most important issues faced by their culture, reflected their lifestyle and way of functioning and served as a vehicle for their myths, their tales and their history.

Regardless of whether an ethnic language reached a written form in the early Middle Ages (e.g. Breton), during the Reformation (e.g. Sorbian) or as late as the 20th century (Kashubian), writing did not become the dominant medium in those communities for a long time, while the institutions of writing did not interfere with the stability and continuation of traditions and customs or the constancy of language in which all affairs of the group were conducted. For minority cultures, writing arrived from the outside and remained the domain of the educated few who were in contact with representatives of the dominant culture, frequently soaking up its ideals, or outsiders who entered the ethnic community, subordinating it to the rules imposed by the written culture – nationality, legal systems and taxation (Goody, 1986). The ethnic world changed with the appearance of writing institutions. The greatest turning point for the continuity of ethnic cultures came with the arrival of the most important institution of written culture – schools.

The general education system permanently changed the unilingual world. The dominant language was intended to serve as the only communication tool, and the aim of the institution itself was to convert peripheral and separate cultures into elements of the political body. Although language policy varied between individual countries (such as France, Germany or Poland), the majority of representatives of minority cultures emerged as ethnically crippled, frequently harbouring a sense of inferiority in comparison to the dominant culture. A mass shift to the dominant language, migration to cities and lifestyle changes, usually going hand-in-hand with renouncing one's own ethnic roots, were common phenomena during the first half of the 20th century.

The latter half of that century proved to be the most challenging period for many minority cultures and languages. On the one hand, ethnic and linguistic minorities entering the world of mass media (radio and television) were forced to quickly adopt the national language. Propagation of new lifestyles, access to the same standards and attractiveness of the dominant and popular cultures led to rural communities becoming abandoned. Populations were moving to cities, quickly renouncing their burdensome ethnic identities and their languages, incomprehensible to others. It also meant that elements of the outside world increasingly encroached on the communities with the advent of industrialization and new technologies – especially radio and television – fracturing them, dividing them into those who remained part of the 'past' vs. those striving for 'progress'. Minority languages were increasingly being pushed to the margins, slowly ceasing to fit the world people actually lived in. They did not adapt to changing needs and customs, and new concepts were being linguistically serviced by the dominant language. This brought about a quick 'folklorization' of ethnic cultures and their languages (Fishman, 1987).

Second Wind for Minority Languages

However, the increasingly marginalized ethnic communities and minority languages gained an unexpected lifeline. Human rights and anti-discrimination movements, dominant since the aftermath of WWII, strengthened minority groups, who had been demanding a change in attitudes since the mid-19th century and who were warning of their woeful situation and inevitable demise. Ethnic activities occurring in Europe since the mid-19th century led to the formation of a trend defined by Smith as *ethnicism*, 'a collective movement, whose activities and efforts are aimed at resisting perceived threats from outside and corrosion within, at renewing a community's forms and traditions, and at reintegrating a community's members and strata' (2007: 50). The desire to protect their own cultures and traditions meant that minority cultures, for years suffering humiliation and being pushed to the sidelines, started to regain their sense of 'rightness and value of the *ethnie's* revelations and life-style' (Smith, 2007: 50).

Linguistic and ethnic revival, blossoming during the 1960s, led to an increased self-awareness among members of many minority cultures, as well as a movement to force governments to take steps in order to regulate such groups' uncertain status.

One major success achieved by minorities was the introduction of their languages into schools, and ensuring them a place in public media (now guaranteed by the European Charter for Regional or Minority Languages). The presence of minority languages in modern media is now regarded as a necessity. Stephen H. Riggins wrote, 'What better strategy could there be for ensuring minority survival than the development by minorities of their own media conveying their own point of view in their own language?' (Riggins, 1992: 3; see also Browne & Uribe-Jongbloed; Jones; Cormack in this volume). Although we are aware that the media (and the education system) functioning in the minority language reflect the system inherited from the dominant culture (Hinton, 2001: 182) and we are unable to clearly assess the impact of the media on minority languages (Browne, 1996: 169; see also Browne and Uribe-Jongbloed and Cormack in this volume), we are conscious that the absence of minority languages in the media that people use to communicate will bring their eventual demise. That is why the role of minority languages functioning in digital media must not be underestimated. Not only is there a place for them in cyberspace but also the internet itself allows the creation of a new type of 'local communities', which may wish to use a minority language as a means of communication or at least a symbol of belonging to and identifying with a minority culture.

Changes in the Kashubian Language

At this point, it will be worth functionalizing the scheme outlined above by looking at how changes to the media have occurred in the Kashubia region in Poland and how they affected the Kashubian language.

The present situation of Kashubian is complicated. On the one hand, the intergenerational transmission of this language has broken down, fewer and fewer people are using it in everyday life, in private communication with other members of the ethnic community and with family, friends and neighbours. Statistical data (Mordawski, 2005) indicate that there are now about 500,000 people who identify themselves fully or partly with the Kashubian group, 60% of them can speak the Kashubian language, but only about 80,000 use it in everyday life. Most of those who know Kashubian belong to the older generation. The middle generation knows the language but rarely uses it outside of the family, whereas the younger generation has passive or no knowledge of Kashubian before going to school. A 100 years ago, all the members of the Kashubian community knew the language. There are many reasons for this breakdown – the status of the language, the linguistic policies followed by the state and the place of the minority language in the education system, media, government, etc. (Edwards, 1992). In the case of the Kashubian language, the most important reason for language shift was a change in lifestyle – the Kashubs, a rural farming and fishing community, became fragmented when many of their members left the villages, moved to the cities and worked in different domains. To adapt and to function in their new environment, they switched to the dominant language. The age-old fabric of the community disintegrated. In the late 20th century, Kashubs ceased to differ in terms of lifestyle and dress from the surrounding Poles and neighbouring Germans, although they were still distinct in terms of habits and language at the outset of the 20th century.

Kashubs inhabit a border zone that has for centuries been subject to rivalry between Poland and Germany. Both countries have pursued assimilating policies in the area. The real change in the situation of the Kashubian language took place in communist-era Poland (1945–1989). The state linguistic policies during this period led many Kashubs to intentionally abandon their ethnic roots and their language as the most important marker of their cultural identity. During this era the use of the Kashubian language was forbidden not only in public life but also in schools. Children who used the minority language in school were reprimanded, ridiculed and suffered corporal punishment from teachers, who were obliged to force them to use the Polish language. In a socialist country, there was no place for a multicultural system or for any type of distinction; everybody quite simply had to be the same. All these factors weakened the intergenerational transmission of the Kashubian language.

Kashubian on the Traditional Media

While the Kashubs were able to live in the world of their own living spoken word, their language developed and retained a strong position as the key tool of communication, lifestyle and the conveying of traditions, values and culture. The Kashubs formed a strong community based on close and immediate ties and face-to-face relationships. However, the lifestyle changes brought about by the necessity to move from the oral to the written and even printed word (into cities with their institutions, schools, bureaucracies and armies) caused destruction of the unifying ties on the one hand and a weakening of the minority language's position on the other hand. As a language where the first (literary only) texts were created as late as the second half of the 19th century, Kashubian was not a language of the printed word. In those spheres, it was necessary to use the dominant languages – Polish or German. Kashubian was being marginalized and pushed to the fringes – purely into the private sphere. The era of new media (radio and television) deepened this chasm further – all contents in those media were transmitted in the dominant languages and Kashubian was more and more folklorized until it was pushed into a very narrow band of contacts.

The change occurred slowly, beginning with the collapse of communism in 1989. Kashubian organizations started to develop and to act for the preservation of the Kashubian language and for the Kashubian ethnic community. The rights of Kashubs gradually gained legal footing, at first in the Polish 'Act on the National and Ethnic Minorities and Regional Language' (which gives the Kashubian language official recognition as a regional language in Poland) and then in the European Charter for Regional or Minority Languages (Council of Europe, 1992; ratified by Poland in 2009). Over the past 20 years, therefore, Kashubian has turned from a rejected dialect into a government-protected regional language with many measures aimed at preserving it: Kashubian language signs and street names have appeared; Kashubian has been included in the school education programme in the region (although, unfortunately, not as a language of teaching or as an essential subject for every child, but as a foreign language taught 3 hours per week at parents' explicit request); in some localities, Kashubian is recognized as an official language in which Kashubs may settle their administrative affairs; courses have been organized for Kashubian language teachers and for public officials; and last but not least – Kashubian has appeared in the new media. At first it appeared in the press and in books, then it began its development on the radio (first on the local state station 'Radio Gdańsk' for a few minutes a day, but since 2004 on the private 'Radio Kaszëbë' station broadcasting only in the Kashubian language). Things have not been as good in TV broadcasting, where Kashubs have very little airtime, amounting to about half an hour a week (Obracht-Prondzynski, 2007: 29–31).

Kashubian on the Internet

Radio and television have a very different kind of influence than the internet, which is based on interactivity, keeping in contact and the creation and exchange of new types of social communities. In those communities, relationships somewhat resemble those from the oral world (this would be an interesting notion to explore further, although there is not enough space for it in this short chapter). Let us cast an eye over the changes that have occurred in the Kashubian world since the advent of the internet.

The language taught in the educational system and used in official media needed codification and standardization. A reform of Kashubian was completed in 1996. Since then there have been special projects to popularize this new version of the language. However, as in many places where a minority language becomes standardized, a problem arose in the Kashubian lands: the oldest generation, for whom Kashubian was the first language of contact with family, neighbours and friends and was used in everyday life, complained that the Kashubian standard language was artificial and claimed not to understand it; reading in this language was difficult for them. On the other hand, the younger generation, who have a passive knowledge of Kashubian (they are able to listen to conversations in the Kashubian language between their grandparents or parents, yet respond in Polish), learn the newer standard language which exists in the media, in the schools and in legal acts, but not in local community life. The oldest and the youngest generation therefore cannot (or do not wish to) understand each other speaking the same language.

These assertions are based on Kashubians' statements (though I have met with similar feelings regarding the Breton language during field studies in Brittany). However, in-depth linguistic and sociolinguistic studies are required to show to what extent the Kashubian language used by young people within their own communities corresponds to the language they learn at school. My initial studies show that among themselves young people use their own blend of Polish and Kashubian languages. Because both languages belong to the same language group (Western Slavic) and are closely related, people who know Kashubian 'by ear' or 'from school' often create new forms using Polish words pronounced with a Kashubian accent[2] or with Kashubian endings. This new language is all the more distinctive when we are dealing with forms and practices that require writing. In writing, young people use specifically Kashubian letters absent from the Polish language: 'ã', 'é', 'ë', 'ò', 'ô' and 'ù'. This gives the listener or reader the impression of interacting with Kashubian. However, from a formal perspective such language can be referred to as 'Kashubified Polish' at most.

The biggest problem with Kashubian was that the young people who learn it rarely use it outside of lessons or special places (meetings of the Kashubian community, events organized by Kashubian cultural organizations, etc.), choosing to communicate with their surroundings and intimates in the dominant language (Mordawski, 2005; Synak, 1998). In this situation, the appearance of the Kashubian language on the internet has entailed a major change in its situation and position. The internet has provided the opportunity to use Kashubian outside the oral sphere – prior to the rise of the internet, Kashubian writing was reserved to a narrow band of experts.

The status of minority languages online is purely up to the people who use them in that sphere. The internet is the most democratic of existing media: everyone has equal access to the content,[3] and everyone is able to post writings online, create new pages and use the opportunities provided by other media existing within the internet (cf. Bolter & Grusin, 1999). At present, the internet is dominated by English, and the position of all other languages (including major national languages) is threatened. However, this trend is slowly changing. The main benefit offered by the internet to minority languages is its varied functionality, which societies can use for their own purposes. Studies indicate that young Kashubs use their language online in contact with the people they use it with in other situations. If the contact language is the dominant language – Polish – it will also be used in online communication. However, the internet also provides space for societies being created and existing online. At least some of those groups wish to communicate in the minority language, at times to show off, to prove their 'uniqueness', and at other times because that is how they communicate with friends 'from real life'. Many young people using Kashubian online claim that they are looking for a new identity, that they do not want to be like the others and that using Kashubian creates this distinctiveness. The fact remains that using certain pages in the minority language is unlikely to produce a major linguistic shift among young people; their main language is likely to remain the national language or – in international contacts – English. However, their attitude towards the minority culture, and thereby the minority language, may well change.

Concluding Remarks

Speaking most broadly, the rise of the internet has been very advantageous for the Kashubian-speaking community, especially for the young. First of all, it has led to an increase in the prestige of the language: if Kashubian can be used online, it cannot be so inferior and unsuitable after all (Buszard-Welcher, 2001: 337). Second, the internet has facilitated the use of Kashubian in different kinds of direct and passive communication: in oral form (internet radio, TV, short videos on YouTube – even if this kind of use is still limited, there is every indication that its popularity will continue to increase), in passive written form (increasing numbers of bilingual websites or sites written solely in the minority language – local government sites, Kashubian or tourist organizations) and in active written form (blogs, forums, etc.) It is notable that this is the first time Kashubian has been widely used in such forms. •

The internet has made it possible for young people to meet one another remotely. Within some internet forums, virtual Kashubian communities have been created: young people communicate, exchange remarks about Kashubian culture and its functions in the modern world and find other people to whom Kashubian culture and language are also important. The position of the Kashubian language in these contacts is important, even if it is not the same language as children are taught in schools.

The internet is mainly a tool for creating one's identity, building proximity with others, learning and deepening lifelong passions. The chance to join groups or societies provides new opportunities for the Kashubian language and culture by increasing interest in them and generating new societal engagement. It creates spaces where the use of Kashubian is 'natural'. The internet allows online activists to arise – the new medium provides them with an infrastructure that is elastic (it is simple to adapt to a local context), non-hierarchical (it allows people to meet and talk on equal footing) and scalable (new people are able to join projects to change and improve them). If a language becomes the subject of such activities, its very existence may end up being revolutionized. This is because the internet creates new societal forms in which the language remains the most important communication tool. The internet changes culture and ways of participating in it. In the digital world, it is necessary to share, to multiply culture and to interact. All these spheres are an inherent part of young people's lives. If living as a cultural minority would mean being separated from them, the language would stand no chance to develop and so would not become a part of the lives of the young and subsequently older people.

Notes

1. 'Most artful Theuth, while one person is able to create the products of art, another is able to judge what harm or benefit they hold for those who intend to use them. Now you, the father, of letters, as a result of your affection for them, are stating just the opposite of what their effect will be. If people learn them it will make their souls forgetful through lack of exercising their memory. They'll put their trust in the external marks of writing instead of using their own internal capacity for remembering on their own. You've discovered a magic potion not for memory, but for reminding, and you will offer your pupils apparent, not true, wisdom'. (Plato & Cobb, 1993, *Phaedrus*, 274e–275b).
2. In Polish, word accent usually falls on the second to last syllable; in Kashubian (dependent on dialect) it falls on the first, second to last, or any syllable.
3. The internet's perceived democracy is only virtual, however (cf. Cunliffe, 2007: 133). That is why the text refers only to the situation faced by minorities living in Europe.

References

Bolter, J.D. and Grusin, R.A. (1999) *Remediation: Understanding New Media*. Cambridge, Mass.: MIT Press.

Browne, D.R. (1996) *Electronic Media and Indigenous Peoples: A Voice of Our Own?* Ames, Iowa: Iowa State University Press.

Buszard-Welcher, L. (2001) Can the web help save my language? In L. Hinton and K.L. Hale (eds) *The Green Book of Language Revitalization in Practice* (pp. 331–345). San Diego: Academic Press.

Council of Europe (1992) European Charter for Regional and Minority Languages. Strasbourg: Council of Europe.

Cunliffe, D. (2007) Minority languages in the internet: New threats, new opportunities. In M. Cormack and N. Hourigan (eds) *Minority Language Media: Concepts, Critiques, and Case Studies* (pp. 133–150). Clevedon: Multilingual Matters.

Edwards, J. (1992) Sociopolitical aspect of language maintenance and loss: Towards a typology of minority language situations. In W. Fase, K. Jaspaert and S. Kroon (eds) *Maintenance and Loss of Minority Languages* (pp. 37–54). Amsterdam: John Benjamins.

Fishman, J.A. (1987) Language spread and language policy for endangered languages. In J. Alatis (ed.) *Proceedings of the Georgetown University Round Table of Languages and Linguistics* (pp. 1–15). Washington: Georgetown University Press.

Goody, J. (1986) *The Logic of Writing and the Organization of Society*. Cambridge: Cambridge University Press.

Goody, J. and Watt , I. (1963) The consequences of literacy. *Comparative Studies in Society and History* 5(03), 304–345. doi: doi:10.1017/S0010417500001730.

Hinton, L. (2001) Teaching methods. In L. Hinton and K.L. Hale (eds) *The Green Book of Language Revitalization in Practice* (pp. 179–190). San Diego: Academic Press.

McLuhan, M., Fiore, Q. and Agel, J. (1967) *The Medium is the Massage*. Harmondsworth: Penguin.

Mordawski, J. (2005) *Statystyka ludności kaszubskiej: Kaszubi u progu xxi wieku*. Gdańsk: Instytut Kaszubski.

Obracht-Prondzynski, C. (2007) *The Kashubs Today: Culture – language – identity*. Gdańsk: Instytut Kaszubski.

Ong, W.J. (2002) *Orality and Literacy: The Technologizing of the Word* (New ed.). London: Routledge.

Plato and Cobb, W.S. (1993) *The Symposium and the Phaedrus: Plato's erotic Dialogues*. Albany: State University of New York Press.

Riggins, S.H. (1992) The media imperative: Ethnic minority survival in the age of mass communication. In S.H. Riggins (ed.) *Ethnic Minority Media: An International Perspective* (pp. 1–20). Newbury Park: Sage.

Smith, A.D. (2007) *The Ethnic Origins of Nations*. Oxford: Blackwell Publishing.

Synak, B. (1998) *Kaszubska tożsamość: Ciągłość i zmiana. Studium socjologiczne*. Gdańsk: Wydawnictwo Uniwersytetu Gdańskiego.

8 The Welsh Language on YouTube: Initial Observations

Daniel Cunliffe and Rhodri ap Dyfrig

Introduction

It is often claimed that the internet, along with the falling cost of production technologies, holds great potential for minority languages (Cunliffe, 2007; see also the other chapters in Part 2). It is suggested that it can break down barriers to production and distribution, giving opportunities for minority language media producers to be seen and heard whereas they were previously limited to the hard economics of traditional commercial media or the possibility of government subsidy.

The online video community YouTube was launched in 2005. In February 2011, YouTube was the third most visited website by UK users (behind Google UK and Facebook) and accounted for more than 2% of UK website visits (Experian Hitwise, 2011). YouTube invites the user to 'Broadcast Yourself' but it is by now much more than a place for personal publishing, providing a huge base to bring users into other Google services and a web platform for professional media producers of all kinds.

YouTube supports the existence of a number of different group types, for example taste communities and brand communities (van Dijck, 2009) and appears to provide the possibility for minority language speakers to create their own media space in their own language. Such a media space would support a variety of usages including consuming, participating (user-to-user or user-to-content) and producing (Shao, 2009), thus supporting language use in a variety of forms.

The Welsh language, *Cymraeg*, has featured on YouTube since its early days and it is not difficult to find Welsh language material on it. But it is not clear to what extent the material is fulfilling the same functions as it is for other, larger languages. Can it be said that there is a distinct and vibrant Welsh language media space on YouTube that provides a serious alternative to traditional broadcast TV and film? Has it widened the range of material and perspectives available to Welsh speakers?

YouTube is a vast database of video content and finding material can be difficult. There are other technical, linguistic, cultural and socioeconomic factors that can militate against Welsh language content finding an audience, or finding its way onto YouTube at all. The social structures and norms of YouTube and the interactions that take place around content are other factors that need to be taken into account when looking at Welsh language use on the service.

This chapter presents an initial study, examining and characterizing the use of the Welsh language on YouTube. The paper first discusses methodological issues associated with sampling language-specific videos on YouTube and investigates how language is signalled on Welsh language videos. It then provides a qualitative and quantitative analysis of a sample of 533 Welsh language videos. Finally, it takes a brief look at social networks within YouTube and some associated issues related to language.

Sampling Welsh Language Videos

Difficulties in sampling YouTube have been noted by several authors (e.g. Cheng et al., 2008; Landry & Guzdial, 2008). Approaches to sampling have included keyword search (e.g. Conway & McInerney, 2008), either making use of YouTube's various popularity ratings (e.g. Landry & Guzdial, 2008) or taking sample points and then crawling links within YouTube (e.g. Cheng et al., 2008). Searching for videos in a particular language – especially a minority language – is further complicated by the fact that language is not well represented within YouTube.

Perhaps, the most efficient way to generate a 'realistic' sample of Welsh language videos would be to follow actual user behaviour of Welsh speakers; however, no user behaviour data of this type exists. As an alternative approach, YouTube's location search was used, based on three such searches focused on population centres in South, West and North Wales. This generated a sample set of 1049 videos; however, only 2 of these were Welsh language videos, so this was not considered a satisfactory way to generate a sample set.

The sample set was finally generated by performing a key word search on *cymraeg* (the Welsh language) along with the mutated, or conjugated, forms of the same word (*gymraeg, chymraeg* and *nghymraeg*). A total of 1159 results were returned, 3 for *chymraeg*, 1 for *nghymraeg*, 155 for *gymraeg* and 1000 (the maximum number of results that can be returned) for *cymraeg*. Deleting videos returned in more than one search removed only two, indicating that searching for the mutated forms can identify a number of videos that would not otherwise be found. Removing duplicates left 878 unique videos. It is not clear why the search returns so many duplicate results and this limits the effectiveness of this approach to sampling. An analysis identified 627 videos to have featured the Welsh language. Videos containing only very limited or no Welsh were excluded. Those which featured Welsh text, captions or subtitles were included.

Four scenarios were identified in which the term *cymraeg* (or a mutated form) was associated with non-Welsh language content.

The most common scenario was the use of the term to denote videos relating to Wales, rather than to the Welsh language. For example, the video 'John Prescott – Gethin Animation #16' is tagged with 'gethin animation wales welsh cymru cymraeg politics politician labour prescott john prescott blair funny baublebob' even though it does not feature the Welsh language. It may be that *cymraeg* has been used incorrectly as the translation for 'Welsh' (in the sense of nationality), rather than the correct translation *Cymreig*, or that it has been used deliberately in order to attract searches for *Cymraeg*, in the belief that the videos would be of interest.

The second scenario is fairly rare, with both title and tags signalling that the video is in Welsh, but it is actually referring to a Welsh-medium school.

Title: Ysgol Gyfun Gymraeg Glantaf
  Account: **worthalot2**
  Tags: Ysgol Gyfun Gymraeg Glantaf

The third scenario is rare and features the use of *cymraeg* as deliberate tagging spam. For example, the video 'Breaking news: Sri Lanka Genocide History Repeating Itself' is tagged with

gaza Isrial Brezhoneg Cymraeg Dansk Deutsch Bahasa Indonesia Italiano ქართული Nederlands Nedersaksisch 語 Norsk (bokmål) Polski РусскийSlovenčina Svenska 文 state terrorism stop genocide freedom massacre protest sky breaking news human rights UN red crickets cross black war refugee Colombo MPs political live free watch india nadu chennai songs part rap speech support rajini kamal simbu fan press movies journalist BCC fighters

Why language names, especially minority language names, should be used in this way is unclear, although the order and range of languages indicates that it may have been cut and pasted from Wikipedia.

The fourth scenario, which is also rare, is when *cymraeg* occurs as part of a user account name, for example 'MrCymraeg' and 'Gymraeg'.

Signalling Welsh Language Content

Given that YouTube provides no specific means for a user to indicate that a video they have uploaded is in Welsh, they are forced to rely on existing mechanisms to include linguistic metadata, that is tags, titles and descriptions. Similarly in the absence of a built-in mechanism for filtering by language, users must rely on other mechanisms, such as YouTube's recommender system and search facility, to locate content in their language. As these are based on tags, titles and descriptions, this metadata plays an important role in finding relevant videos (Lange, 2008). In contrast to other social platforms which employ tagging systems, YouTube also does not allow collaborative tagging (i.e. allowing other users to add to the tags on a video) (Greenaway *et al.*, 2009), meaning that untagged or 'badly' tagged videos cannot be amended by other users who are aware of the limitations of finding videos in a given language.

In the sample, examples were found of all of these being used to explicitly indicate Welsh language content, with tags and titles being the most used. Some illustrative examples are presented here.

- *English language title, including explicit language signal in Welsh.* Tags bilingual, but not explicitly signalling language.

  Title: New Motorcycle Cymraeg
  > Account: **NorthWalesRCRP**
  > Tags: North Wales Roads Casualty Reduction Partnership Partneriaeth Lleihau Anafiadau Ffyrdd Gogledd Cymru

  Welsh language title, including explicit language signal in Welsh. Welsh-language tags, including explicit language signal in Welsh.

  Title: Newyddion Byd Amaeth Fersiwn Cymraeg
  > Account: **ffermio**
  > Tags: Bwletin W3 cymraeg

- *English language title, including explicit bilingual language signal.* Tags almost entirely in English, not explicitly signalling language.

Title: Plaid Cymru - Party Political Broadcast 2006 (Cymraeg/Welsh)
Account: **rhysllwyd**
Tags: Plaid Cymru ppb political broadcast wales hope labour cymru

Bilingual title, no language signal. Tags bilingual, not explicitly signalling language. The only language signal is contained within the description.

Title: The Last Days of Mynyddcerrig School | Diwrnodau Olaf Ysgol
Account: **heddgwynfor**
Description: heddgwynfor — 07 February 2008 — A documentary by[...] showing how the closure of a Welsh medium village school affects pupils, teachers and the community. Lleucu filmed during the last week of Ysgol Mynyddcerrig, Carmarthenshire in July 2007 ///////////////////////////////// CYMRAEG: Ffilm ddogfen gan [...] yn dangos effaith cau ysgol bentrefol ar y disgyblion, yr athrawon a'r gymuned. Bu Lleucu yn ffilmio yn ystod wythnos olaf Ysgol Gynradd Mynyddcerrig, Sir Gaerfyrddin ym mis Gorffennaf 2007. Fersiwn Gymraeg heb is-deitlau yma – http://youtube.com/watch?v=vf8pxzC_MPE
Tags:
ysgol gynradd mynyddcerrig mynydd cerrig cau small school closure wales cymru carmarthenshire

English language title, no language signal. Tags bilingual, explicitly signalling language.

Title: Welsh Premier League – Connah's Quay Nomads v Neath 25/08/07
Account: **Peldroedcymru**
Tags: Wales Welsh Cymru Cymraeg Peldroed Football Pel Droed

As the examples illustrate, while tags, titles and descriptions were all used to signal language, their use was highly inconsistent, with all or some being used in different videos. An examination of videos not in the sample suggests that there are many which do not have any language signalling and that explicit language signalling may actually be the exception rather than the rule.

Mechanisms such as related videos will not pick up relationships based on language, unless it is indicated in the tags, title or description. Bilingual users may not consider language to be a useful measure of relatedness anyway as it cuts across topics. Users may also be able to make judgements on the basis of personal knowledge of the account or titles of other videos uploaded by the account. However, it may be possible to tell if a video is in

Welsh only by actually watching it. YouTube provides no real support for a Welsh language media space, and there is no easy way to gain an overview of Welsh language content or producers.

Analysis of the Sample

In order to focus on content aimed at Welsh speakers, videos which were targeted at Welsh learners or were produced by Welsh learners were excluded from further analysis. This removed 72 videos, almost 11.5%. This high percentage is the result of search bias as videos related to language learning are likely to mention language in the title or tags as it is a salient characteristic of the content. Two more videos were removed from YouTube before the analysis was performed. This left a total of 533 videos in the sample set for further analysis.

The quality of the 553 videos in the sample varied greatly, from almost unintelligible mobile phone footage taken in nightclubs to extracts from broadcast quality programs. A subjective analysis of the quality of the videos in the sample was performed. Videos were classified as 'homemade', 'professional' or 'TV', though these are better understood as points on a continuum with overlapping and imprecise boundaries. Homemade videos included mobile phone footage and parents' videos of school concerts. It also included homemade music videos to accompany professionally produced music and screen captures demonstrating software. The professional category included promotional videos. Videos in this category were often distinguished from homemade videos by superior audio quality and lighting. The TV category included content taken from TV or film.

Of the 533 videos in the sample, 269 were categorized as homemade, 112 as professional and 172 as TV. This suggests a roughly equal split between amateur production (what might be considered 'authentic' user-generated content) and production featuring at least a degree of professionalism. In some cases, these videos might not otherwise have had access to such a wide-reaching distribution platform, but in other cases YouTube was being used by organizations which had access to traditional TV or radio.

In order to gain an overview of the topics covered in the sample, a content analysis was performed. The categories shown in Table 8.1 are non-exclusive and only the largest categories are shown.

As expected given the sampling method, there is a significant bias towards videos where the language is important in terms of characterizing and describing the content, for example Welsh language music, Welsh

Table 8.1 Content analysis

Music (290)	Choir: 33; voice: 30; contemporary: 206
Art and culture (60)	Poetry, art, drama, dance and history
Narrative (57)	Personal films (typically homemade)
Activism (37)	Mainly language, education and rural
Environment and Human rights (36)	Majority from the Equality and Human Rights Commission
Sport (25)	Football: 21 (all TV) ; rugby: 2; wrestling: 2
Politics (21)	Mainly party broadcasts and promos
Information technology (14)	Majority software demos
Religion (7)	Mostly prayers and psalms in Welsh

language versions of political broadcasts, Welsh language activism and so on. Therefore, it may not be representative of the totality of the Welsh language content on YouTube.

The sample was also analysed quantitatively; however, meaningful comparisons with other reported figures (such as in Cheng *et al.*, 2008; Landry & Guzdial, 2008) are difficult, because they often depend to some extent on the most popular videos to generate their sample set, giving them an inherent bias.

Figure 8.1 shows the number of videos uploaded over time. Comparing the yearly uploads on the right of the graph suggests that the sharp rise in the number of uploads may be levelling off.

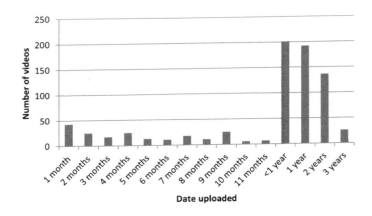

Figure 8.1 Number of video uploads by date

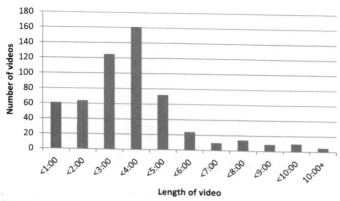

Figure 8.2 Length of videos

As can be seen in Figure 8.2, the large majority of videos are less than 4-minute long. The shortest video had a duration of 0:07 and the longest was 10:24. The overall pattern would appear to be similar to the distribution observed by Cheng *et al.* (2008). Cheng *et al.* suggest that the peak length of between 3 and 4 minutes can be explained by the typical length of a 'music' category video; it may be that a similar explanation can be applied to the data in Figure 8.2. Landry and Guzdial (2008) reported a similar average video length of 3.71 minutes.

Figure 8.3 shows that the majority of the videos in the sample were rated, and the vast majority of those rated were rated highly, with an average rating of 4.5. In their study, Landry and Guzdial (2008) found an average rating of 3.59. In the present sample, it is not clear if users only

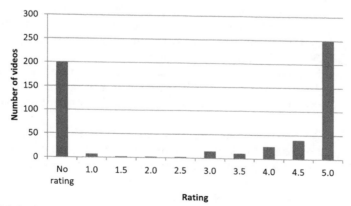

Figure 8.3 Rating of videos

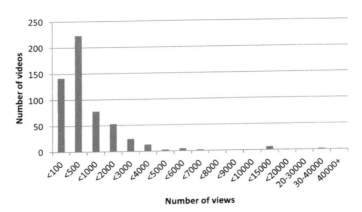

Figure 8.4 Number of views per video

bothered to rate videos they liked or the videos uploaded genuinely deserved a high rating, or whether some other factor was at play.

Figure 8.4 shows that the majority of videos were viewed less than 500 times. The number of views ranged between zero for a video which had been uploaded '3 days ago' and 162,821 for a video that had been uploaded '3 years ago'. The video was entitled 'Iraqi torture' and described as 'iraqi torture shot with with [sic] sa80 assault rifle' which might explain the high number of viewings. The video in fact featured a person being shot with an air rifle, presumably as a prank. The video appears to have attracted a large number of negative and aggressive comments, perhaps due to the mismatch between the title and the content or the nature of the content itself.

Other videos with particularly high number of views were one entitled 'Calon Lan' featuring a rendition of a popular Welsh language hymn (34,094 views, uploaded 2 years ago) and one entitled 'PlaidTV – Cymraeg/Welsh Language broadcast' a Welsh language political video produced by Plaid Cymru (35,750 views, uploaded 1 year ago).

Figure 8.5 shows that most of the user accounts featured in the sample had uploaded only one video which appeared in the sample. It should be noted that they may have uploaded other videos that did not appear in the sample.

Of the 9 accounts that had uploaded more than 10 videos included in the sample, 4 uploaded predominantly music, 2 predominantly politics and language activism, 1 human rights, 1 music and 1 combined music and language activism each. Again it should be noted that this is likely to be partly an artefact of the sampling method and patterns of tagging, titling and describing videos.

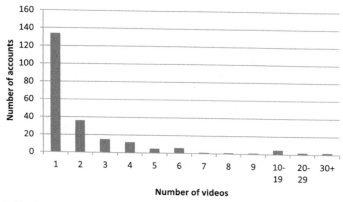

Figure 8.5 Number of videos uploaded per account

Exploring Social Networks

Social networks have been identified as important in the development of language norms, particularly in opposition to the standard (majority) norms (Wei, 2000). It has also been suggested that networks of strong ties support minority language speakers in resisting pressures towards language shift (Milroy, 2001; Wei, 2000). Morris (2007) observes that the greater the density of Welsh speakers in the social network of young Welsh speakers, the greater the opportunity and tendency for members of that network to use Welsh.

A number of researchers have mentioned the significance of the social networking features of YouTube (e.g. Conway & McInerney, 2008; Lange, 2008) and some have explicitly considered its role in maintaining cultural identity (e.g. Yang, 2008). Haridakis and Hanson (2009) suggest that while some people watch YouTube for same reasons as they view TV, for others there is a distinctly social aspect to YouTube. They suggest that YouTube supports seamless movement between traditional watching of mediated content and interpersonal social activity. However, a study of over 1 million YouTube users by Cheng et al. (2008) found that 58% had no Friends. They suggest that social networking among users has less impact than the network existing among related videos, which are based on tags, titles and descriptions. Therefore, if tags, titles and descriptions contain linguistic metadata, they will be important in defining networks of videos related by a common language. However, the social networking features of YouTube may also help users locate content in their language, for example, that has been produced by friends.

Table 8.2 Social network analysis

	Comments		Friends			Subscribers			Subscriptions		
	W	W̶	W	W̶	?	W	W̶	?	W	W̶	?
Chwyrligwgan	4	2	7	4	–	14	11	1	11	6	–
CYMRAESYGORAU	2	–	3	2	4	–	1	1	–	–	–
femtaffy1967	1	2	4	3	–	2	2	–	2	1	–
peldroedcymru	–	5	1	–	3	13	35	8	5	3	–
Supgav	3	1	2	–	–	2	8	3	–	9	–

In order to form an initial impression of language use in the social networks of users on YouTube, five accounts were selected at random from the sample set. The comments on each of the accounts were examined and classified as either using Welsh (W) or not using Welsh (W̶). The accounts of Friends and Subscribers were then examined and, on the basis of the account information, the language used for comments on the account page and the language of the videos they uploaded, these connections were categorized as Welsh used (W), apparently no Welsh used (W̶) or unknown (?). Finally, the subscriptions of each of the five accounts were examined and categorized in the same way.

While the results shown in Table 8.2 must be treated with caution due to the very small sample size, they nonetheless suggest that the social networks are bilingual not only in terms of content consumed (as might be expected for bilingual users) but also in terms of audience. It is particularly interesting to note the numbers of apparent non-Welsh speakers who are subscribers to accounts which uploaded Welsh language content, although this could be due to YouTube users engaging in the practice of collecting subscribers to their own channels rather than any particular interest in the content.

Following the connections in the social networks of accounts which upload Welsh language content may also provide an alternative way of sampling Welsh language content, though the characteristics of the networks may make it sensitive to the initial starting points.

Presenting Linguistic Identity

While it was not examined systematically, it was clear that the extent to which account information indicated whether a user was a Welsh language speaker varied considerably. In many cases, it was not mentioned at all.

In some cases self-identification as a Welsh speaker was explicit:

'Hey. My names Sion. Wondering how you say it? Same as Sean, Shaun in English. Im Welsh. Proud. Can Speak 2 languages fluent. English obviously as one, and Welsh. Gallu Siarad Cymraeg.'

Or, was made explicit by the use of Welsh:

Hey, I'm [...] a Guy from a Place in North Wales called Blaenau Ffestiniog. I Love music! I Love to sing! I can play a little piano a bit of guitar and I can play the bass guitar. Im in two choirs one Youth choir (Ysgol Glanaethwy) and one Male voice choir (Cor Y Brythoniaid). I can get very bored this would explain most of my videos. (Y) - - - - - - - - - - - - Hei, [...] dwi ac rwyf yn dod o bentre yng ngogledd Cymru or enw Blaenau Ffestiniog. Dwi yn Caru Cerddoriaeth! Dwin Caru Canu!Rwyf yn medry chware dipyn bach o biano a gitar a rwyf yn medry chwara y gitar fas. Rwyf mewn ddau gor, Cor Meibion (Cor Brythoniaid) ac Cor Ieuienctid (YsgolGlanaethwy). Mae hi yn medry bod yn ofnadwy o ddiflas weithia ac mae hynu yn eglyro lot o fy fidios. (Y)

In others, it was implicit, for example suggested by book or music favourites:

Music:

Aly&Aj, Brigyn, Celine Dion, Celt, Colbie Caillat, Connie Fisher, Duffy, Einir Dafydd, Elin Fflur, Eva Cassidy, Fflur Dafydd, Gemma, Green Day, Gwawr, Gwibdaith, Gwyneth Glyn, Heather Dale, Katy Rose, Kellie Pickler, Kelly Clarkson, Lady GaGa, Leona Lewis, Mariah Carey, Meinir Gwilym, Mirain Haf, Nerina Pallot, P!nk, Pixie Lott, Sara Mai, Tara Bethan, Taylor Swift, Tebot Piws, We the Kings,

Books:

9 Mis (Caryl Lewis), P.S. I love you (Cecelia Ahern), Pili Pala (Catrin Dafydd), Y ferch dawel (Marion Eames), Hi yw fy ffrind (Bethan Gwanas), The boy in stripped pyjamas (John Boyne), The way I see it (Nicole Dryburgh), Before I die (Jenny Downham)

Account names also sometimes suggested a knowledge of the Welsh language, for example Peldroedcymru (football Wales); YDysgwrAraf (the slow learner); Ubuntucymraeg (Welsh-language Ubuntu); LicioHwn ([I] like this). Though as noted in Section 8.3, this is not necessarily a reliable indicator.

Considering Audience

The results of the analysis suggested that the social networks are bilingual. Thus, YouTube appears to be an environment in which non-

Welsh speakers may come into contact with Welsh language content and may choose to subscribe to accounts which upload such content. However, this does not appear to be a barrier to the uploading of Welsh language content and in some cases the non-Welsh-speaking audience was explicitly acknowledged in the description of a video:

> This is a short clip of the beginning of our GCSE Drama performance. If you don't understand the language it's because it's welsh.
> A very long time ago. Most of you watching will most probably not understand, mainly because it's in Welsh, my home language, and two, it was a close friend joke type thing.

In some cases this included a translation of the Welsh:

> This was well fun :] Elin tells me to close my legs lmao

Other examples included translations of song lyrics and bilingual or English language descriptions of Welsh language videos.

Conclusions

The study presented here has attempted to characterize the Welsh language media space on YouTube and to explore some of the methodological issues and research questions raised. While there is a clear bias in the sampling technique used, the sample generated has facilitated some initial observations. Further research is needed, for example, into user behaviour and motivations and identity performance. A method for generating more representative samples is also required; perhaps, snowball sampling based on the social networks of users and of videos might be a useful approach.

While there is undoubtedly a quantity of Welsh language material on YouTube, it is difficult to argue on the basis of this sample that there is a coherent Welsh language media space. First, because of YouTube's limited support for language and the inconsistent and ad-hoc ways in which linguistic metadata are included in tags, titles and descriptions; second, because of the apparently bilingual nature of the social networks. It appears that many Welsh speakers are relatively unconcerned that their Welsh language content uploaded to YouTube may be viewed by non-Welsh speakers, thus maybe audience is less of an inhibiting factor for Welsh language use in YouTube than it perhaps is in blogging. This may reflect a distribution model based more on viewing videos on other social networks and on the consumption of individual videos rather than on a traditional producer–consumer relationship where maximizing the audience might be seen as a primary concern and the concept of a channel is more dominant. The audiovisual nature of YouTube and the predominance of music content also permit language to be less of a critical issue in comparison to blogging.

The limited use of social networking functionality on YouTube also suggests that coherent linguistically hermetic media spaces may not be an obvious feature in any of the languages which are not yet officially supported by the site. This is compounded by the gradual phasing out of YouTube groups (collaborative spaces for aggregating videos around a theme), which has greatly diminished the ability to create user-generated media spaces within the site. Nevertheless, the use of YouTube videos beyond the site through embedding is not covered in this study and it may well be the case that videos are used in wholly Welsh language media spaces elsewhere.

Concerns have been expressed about the impact of YouTube on traditional television viewing (Waldfogel, 2009); however, it is difficult to judge the impact of Welsh language material on YouTube upon traditional Welsh language broadcasters. In light of figures in the Ofcom Communications Market Report (Ofcom, 2010) noting that television viewing amongst adults aged 16–24 years has dropped steadily since 2004, while there has been a steady rise in total audience for YouTube, one might suggest a correlation and infer that young adults are moving their viewing habits to online. Given the difficulties surrounding Welsh language content discovery on YouTube, might those viewers merely be leaving S4C for English language material online? This kind of gap raises issues about how best to increase the visibility of Welsh language content online. That being said, the monthly hours spent watching television still far outweighs those of online videos for now. Certainly, Welsh language videos on YouTube generally are not yet reaching the same kinds of audiences as S4C, with only rare exceptions. One could say that the relatively small quantity of 'official' material from traditional broadcasters may be problematic in the future, although much of the Welsh language online viewing may be taking place on proprietary distribution platforms such as S4C's Clic.

Given the lack of a clearly defined Welsh language media space on YouTube, it is not clear how those wanting to promote the Welsh language make best use of YouTube, either in terms of activists' activities or in terms of language policies. YouTube is one of a number of technologies that have potential to benefit the Welsh language and other minority languages, and it has certainly provided a space for user-generated Welsh language media, expanding the range of material available. However, it remains to be seen whether it can have mainstream impact without further input from broadcasters and coordinated efforts to promote videos.

References

Bolter, J.D. and Grusin, R.A. (1999) *Remediation: Understanding New Media*. Cambridge, MA: MIT Press.

Browne, D.R. (1996) *Electronic Media and Indigenous Peoples: A Voice of Our Own?* Ames, Iowa: Iowa State University Press.

Buszard-Welcher, L. (2001) Can the web help save my language? In L. Hinton and K.L. Hale (eds) *The Green Book of Language Revitalization in Practice* (pp. 331–345). San Diego: Academic Press.

Conway, M. and McInerney, L. (2008) Jihadi video and auto-radicalisation: Evidence from an exploratory YouTube study. *Proceedings EuroISI 2008 – First European Conference on Intelligence and Security Informatics* (pp. 108–118). Esbjerg, Denmark.

Council of Europe (1992) *European Charter for Regional and Minority Languages*. Strasbourg: Council of Europe.

Cunliffe, D. (2007) Minority languages in the Internet: New threats, new opportunities. In M. Cormack and N. Hourigan (eds) *Minority Language Media: Concepts, Critiques, and Case Studies* (pp. 133–150). Clevedon: Multilingual Matters.

Cheng, X., Dale, C. and Liu, J. (2008) Statistics and social network of YouTube videos. Paper presented at the Proceedings of the 16th International Workshop on Quality of Service, Enschede, The Netherlands.

Edwards, J. (1992) Sociopolitical aspect of language maintenance and loss: Towards a typology of minority language situations. In W. Fase, K. Jaspaert and S. Kroon (eds) *Maintenance and Loss of Minority Languages* (pp. 37–54). Amsterdam: John Benjamins.

Experian Hitwise (2011) Data Center: Top sites & engines: Data for four weeks, ending 12 February 2011, accessed 18 February 2011. http://www.hitwise.com/uk/datacentre/main/dashboard-7323.html.

Fishman, J.A. (1987) Language spread and language policy for endangered languages. In J. Alatis (ed.) *Proceedings of the Georgetown University Round Table of Languages and Linguistics* (pp. 1–15). Washington: Georgetown University Press.

Goody, J. (1986) *The Logic of Writing and the Organization of Society*. Cambridge: Cambridge University Press.

Goody, J. and Watt, I. (1963) The consequences of literacy. *Comparative Studies in Society and History* 5 (03), 304–345. doi: 10.1017/S0010417500001730.

Greenaway, S., Thelwall, M. and Ding, Y. (2009) Tagging YouTube – A classification of tagging practice on YouTube. *Proceedings of the 12th International Conference on Scientometrics and Informetrics* (pp. 660–664). Rio de Janeiro, Brazil. Retrieved from http://www.sakcreations.co.uk/docs/TaggingYouTube-pp.pdf.

Haridakis, P. and Hanson, G. (2009) Social interaction and co-viewing with YouTube: Blending mass communication reception and social connection. *Journal of Broadcasting & Electronic Media* 53 (2), 317–335.

Hinton, L. (2001) Teaching methods. In L. Hinton and K.L. Hale (eds) *The Green Book of Language Revitalization in Practice* (pp. 179–190). San Diego: Academic Press.

Landry, B.M. and Guzdial, M. (2008, 21 April 2011) Art or circus? Characterizing user-created video on YouTube. School of Interactive Computing Technical Reports; GT-IC-08-07. Accessed 21 April 2011. http://smartech.gatech.edu/bitstream/handle/1853/25828/GT-IC-08-07.pdf.

Lange, P.G. (2008) Publicly private and privately public: Social networking on YouTube. *Journal of Computer-Mediated Communication* 13 (1), 361–380. doi: 10.1111/j.1083-6101.2007.00400.x.

McLuhan, M., Fiore, Q. and Agel, J. (1967) *The Medium is the Massage*. Harmondsworth: Penguin.

Milroy, L. (2001) Bridging the micro–macro gap: Social change, social networks and bilingual repertoires. In J. Klatter-Folmer and P. Van Avermaet (eds) *Theories on Maintenance and Loss of Minority Languages: Towards a More Integrated Explanatory Framework* (pp. 39–64). Munster: Waxman.

Morris, D. (2007) Young people's social networks and language use: The case of Wales. *Sociolinguistic Studies* 1 (3), 435–460.

Ofcom (2010) Communications market report, accessed 21 April 2011. http://stakeholders.ofcom.org.uk/binaries/research/cmr/753567/CMR_2010_FINAL.pdf.

Ong, W.J. (2002) *Orality and Literacy: The Technologizing of the Word* (New edition). London: Routledge.

Plato and Cobb, W.S. (1993) *The Symposium and the Phaedrus: Plato's erotic dialogues*. Albany: State University of New York Press.

Riggins, S.H. (1992) The media imperative: Ethnic minority survival in the age of mass communication. In S.H. Riggins (ed.) *Ethnic Minority Media: An International Perspective* (pp. 1–20). Newbury Park: Sage.

Shao, G. (2009) Understanding the appeal of user-generated media: A uses and gratification perspective. *Internet Research* 19 (1), 7–25.

Smith, A.D. (2007) *The Ethnic Origins of Nations*. Oxford: Blackwell Publishing.

Synak, A.D. (1998) *Kaszubska tożsamość: ciągłość i zmiana. Studium socjologiczne*. Gdańsk: Wydawnictwo Uniwersytetu Gdańskiego.

van Dijck, J. (2009) Users like you? Theorizing agency in user-generated content. *Media, Culture & Society* 31 (1), 41–58. doi: 10.1177/0163443708098245.

Waldfogel, J. (2009) Lost on the web: Does web distribution stimulate or depress television viewing? *Information Economics and Policy* 21 (2), 158–168. doi: 10.1016/j.infoecopol.2008.11.002.

Wei, L. (2000) Towards a critical evaluation of language maintenance and language shift. *Sociolinguistica* 14, 142–147.

Yang, E. (2008) Recreating Hmong history: An examination of www.youtube.com videos. *Amerasia Journal* 34 (3), 19–36.

9 Learning Communities Mediated through Technology: Pedagogic Opportunities for Minority Languages

Niall Mac Uidhilin

Introduction

This chapter argues that the recent alignment of key pedagogical and technological developments have the potential to revolutionize learners' experiences within learning environments. For minority languages, this presents both a challenge and an opportunity. The challenge is that dominant languages are becoming even more pervasive as new forms of media and technology enter into our daily lives. The opportunity is that new technologies have lowered the barriers to producing and publishing many forms of content and have enabled many-to-many communication and collaboration. The chapter outlines the theoretical underpinnings of collaborative learning and how these affect language and literacy learning. The field of 'New Literacy Studies' is then discussed and how this field has particular relevance for minority language communities. Some of the uses of Web 2.0 technologies in relation to language and literacy development are highlighted. The chapter concludes with an example of how these technologies could be used to forge links between a school and its wider community.

In a study by Moll & Whitmore (1993) of a third grade bilingual classroom (English and Spanish) undertaken in the U.S., a major instructional goal of the teacher was to make the classroom a highly literate environment.

Eschewing traditional models based on fixed texts transmitted in stages, she organised literature groups according to the interests and choices of the children, and provided them with frequent opportunities to mediate each other's learning through shared literacy experiences. The teacher would help the children attempt more difficult materials with the aim of expanding their abilities. She would also ensure that the children developed strong literacy skills in their first language to serve as a basis for second language development.

Part of the children's day was spent working on both individual and collaborative projects based on a theme chosen by the class. Based on these themes, the teacher would gather together a wide variety of literacy resources (books, posters, pieces of art and artefacts) in both languages to support research. She would also encourage the children to bring objects of interest and value to them from home. No limit was placed on what the children could learn about a theme; in fact they were encouraged to stretch their abilities. Both the process of learning and the completed project were equally valued. An essential factor that contributed to the success of the classroom was the control given to the children in relation to their learning experience. Each theme culminated with the production of an artefact or presentation and the children also completed a referenced report which was submitted to the school library.

This vignette illustrates the types of pedagogical approaches that a teacher with a sociocultural perspective would use to engage young learners with language and literacy in a multilingual and multicultural classroom. There are greater overheads involved in such an approach in terms of preparation, administration and assessment compared to a more traditional drill-and-practice routine.

This chapter argues that similar interventions to this one have become much easier to implement due to the recent alignment of key pedagogical and technological developments. Different fields of research such as Computer-Supported Collaborative Learning (CSCL) (Koschmann, 1996) and Network-Based Language Teaching (NBLT) (Kern & Warschauer, 2000) recognize that social learning practices mediated through technology have the potential to revolutionize learners' experiences within learning environments. This is true now more so than ever, as these practices have become the norm for many people to consume and produce information:

Millions of people now interact through blogs, collaborate through wikis, play multiplayer games, publish podcasts and video, build relationships through social network sites, and evaluate all the above forms of communication through feedback and ranking mechanisms. (Warschauer & Grimes, 2007: 1)

For minority languages, this presents both a challenge and an opportunity. The challenge is that dominant languages are becoming even more pervasive as new forms of media and technology enter into our daily lives. In the case of Irish, a language in near-terminal decline as a native language (Ó Giollagáin et al., 2007), the omnipresence of English language media (among other factors) is having a corrosive effect on the linguistic habits of young native speakers (Ní Shéaghdha, 2010; Ó Curnáin, 2009). The opportunity is that new technologies have lowered the barriers to producing and publishing many forms of content and have enabled many-to-many communication and collaboration (Warschauer & Grimes, 2007). Research underpinning these new literacies views them as a set of social and critical practices that empowers learners to engage their identities and their prior knowledge with literacy and society.

The chapter will outline the theoretical underpinnings of collaborative learning and how these affect language and literacy learning. The field of 'New Literacy Studies' is then discussed and how this field has particular relevance for minority language communities. The chapter then discusses some of the uses of Web 2.0 technologies in relation to language and literacy development and concludes with an example of how these technologies could be used to forge links between a school and its wider community.

Collaborative Learning

Collaborative learning has been motivated by various theories based on a sociocultural perspective emanating from the writings of Russian psychologist Lev Vygotsky. Vygotsky worked in the early 20th century but his writings only came to prominence in the Western world towards the end of the century gone by. His writings attempted to develop a theory of the human mind in social, cultural and historical terms. He identified cultural artefacts, such as speech and language, as tools that are crucial in shaping thought and action. One of the most important elements in Vygotsky's approach to pedagogy is the *Zone of Proximal Development (ZPD)* which establishes the ways in which instruction can lead to development – represented by the enhanced capabilities of a learner working in the presence of a more skilled peer or teacher (Vygotsky, 1978).

Building on sociocultural theory, a number of studies have been conducted in recent years by anthropologists, sociologists and psychologists into how groups of people function in everyday settings. The physical and social environments were found to be an integral part of the cognitive activities of the groups. Lave and Wenger (1991) used the term *situated learning* to describe how knowledge, tasks and responsibilities are distributed among practitioners within diverse *Communities of Practice (CoPs)* situated in a particular social context. They use the term *legitimate peripheral participation* to describe how newcomers (or *apprentices*) to these CoPs gradually earn the knowledge and skills required to fully participate as members in the community.

Language and Literacy Development

In analysing the vignette at the start of the chapter, Moll and Whitmore (1993), stressing the importance of language in Vygotsky's theories, argue that the ZPD should not be thought of as a characteristic of the child or of the teaching, but of the child engaged in collaborative activity within specific social (discourse) environments. They propose that the sociocultural system within which children learn should be thought of as a 'collective' zone of proximal development. They claim that the interdependence of adults and children, and how they use social and cultural resources, is central to a Vygotskian analysis of instruction.

Language acquisition is likely to take place whenever learners interact with fluent speakers under conditions of legitimate peripheral participation. In a dedicated learning environment, where a form of *cognitive apprenticeship* takes place, the effectiveness of the interactions depends on the master's ability to manage a division of participation that provides for growth on the part of the apprentice (Brown *et al.*, 1989; Hanks, 1991; Lave & Wenger, 1991; Oxford, 2008).

Hanks (1991) goes on to suggest that the way to maximize learning is to perform rather than to talk about it. As fluency in a language is one of the most basic skills required to participate in society, discourse production should be viewed as a way of engaging a learner/apprentice in social and cultural practice rather than simply as a structure in which engagement takes place.

New Literacies

The attainment of competence in *literacy*, as opposed to simply *reading and writing*, has assumed much greater importance in recent times. This has been due to factors such as the prominence of Freire's work within critical pedagogy, the alleged literacy crisis of the 1970s in the United Sates and the increasing influence of sociocultural theory on pedagogical practice (Lankshear & Knobel, 2006).

The term 'multi-literacies' was coined by a group of specialists in education, critical literacy and discourse analysis who came together in the mid-1990s to discuss the future of literacy pedagogy. The pedagogy of muti-literacies focuses on how cultural and linguistic diversity and the emergence of new paradigms of literacy through ICT are changing the landscape in terms of what it means to be literate in the modern world. Learners need an extended skill set on top of traditional literacy skills to be able to navigate this new multimodal landscape. This includes developing critical literacy skills (Kalantzis & Cope, 2008; The New London Group, 1996).

Traditionally, literacy has been viewed from a cognitive perspective related to attaining competence in reading and writing. The word 'new' has been recently placed before both 'literacy' and 'literacies' to indicate opposition to this traditional view of literacy. Lankshear and Knobel (2006) identify both a *paradigmatic* and an *ontological* interpretation of the use of 'new' in relation to literacy.

The *paradigmatic* refers to 'New Literacy Studies' which views literacy from a sociocultural perspective – as a social practice that is situated within a physical and social environment (Gee, 2008, 2010; Lankshear & Knobel, 2006; Street, 2008). Within different environments, the practices change with emphases on different aspects of literacy – oral, written, multimodal (any combination of words, images, sounds or motion), formal, informal, etc. For example, the literacy practices involved in classroom discourse (typically, oral and written discourse using more formal academic language) would tend to differ from those in an online social network (typically, written and multimodal discourse using more informal language).

The *ontological* refers to the nature of how literacy has changed in recent years. Lankshear and Knobel (2006) suggest that there are two aspects to this. The first has to do with the emergence of technologies that have enabled the wide availability of 'post-typographic' forms of literacy and literacy production that are significantly different from conventional literacies. The second aspect refers to there being a different ethos involved with new literacies. They tend to be more participatory, collaborative and distributed, but less published, individuated and author-centric than conventional literacies.

From a sociocultural perspective, literacy practices are viewed as intersecting with our personal identities. The degree to which we invest our identities in literacy practices varies according to how meaningful they are to our personal interests and goals. Successful school learners tend to invest much of their identity in the literacy practices in school. The reason some learners fail to engage with traditional literacy skills is often not because of poor cognitive ability but because of the fact that the literacy instruction they experienced in school failed to ignite any significant degree of identity investment in that literacy practice. The same students will often significantly invest their identities with highly developed literacy practices outside of school because they engage with their personal interests (Pahl & Rowsell, 2005).

Cummins (2005: 150) suggests that learners' creation of 'identity texts' can lead to much stronger literacy engagement:

> Identity texts refer to products of students' creative work or performances carried out within the interpersonal space orchestrated by teacher–student interactions. (...) When students share identity texts with multiple audiences (peers, teachers, parents, grandparents, sister classes, the media, and so on) they are likely to receive positive feedback and affirmation of self in interaction with these audiences.

He goes on to suggest that technology can facilitate such texts:

> Although not always an essential component, technology acts as an amplifier to enhance the process of identity investment and affirmation. It facilitates the production of these texts, makes them look more accomplished and expands the audiences and potential for affirmative feedback. (Cummins, 2005: 150)

Gee's (2008) notions of *Discourses* and powerful literacies are particularly valuable in the context of developing critical literacy skills for members of a minority language community. Gee defines *Discourses* as 'ways of being in the world', which integrate words, acts, gestures, attitudes, beliefs, clothes, etc. He emphasizes that language is a central aspect to *Discourses* but that it is not the only aspect and that language uses (which he calls *discourses*, with a small 'd') change according to a particular *Discourse*. Gee suggests that a 'powerful literacy' is one which shows an awareness of one's own *Discourses* and which involves using a 'metalanguage' to analyse and critique a particular *Discourse*. Using powerful literacies can provide the basis for renegotiating *Discourses* and identities within society (Gee, 2008).

From a threatened language point of view, the notion of Gee's *Discourses* is similar to that of Fishman's (2001) notion of language functions, but at an individual level. In trying to reverse language shift, Fishman suggests that the number of language functions using the minority language needs to be increased. By making members of a minority language community aware of their own *Discourses* and by enabling them to compose powerful literacies about them, they can analyse the power relations within their own and other *Discourses*. Examples of this could include analysis of how their primary *Discourse* (home) intersects with their secondary *Discourses* (school, sports clubs, etc.), analysis of the school curriculum and of available learning resources and how these support the needs of native speakers, analysis of how the dominant culture interacts with the minority culture and what effects this has on their identity and the future of the language, etc. This could equip them with the knowledge and power to renegotiate these *Discourses* and their own identities within society.

The recent emergence of Web 2.0 technologies (see below) can facilitate the publishing of such literacies and enable new *Discourses* to emerge from the communities themselves, thus potentially adding to the functions of the language. The participatory nature of these technologies can facilitate dialogue and collaboration on these literacies and could also potentially connect with other minority language communities (see also Uribe-Jongbloed's contribution in this collection) which could ultimately facilitate informed decisions relating to the maintenance of threatened languages and cultures.

Web 2.0 Technologies and Education

Blogs

A blog (shortened form of weblog [Web log]) is an online journal with entries posted in reverse chronological order (Lankshear & Knobel, 2006). Among the millions of blogs in existence in the *blogosphere* since the process to create them was simplified in 1999, two main types of blog have been identified – personal journals and information blogs (for a more developed taxonomy of blog types, see Lankshear & Knobel, 2006). Blogs also differ in structure, from single-author blogs with a simple interface, infrequent updates and little or no commenting to complex multi-author blogs with elaborate interfaces, constant updates and frequent commenting. Most blogs are enabled for reader's comments which can result in a sense of community among bloggers with a common interest (Herring *et al.*, 2005; Warschauer & Grimes, 2007).

Blogs have been increasingly used in education and particularly in language teaching (Warschauer & Grimes, 2007). Initial indications are positive towards the use of blogs within language teaching. The author recently supervised an MA student investigating the use of blogs to support the teaching of Irish in an English-speaking school (Ní Choileáin, 2009). The class was divided into learning groups, each made up of five–six learners of differing language proficiencies. Learners could choose their own topics to write about in the blogs and many wrote personal stories. By the end of the intervention, their writing was clearer, more accurate and better organized and their oral skills had also improved. Looking at the work of other learners and posting and receiving comments motivated them to work on improving their blogs some of which they worked on from home. They quickly realized that by acting as a community, it was easier to solve problems (content-related, linguistic, technical, etc.) collaboratively than individually. The learner's attitude towards Irish became more positive and the collaborative nature of the class resulted in a more cooperative, supportive environment.

Social networks

There are many types of social networks such as those designed for personal networking (e.g. Facebook, Bebo, Ning, etc.), media sharing (e.g. YouTube, Flickr, etc.) and social bookmarking (e.g. del.icio.us, Digg, etc.). It is suggested that long-established patterns of social interaction are being transformed by making many-to-many multimodal communication a societal norm, particularly among young people (see also Cunliffe *et al.*; Johnson; Dołowy-Rybiｃｓka; Wagner in this book). The ability to tag and rate content in these networks contributes to democratization of editorial decisions. What makes the front page on a social network is based on the clicks of thousands of people rather than a conscious decision by an editor. Social networking phenomena often go on to create news in the traditional media. A recent example of this is the sudden rise to fame of the Irish country music phenomenon *Crystal Swing* thanks to a performance on YouTube (Irish Times, 2010).

Researchers of new literacies have looked at literacy activities in social networks. Popular practices include the writing of fan fiction (extending books, TV shows, video games, etc.), the production of videos and music to share (see also ap Dyfrig and Cunliffe in this collection), the *Discourses* that occur in relation to common interests, etc. Most of the literacy practices used in social networks are in out-of-school contexts as social networks are typically banned from use in schools.

Wikis

Wikis are websites that any authorized user (often anonymous) can contribute to. A wiki is usually created to enable a group of people to engage in some form of collaborative knowledge building. In looking at the potential of wikis in education, Warschauer and Grimes (2007: 12) suggest that while computer-mediated communication (such as discussion boards or chat rooms) has served as a powerful medium for developing community and exploring identity, it has, to date proven to be 'a very unsuitable medium for accomplishing many kinds of collaborative work due to the inherent difficulty of arriving at decisions in groups dispersed by space and time'.

The *raison d'être* of Wikis, on the other hand, is collaborative work. Each edit on a wiki is a contribution to a collective work of literacy. In his own teaching, Warschauer found that students working with wikis were more motivated in their work than when using traditional means of assessment. The wiki's ability to track contributors greatly facilitated individual assessment in group projects (Warschauer & Grimes, 2007: 12).

Wikipedia is by far the largest and most well-known wiki with over 15 million articles, over 1 million editors in over 250 languages including many minority languages (Wikipedia, 2010; see also Zachte, 2011). What makes Wikipedia particularly interesting is how the Wikipedia community has evolved since its creation. In an empirical analysis of community activity in Wikipedia, Viégas *et al.* (2007: 1) found that despite rapid growth, 'the Wikipedia community places a strong emphasis on group coordination, policy, and process'.

Brown and Adler (2008) cite the development of Wikipedia as an example of an online community of practice. Novices become trusted members of the community through a process of legitimate peripheral participation. Newcomers begin by applying some minor edits to pages and by observing the social norms of the community. As they begin to show proficiency, other users begin to trust and rely on them until they eventually may achieve administrator status which has increased responsibilities and access to privileged editing tools. In addition to sociocultural aspects, they also focus on structural features of wikis whereby the history of a page and the discussions around its content can be easily reviewed, which they suggest, enables '(...) a new kind of critical reading – almost a new form of literacy – that invites the reader to join in the consideration of what information is reliable and/or important' (Brown & Adler, 2008).

Conclusions

In a traditional classroom, there are limited opportunities for learners to express their identities. Fishman (2001: 14) suggests that many school language efforts are not connected to home–family–community functions and that

> threatened languages must establish both (1) *a priority of functions*, and (2) *a priority of linkages between functions* in order to derive the maximal benefit from their relatively weak resource base and unfavourable resource competitive setting .

Language revitalization efforts need to focus on intergenerational transmission; thus, school interventions should involve their surrounding language community (Ó Laoire & Harris, 2006). As part of my research, I use Web 2.0 technologies to create a learning space that connects learners' primary *Discourse* at home with their secondary *Discourses* at school and with the wider community (see Figure 9.1). Such a space could be used for the collaborative creation of classroom resources, to acknowledge the learners' existing literacy practices, to enable community involvement in the creation of classroom literacies, the creation of identity texts or for the development of powerful literacies in relation to *Discourses* and identity formation (or any combination of these).

The use of digital video and audio can allow learners conduct inquiry-based fieldwork within the community and publish their results in a shared knowledge base. Links with an institution, such as a university, could enable lecturers, students, researchers and learning technologists to support both teachers and learners interactions within the learning space and to contribute their expertise to the knowledge being created.

One of the key factors in the success of any such intervention is its authenticity (similar to the opening vignette). Giving as much control of

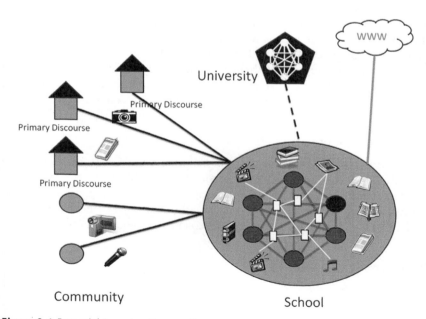

Figure 9.1 Potential Learning Community

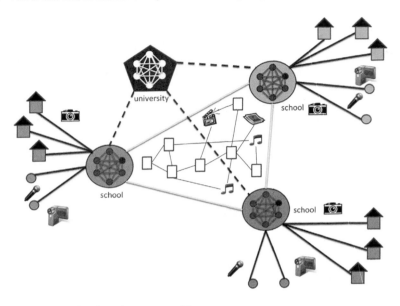

Figure 9.2 Connecting learning communities

content as possible to the learners adds authenticity as it suggests a degree of ownership and real authorship. Linking the school with the community (Figure 9.1) and possibly beyond to other schools (Figure 9.2) provides a real audience, another factor in authenticity. Finally, by setting goals to produce certain types of content or artefacts to certain standards also gives such an intervention a sense of purpose and also a sense of completion.

Acknowledgements

The researcher wishes to thank An Comhairle um Oideachas Gaeltachta agus Gaelscolaíochta for providing support towards this doctoral research, his supervisors Tony Hall and Fíona Concannon, for invaluable support and advice, and Peadar Mac Muiris, Breandán Mac Mathúna and all of his colleagues in Acadamh na hOllscolaíochta Gaeilge, Ollscoil na hÉireann, Gaillimh.

References

Brown, J.S. and Adler, R.P. (2008) Minds on fire: Open education, the long tail, and learning 2.0. *EDUCAUSE Review* 43 (1), 16–32.
Brown, J.S., Collins, A. and Duguid, P. (1989) Situated cognitions and the culture of learning. *Educational Researcher* 18 (1), 32–42.

Cummins, J. (2005) Afterword. In K. Pahl and J. Rowsell (eds) *Literacy and Education: Understanding the new Literacy Studies in the Classroom* (pp. 140–152). London: Sage.

Fishman, J.A. (2001) Why is it so hard to save a threatened language? In J.A. Fishman (ed.) *Can Threatened Languages be Saved? Reversing Language Shift Revisited: A 21st Century Perspective* (pp. 1–20). Clevedon: Multilingual Matters.

Gee, J.P. (2008) *Social Linguistics and literacies: Ideology in Discourses* (3rd edition). London: Routledge.

Gee, J.P. (2010) *New Digital Media and Learning as an Emerging Area and 'Worked Examples' as One Way Forward*. Cambridge, MA: MIT Press.

Hanks, W.F. (1991) Foreword. In J. Lave and E. Wenger (eds) *Situated Learning: Legitimate Peripheral Participation* (pp. 13–23). Cambridge: Cambridge University Press.

Herring, S.C., Scheidt, L.A., Wright, E. and Bonus, S. (2005) Weblogs as a bridging genre. *Information Technology & People* 18 (2), 142–171. doi: 10.1108/09593840510601513.

Irish Times (2010, February 27) Stand by your mam: Cork family rockin' the web, accessed 3 March 2010. http://www.irishtimes.com/newspaper/weekend/2010/0227/1224265257624.html].

Kalantzis, M. and Cope, B. (2008) Language education and multiliteracies. In S. May and N.H. Hornberger (eds) *Encyclopedia of Language and Education* (2nd edition, Vol. 1, pp. 195–211). New York: Springer.

Kern, R. and Warschauer, M. (2000) Theory and practice of network-based language teaching. In M. Warschauer and R. Kern (eds) *Network-Based Language Teaching: Concepts and Practice* (pp. 1–19). New York: Cambridge University Press.

Koschmann, T. (1996) Paradigm shift and instructional technology. In T. Koschmann (ed.) *CSCL: Theory and Practice of an Emerging Paradigm* (pp. 1–23). Mahwah, NJ: Lawrence Erlbaum Associates.

Lankshear, C. and Knobel, M. (2006) *New Literacies: Everyday Practices and Classroom Learning* (2nd edition). Maidenhead: Open University Press.

Lave, J. and Wenger, E. (1991) *Situated Learning: Legitimate Peripheral Participation*. Cambridge: Cambridge University Press.

Moll, L.C. and Whitmore, K.F. (1993) Vygotsky in classroom practice: Moving from individual trasmission to social transaction. In E.A. Forman, N. Minick and C.A. Stone (eds) *Contexts for Learning* (pp. 19–42). New York: Oxford University Press.

Ní Choileáin, A.M. (2009) *An féidir le blagana cur le cumas cumarsáide na bhfoghlaimeoirí dara teanga i sealbhú na Gaeilge?* M.A., Ollscoil na hÉireann, Gaillimh.

Ní Shéaghdha, A. (2010) *Taighde ar Dhea-chleachtais Bhunscoile i dtaca le Saibhriú/Sealbhú agus Sóisialú Teanga do Dhaltaí arb í an Ghaeilge a gCéad Teanga*. Baile Átha Cliath: An Chomhairle um Oideachas Gaeltachta agus Gaelscolaíochta.

Ó Curnáin, B. (2009) Mionteangú na Gaeilge. In B. Ó Curnáin (ed.) *Léachtaí Cholm Cille XXXIX – Sochtheangeolaíocht na Gaeilge* (pp. 90–153). An Sagart: Maigh Nuad.

Ó Giollagáin, C., Mac Donnacha, S., Ní Chualáin, F., Ní Shéaghdha, A. and O'Brien, M. (2007) *Comprehensive Linguistic Study on the Use of Irish in the Gaeltacht*. Dublin: Stationery Office.

Ó Laoire, M. and Harris, J. (2006) *Teanga agus Litearthacht i mBunscoileanna ina bhfuil an Ghaeilge mar mhéan: Athbhreithniú ar an Litríocht*. Baile Átha Cliath: CNCM.

Oxford, R. (2008) Conditions for second language (L2) learning. In N. Van Deusen-Scholl and N. H. Hornberger (eds) *Encyclopedia of Language and Education* (2nd edition, Vol. 4, pp. 41–56). New York: Springer.

Pahl, K. and Rowsell, J. (2005) *Literacy and Education: Understanding the New Literacy Studies in the Classroom*. London: Paul Chapman.

Street, B.V. (2008) New literacies, new times: Developments in literacy studies. In B.V. Street and N.H. Hornberger (eds) *Encyclopedia of Language and Education* (Vol. 2, pp. 3–14). New York: Springer.

The New London Group (1996) A pedagogy of multiliteracies: Designing social futures. *Harvard Educational Review* 66 (1), 60–93.

Viégas, F.B., Wattenberg, M., Kriss, J. and Ham, F.V. (2007) Talk before you type: Coordination in Wikipedia. Paper presented at the 40th Annual Hawaii International Conference on System Sciences (HICSS'07), Big Island, Hawaii.

Vygotsky, L.S. (1978) *Mind in Society: The Development of Higher Psychological Processes.* Cambridge, MA: Harvard University Press.

Warschauer, M. and Grimes, D. (2007) Audience, authorship, and artifact: The emergent semiotics of web 2.0. *Annual Review of Applied Linguistics* 27, 1–23. doi: 10.1017/S0267190508070013.

Wikipedia (2010) Wikipedia, Accessed 19 March 2010. http://en.wikipedia.org/wiki/Wikipedia.

Zachte, E. (2011) Growth pr Wikepedia wiki [Online Flash Animation], Accessed 8 June 2011.

10 Enhancing Linguistic Diversity through Collaborative Translation: TraduXio, an Open Source Platform for Multilingual Workflow Management in Media

Philippe Lacour, Any Freitas, Aurélien Bénel, Franck Eyraud and Diana Zambon

Introduction

This paper addresses linguistic diversity from the perspective of (collaborative and web-based) translation. Understanding language pluralism as an opportunity rather than a 'barrier', translation becomes one of the key tools for both promoting and preserving cultural and linguistic diversity. The rapid development of information and communication technologies (ICT) during the past two decades has also brought important changes to the way translation is conceptualized and effectively done. ICT tools, most notably the internet, have moreover increased the presence and visibility of a variety of languages on the web, thus leading to a de facto challenge to the 'all in English' norm.

In a context of increasing media convergence, content may be conveyed not only in different ways but also in many different languages – to different audiences. The spread of multilingual content sites and localization strategies have only reinforced such trend and considerably boosted the relevance of translation on, for and through the web.

As the demand and need of translation thus increase, different tools have been developed either to facilitate or to speed up translation processes. If some of these tools provide interesting results, these are fairly limited to the realm of technical, 'mass consumption' translation. Literary and other types of complex, culture-laden translation are ineffectively approached or simply left aside. What is more, these tools often fall short of providing satisfying solutions when it comes to *multilingual* translation.

In the following sections, we will discuss different aspects of the ICT revolution applied to the field of linguistic diversity in a context of media convergence. The first three sections examine the development of a linguistic diversity 'norm' (on and beyond the web) and issues related to media convergence and technological development. From Section 10.5 onwards, we will present and explore the *TraduXio* project: an innovative platform for collaborative translation that offers an alternative approach to multilingual e-translation.

The Spread of Linguistic and Cultural Diversity 'Norm'

In the past two decades, the preservation and promotion of world's 'biocultural' diversity have gained unprecedented force in the international arena (see, for instance, Maffi, 2001; and some of the contributions to this book). The awareness that not only ecosystems but also people, cultures and languages need to be safeguarded, and their variety furthered, is now recognized as one of the most pressing goals to be achieved through international cooperation and action.

The 'all in English' norm – based on the belief that the spread of English language should dissolve linguistic 'barriers' – has been thereby progressively challenged by the idea that linguistic pluralism should not be seen as a 'problem'. Linguistic diversity advocates do not, in fact, deny the importance of having a shared language (such as English, Chinese or Russian). They stress, on the other hand, that the 'one language only' perspective can be potentially dangerous, especially when taken to its extreme. Above all things, they highlight that the diversity of languages constitutes a reflection of the world's (cultural) plurality and call that political actors ensure that such variety might continue to exist and flourish.

This alternative dimension of globalization – that emphasizes particularities instead of compelling towards further homogenization – has been indeed central to many 'civil society' movements (see, for example, the journalists' movement Plus d'une langue, 2011), not only in the area of cultural/linguistic diversity. More recently, linguistic diversity has also reached the agenda of states and international organizations of different sorts, giving new force to the topic.

Multilingualism has been placed, for instance, as one of the key priorities of UNESCO. Its 'Convention on the Protection and Promotion of the Diversity of Cultural Expressions' (UNESCO, 2005a; in force since 2007) was actually one of the first major steps towards the recognition of multilingualism at the international level, for it acknowledged the specific nature of cultural productions as carriers of 'identity, values and meaning' (UNESCO, 2005a: 3). The declaration is actually one of the three pillars of the preservation and promotion of creative diversity (together with the 1972 Convention concerning the protection of world cultural and natural heritage and the 2003 Convention for the preservation of the intangible cultural heritage), and constitutes the basis of the organization's actions in the field.

The promotion, protection and preservation of the diversity of languages and cultures have also been embraced by the European Union. Member states and European institutions have thus been required to fully embrace these ideas, either by encouraging or by assisting citizens in acquiring language skills. Considering languages as 'an integral part of cultural identity', the EU decided to go a step further and proclaimed 2008 the 'European Year of Intercultural Dialogue' (http://www. interculturaldialogue2008.eu/?L=0).

E-Diversity: Digital Technologies for Promoting (Language) Learning, (Knowledge) Transfer and (Cultural) Dialogue

In parallel to the development of this linguistic diversity 'norm', another important transformation has been taking place at the international (transnational) sphere. The rise of information and communication technologies (ICTs), in particular in the field of education (Information and Communication Technologies for Education – ICTE), has brought new (more inclusive) forms of knowledge production, transfer and sharing – as well as alternative tools for political *action*. This process has been particularly felt within the humanities and other areas of human sciences. Initiatives such as Wikipedia, the Open Access Initiative and the multiplication of digital libraries worldwide are only a few examples of such trend – organizations, institutions and universities have also been trying to apply some of these Web 2.0 concepts (for a critical overview, see Lacour & Freitas, 2011).

The spread of collaborative technologies has, in fact, enhanced the possibilities of co-writing and editing (shared documents and bibliographies, wikis), watch (shared aggregators, social tagging, social search engine), networking (social networks of different sorts) and content management (forums, chats, polls, newsletters). All in all, the development of freely accessible, collaborative, inter-subjective, web-based technologies have launched a kind of 'smooth revolution' in the way not only single individuals but also institutions produce, reproduce and share knowledge and culture; a 'revolution' that is all the more relevant since it comprises virtually the whole World Wide Web.

Growing flows of digitized data have moreover facilitated public *access* to all sorts of information – some, not always intended to become public, as is the case of the 'Wikileaks' website. Individuals and groups not only have received a facilitated access but also have been enabled to produce and publish information, leading to important questioning of the role and legitimacy of journalists (and media actors in general). In fact, the impact of this ICT (r)evolution both on the media and on other dimensions of human life (learning, socializing, working, playing and so on) has only begun to be assessed.

If, initially, content (re)production on the web reflected the prevalence of the 'all in English' norm, researchers have been showing that the web has also progressively become a multilingual space. Data show that English has been actually losing space to other languages and is no longer the 'lingua franca' of the web. In this way, if by the mid-1990s, 80% of web pages were created in English, in 2005, English language content production counted no more than 35% of the World Wide Web (UNESCO, 2005b). The internet is hence more and more a multilingual (cyber) space (Crystal, 2001; Pimienta *et al.*, 2001).

This trend should be reinforced by the development of ICT within the so-called BRIC countries – Brazil, Russia, India and China. Their impressive economic expansion, allied to their technological development, political weight, demographic growth and (at least in the case of China and India) multilingual configuration should lead them to play an important role in the ICT and linguistic diversity issues. In fact, the expansion of the internet in these countries (particularly China), not only in terms of number of users but also in terms of content production, has been the major factor behind the decline of English on the web.

As has been the case in the international political realm, there have also been considerable efforts to support linguistic diversity in the cyberspace – of which Unesco's b@bel, 'café babel' or Presseurop are good examples (see their web presence at http://webworld.unesco.org/imld/babel_en.html;

http://www.cafebabel.com; and http://www.presseurop.eu). The latter two initiatives are, in fact, part of an international trend within media (and cultural) actors which have already started to reflect the importance of language diversity on the web, mostly by proposing multilingual 'versions' of their content. However, these different attempts remain insufficient, particularly when it comes to protecting and/or preserving minority (or endangered) languages. In reality, little (cultural, informative) content has been produced in the thousands of spoken languages in the world. In addition to other barriers (human and financial), speakers of these languages face difficulty in finding appropriate tools to both create content and translate existing information in these languages.

E-Translation: Tackling the Challenge of Multilingualism in a Media Convergence Context

As already mentioned, we have only begun to imagine the possible uses of new technologies for the preservation and the concrete promotion of cultural and linguistic diversity. Digital and cultural cooperation policies worldwide – especially scientific ones – remain too often at the national or supranational levels. This means above all that initiatives and decisions are considerably 'top-down' (like the many 'European framework programmes') and that little room is left open to the creativity of individual users or communities.

On another level, many organizations are eager to constitute transnational and dynamic networks, based precisely on the principle of sharing, collaborating and the 'localization' of their websites on different languages. If they can benefit from the various, but still developing, collaborative technologies, these grassroots and 'bottom-up' initiatives are soon confronted with the challenge of multilingualism. This is particularly so for those based on or directed to a European public – or audience. Indeed, new technological and practical challenges arise then from these efforts to 'go multilingual'. The first one is the growing demand for *precise* and *accurate* translation, able to convey the text's 'message' with all the 'cultural specificities' embedded in it. The second challenge is the *management* of such multilingual content. In fact, once a text is translated, the actual flow of content becomes wider, and administering this diversity can be a major difficulty for media actors if not processed appropriately.

At the time of media convergence, there is a clear need of a tool (and a platform) for the 'long tail' of translation, which would allow media actors to keep up with the news world wide, connect with other actors or individuals who share their views, worries or simply an interest for the same themes. This tool should above all empower these actors and give them a more active role in both sharing and producing information in different languages on a transnational basis.

Media convergence can be defined as the *new cultural processes occurring among different media organizations, creating new audiences and producers of communication and regenerating the public sphere in all its diversity* (for more discussion on convergence, see the contributions by Jones and by Uribe-Jongbloed in this volume). Within this general trend, one must immediately stress the importance of the World Wide Web, which is both the arena and the medium through which interactions of all sorts take place. Indeed, the web can support and, thus, allow for the most creative combination of several forms of media (radio, TV, photo, music, texts, etc.). Within this ever-evolving, web-based *converged* media, the (re-)production of language(s) and plurilingual practices – as we have briefly described above – also play a crucial role.

The adoption of a 'lingua franca', as detailed earlier, is not the appropriate answer to tackle the challenge of multilingualism – both in and outside the web. Instead of focusing on the 'dissolution' of plurality by the adoption of the 'all in English' norm, we hold, on the contrary, that translation should be put at the centre of policy and political action. Translation, in particular, multilingual translation should hence be promoted as a way to preserve language diversity, while ensuring effective communication and accurate exchange of information among these different media actors. In the context of technological development, translation, and translators alongside, has been considerably empowered by the spread of the collaborative, ICT tools.

E-translation is also at the bottom of processes of dissemination of culture, such as those engendered by immigrants and diasporas world wide. Its role and application in other fields are countless – and all of crucial importance. In the area of science and society, one could consider the role of translation in leveraging multilingual content concerning sustainable development. In the cultural domain, one could imagine to disseminate works of art though the translation of biographical data. Groups of actors – or artists of different sorts – can moreover be empowered with the capacity to (re)translate classical plays, or create alternative adaptations of existing ones (see, for example, http://sondes. chartreuse.org/document.php?r=61&id=137).   More   importantly, managing multilingual translation content can also be used to sustain minority languages on the web.

Numerous technological efforts have been dedicated to the development and improvement of automatic translation. However, this orientation is still tantamount to considering linguistic diversity as an obstacle to communication, a hindrance to be surpassed by cutting through semantics as quickly as possible. Though 'rational' and 'pragmatic' at first sight, the idea is comparable to efforts to building a highway in a very hilly landscape: one might not necessarily want to 'go faster' and lose all the pleasure of discovering new paths or uncovered aspects of the site while hiking. To be sure, in the same way that there is no real contradiction between driving a car and taking a walk, there is no exclusive alternative between automatic (*fast*) and precise (*slow*) translation: both are interesting and valuable and should therefore be considered complementary.

Yet, little has been said or effectively done to transform the potential of technologies for precise translation into concrete tools. *TraduXio* comes, in fact, to fill this gap, offering an innovative solution to support collaboration and translation through the web. In the following sections, we should detail the philosophy and actual scientific, technical and legal implications of *TraduXio*.

The TraduXio Project: A New Approach to Collaborative, Multilingual E-Translation

With the increasing need for, and interest in, translation, different tools have been developed in these past decades particularly to boost translation processes. Even if they provide quite interesting solution, we claim that none has gone as far as *TraduXio*, particularly in the field of multilingual, collaborative translation. Employing one of the most original solutions available in the area of web-based translation, *TraduXio* presents a number of advantages when compared to existing devices (Bénel & Lacour, 2011; Lacour *et al.*, 2010).

In a nutshell, *TraduXio* is a *free, open source, web-based, collaborative and computer-assisted translation tool, developed with innovative technology (a new 'Translation Memory' device)*. *TraduXio* has been developed by the Zanchin NGO, in collaboration with the University of Technology of Troyes, with the support of the UNESCO and the International Organization of 'Francophonie', among other partners. Inspired by the strong collaborative spirit of Web 2.0, and available to different audiences, the software has the vocation to become a mechanism of general interest – a true 'common good'. Though it has first been out to the test in the field of education, *TraduXio* has a tremendous potential for online media, as well as artistic and educational, projects.

TraduXio uses Translation Memory technology in an alternative way. The originality of the software resides in its certain functionalities – besides the already mentioned ones (freeware, open source, collaborative and designed to cultural texts). Traditional computer-assisted translation tools, especially Translation Memories, are limited to two languages (source/target), thus enforcing a 'star' system, in which a privileged language is set at the centre – one only, and always the same. In this device, like the Google Translator's toolkit (available at http://blogoscoped.com/archive/2008-08-04-n48.html), for instance, one can only go from language B to language C, through language A at the centre: English (see Figure 10.1).

TraduXio, on the other hand, enables *multilingual* translation, through the comparison of different versions of the same text. In this case, a translated text is not considered an independent segment but rather a version of the initial text in another language. *TraduXio*'s inner structure is therefore a *serial* system (see Figure 10.2), and not a star one. Also, the

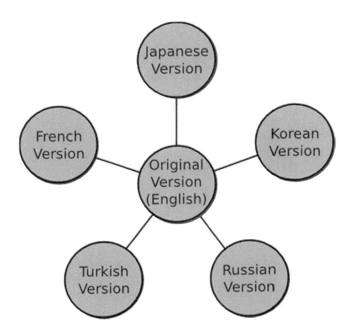

Figure 10.1 Star system (e.g. Google Translator's toolkit)

original version can be in *any* language, not only one (as in the previous 'star' system).

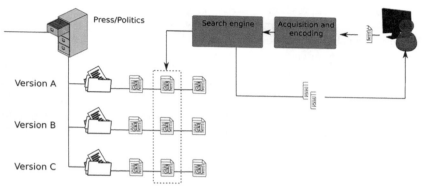

Figure 10.2 The TraduXio Serial System

The serial system allows *multilingual* translations, which are visible at the same time, as the following image illustrates (see Figure 10.3):

Moreover, *TraduXio* offers a better management of the translation context, for proposes a contextualized classification of the source (i.e. classification of the text according to the history, genre, author, etc.). Thanks

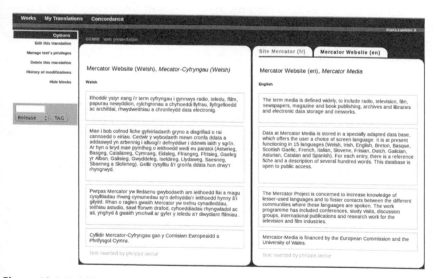

Figure 10.3 Multilingual translation

to this relevant classification device, information can be more easily assessed and treated, thereby helping users finding the appropriate translation for particular words, expressions and so on.

As a collaborative translation software, *TraduXio* is more than a common workbench for digital translators. It is also a network and a platform where translators can meet and create joint projects, exchange ideas, create corpora and glossaries. Few platforms, be they commercial (such as *translated.com*, *proz.com*) or non-profit, offer the conjunction of both services. Google has recently launched a Translation Center (still a beta version), a market place that should include a workbench. However, following the general orientation of Google, such initiative would be certainly profit oriente

TraduXio to whom?

As noted in the preceding paragraphs, the audience for *TraduXio* is potentially quite broad. It can primarily be used by translators, researchers, journalists, students and all those who use concepts and language as a way of theoretically reconsidering empirical practices. Likewise, NGOs, international associations and organizations, research institutions in a wide sense, political actors coming across translation problems, professional stage performers re-working previous translations of a theatre play in order to come up with a new version and so on are also targeted by the project.

Despite the difficulties of establishing the outcomes of such an enterprise, some of its potential impacts can be sketched out. First, *TraduXio* should help empower endangered and minority languages at both the new public (cyber-)space and the academic arena, through an appropriate and open technology. It should moreover efficiently promote linguistic diversity in media, by fostering online plurilingualism or promoting multilingual edition. It would thus reinforce already existing virtual communities of journalists by making experiments of multilingual mutualization ordinary. It would moreover constitute an important tool for a European and international *linguistic policy*, by promoting regional and minority languages across the globe.

On another level, for the software is based on an essentially collaborative technology, it has the vocation to create a diversity of cross cutting network of individuals, for professional or personal reasons. Putting people in contact and fostering inter-cultural (linguistic) dialogue is actually one of the most relevant objectives one can expect *TraduXio* to reach.

TraduXio and intellectual property rights: The (creative) 'commons' approach

TraduXio is not designed to perform any publishing or editorial functions, but rather to work as a digital workbench and network connecting users/translators worldwide. Translations carried out using *TraduXio* are thus not intended to be published or printed by the web service itself – although authors may personally chose to do so. All content provided by users is integrated into the Translation Memory, which is the foundation and the real differential of the tool. *TraduXio* is hence based on a 'mutualization' logic in order to create (non-financial) value. Its vocation is to become a 'commons' (like Creative Commons or Wikimedia Commons) on a not-for-profit basis.

The non-commercial and 'communitarian' dimension of the tool does not imply that the resulting translations will belong to the public domain. To begin with, users can manage the *privilege* of other users over its own work. In this way, she or he may decide to keep it completely private (thus 'hiding' her/his work) or to 'go public' and fully share it with the community. Privileges management is adapted to users' goals and is hence open to modification whenever she/he decides to change it, as the image in Figure 10.4 illustrates.

Users might also decide to share their work with certain, selected users (or community) which might then be entitled to certain functionalities (e.g. read, edit, etc., as shown on Figure 10.6).

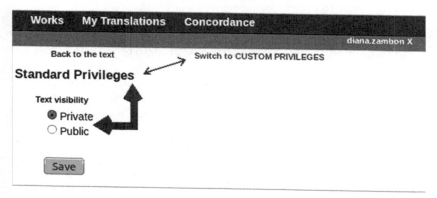

Figure 10.5 General privileges management

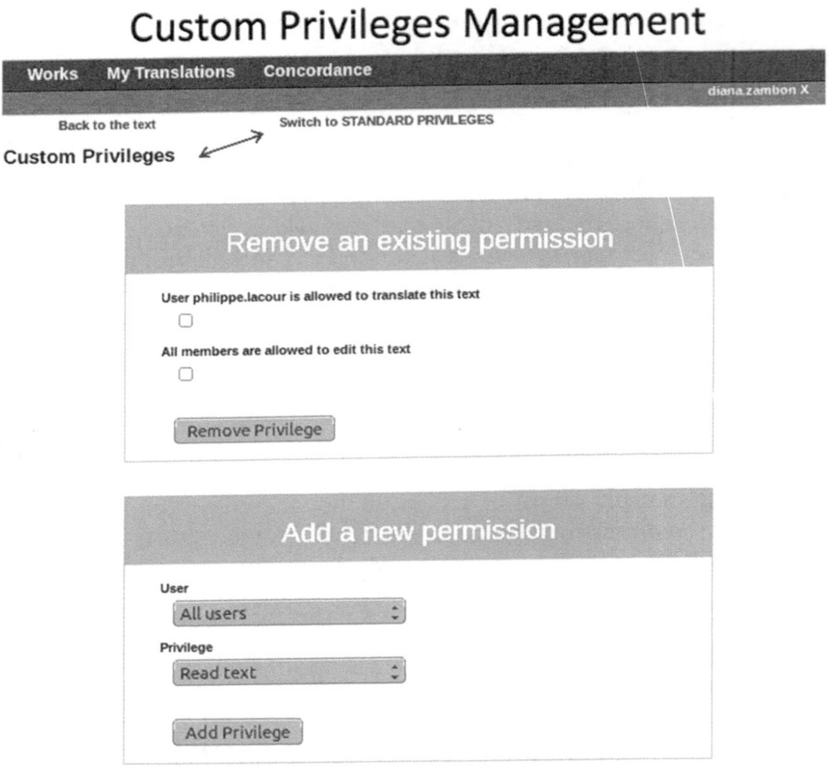

Figure 10.6 Custom privileges management

But more importantly, each translator will indeed be given the possibility to tag their creation with a *legal licence* of her or his choice. The range of rights' attribution goes from full copyright to the public domain. Given the 'sharing-driven' philosophy of the project, and its intent to protect (and ensure) users' rights of ownership, *TraduXio* is particularly close to the 'Creative Commons' (CC) system of licensing.

First conceived by Lawrence Lessig, a law scholar of Harvard University, the CC licences enable a disaggregation of the different properties of ownership rights, thus leaving to the user/author the possibility to 'keep' some (most notably, authorship attribution), while 'opening up' others (e.g. the right to use, reproduce, copy, sell and so on). This particular type of 'open licence' not only represents an alternative to more *traditional* conceptions of (intellectual) property but also provides legal support to those who view translation as a fundamental right (Basalamah, 2009; Lacour & Freitas, 2011).

TraduXio users will be hence encouraged to choose among these different CC licences. It is, however, important to note that they may choose to keep 'full' ownership (a 'strict' copyright licence) if they wish, or even to change the licensing regime over time. Attribution of authority over translations is indeed important since the re-utilization of 'memory matching' depends on the identification of the author of a given semantic creation. Frequent users could thus benefit from a form of public and non-financial recognition (a system of 'points'), which eventually might turn into a sort of professional reputation. The same liberal approach would apply to databases (the Translation Memory constituted through a specific use of *TraduXio*).

Conclusions

The exponential development of ICT of these last decades has simultaneously boosted processes of media convergence and linguistic diversification (on and beyond the web). The multiplication of digitized flows of information in different languages calls for appropriate tools to assist translation processes, while ensuring an efficient management of this multilingual content. Despite the development of different e-translation tools, these are often most suited for 'large consumption', rather technical types of text. An accurate and precise translation, required when source texts are complex (culturally laden), is often not compatible with the solutions proposed by existing translation tools.

In this chapter, we have presented the *TraduXio* project, which has, among its functionalities, the possibility to not only become a 'workbench' for collaborative translation but also to assist the management of multilingual workflow of different sorts. The *TraduXio* environment can thus be adapted to the particular needs of media actors (as well as single individuals or institutions) and thus help organize the administration of texts and other material generated in process of 'localization'.

More than a 'text management' tool, or an e-translation device, *TraduXio* embodies a particular philosophy the 'public good' which wishes to empower individuals (translators, media actors, scholars, NGOs, etc.) and help them share, collaborate and circulate different forms of cultural expressions. *TraduXio* wishes, in other words, to emphasize the importance of translation in an increasingly multilingual context.

References

Basalamah, S. (2009) *Le droit de traduire: Une politique culturelle pour la mondialisation*. Ottawa: Presses de l'Université d'Ottawa.

Bénel, A. and Lacour, P. (2011) Towards a collaborative platform for cultural texts translators. In M. Pierre (ed.) *Virtual Community Building and the Information Society: Current and Future Directions* (pp. forthcoming). Hershey, PA: IGI Global.

Crystal, D. (2001) *Language and the Internet*. Cambridge: Cambridge University Press.

Lacour, P., Bénel, A., Eyraud, F., Freitas, A. and Zambon, D. (2010) TIC, collaboration et traduction: Vers de nouveaux laboratoires de translocalisation culturelle. *Meta* 55 (4), 674–692.

Lacour, P. and Freitas, A. (2011) Translation and the new digital commons. Paper presented at the Trelogy: Translation careers and technologies: Convergence Points for the Future, Paris.

Maffi, L. (ed.) (2001) *On Biocultural Diversity: Linking Language, Knowledge, and the Environment* Washington DC: Smithsonian Institution Press.

Pimienta, D., Lamey, B., Prado, D. and Sztrum, M. (Producer). (2001, 18 May 2011) L5: The fifth study of languages on the Internet. Retrieved from http://www.funredes. org/lc2005/english/L5/L5index_english.html

Plus d'une langue (2011) Plus d'une langue: Informationsportal zum Thema Sprachen, Übersetzungen und Dolmetscher, accessed 18 May 2011. http://www.plus-dune-langue.eu/

UNESCO (2005a) Convention on the protection and promotion of the diversity of cultural expressions, accessed 18 May 2011. http://unesdoc.unesco.org/images/0014/001429/142919e.pdf.

UNESCO (2005b) Measuring linguistic diversity on the Internet. World Summit on the Information Society, UNESCO (ed). Accessed 18 May 2005. http://www.uis.unesco.org/template/pdf/cscl/MeasuringLinguisticDiversity_En.pdf.

11 Experiences of Audience Interaction by BBC Network Radio Producers: Implications for Endangered Language Media

Philippa Law

Introduction

The use of media in the context of endangered languages can increase a language's prestige, offer employment opportunities to minority language speakers and enrich the language's vocabulary so that it remains relevant to a new generation (Cotter, 2001). Now that audiences have come to expect to participate actively in the media (Deuze, 2006), the contemporary broadcasting landscape has opened up new domains of use for endangered languages, offering potential opportunities for language maintenance and revitalization (Cormack, 2007).

For language activists and media practitioners to make the most of these opportunities, it is important to understand the expectations and attitudes of not only the audience but also the producers involved in creating the content. This chapter addresses this issue by considering the effects that a changing media landscape has had on BBC radio producers who have adapted their working practices to incorporate more interactivity in the programmes they produce.

From the perspective of a sociolinguistic researcher with a background in professional media production, I examine some of the benefits and challenges posed by interactive or participatory media content as experienced and described by the production teams in which I have worked. Relating this insider knowledge to previous sociolinguistic studies of language revitalization media projects (e.g. Pietikäinen, 2008), this chapter articulates what can be gained by understanding the motivations of the broadcast practitioners on whom certain language revitalization efforts rely.

Background

In the prevailing media landscape, audiences have come to expect to participate actively in the media (Deuze, 2006). Participation takes many different forms. Audiences can take part in a radio phone-in, for instance, contribute to a debate in an online forum, volunteer at a community radio station or create and upload a video mashup. These are all contexts where discourse and language use come into play; some of them enable audiences in bilingual situations to communicate directly with the broadcaster or other audience members using the minority language. Such interaction may be synchronous or asynchronous, in speech or in writing, a point that I will address further in this chapter.

This new participatory culture within the media has the potential to encourage speakers to use their language in new domains. From a linguistic point of view, the outlook for endangered languages may therefore be more optimistic in communities who are willing and able to embrace the opportunities presented by the contemporary media landscape (for a potential of IT on the internet, see Crystal, 2000: 141–143).

Definitions of terms

The word 'interactivity' has two meanings in radio production. The first is a catch-all term for the provision of online and the other so-called 'new media' content. The second meaning is the more literal sense of enabling the public to interact with a programme's presenter, producer or other members of the audience, with or without the aid of the internet. I use the second definition in this chapter.

Both of these meanings are quite different from the word 'interaction' in sociolinguistics, which typically refers to face-to-face linguistic communication and all it entails (Cotter, 2010: 126; Crystal, 2003: 238). In the context of BBC network radio, interaction between the audience and the broadcaster, or among audience members, is sometimes conducted face-to-face, but is more often conducted at a distance (e.g. online).

Another common term used in radio production is 'user-generated content' (UGC), which refers to any broadcast or published content that has been provided by a member of the audience. Linguistically, UGC covers various genres, including emails, scripted or unscripted 'audio diaries' and visual communication such as photos and drawings.

In this chapter, the term I use most is 'participation', which encompasses various ways that the audience may interact and get involved with content, including UGC.

Aims of this chapter

For language activists and media practitioners to make the most of the apparent opportunities offered by participatory media culture, it is important to understand the expectations and attitudes of not only the audience but also the producers involved in creating the content, since their commitment may be critical to the success of certain minority language media. What are the day-to-day concerns and motivations of producers who incorporate audience participation into their work? And how do these concerns and motivations influence the content they make?

From 2002 to 2009, I worked on a variety of radio and online content at the BBC. This chapter draws on knowledge gained through participant observation within BBC network radio production teams. Examples are taken from two speech radio stations based in London: the BBC World Service and BBC Radio 7. The World Service broadcasts news, factual and entertainment programmes around the world, and Radio 7 – which was re-launched as Radio 4 Extra in 2011, to strengthen its links with BBC Radio 4 – was the BBC's digital radio network for drama, comedy and children.

In the following pages, I examine some of the benefits and challenges posed by participatory media content in my own experience as a network radio producer and as described by other producers. The objective is to make these issues transparent for minority language communities and language activists considering working with the media. The case studies presented also provide ideas for simple forms of audience participation. Minority language communities may wish to assess the suitability of these ideas for use within their own media.

Benefits of Incorporating Audience Participation

In all of the radio production teams I have worked in, producers have described various benefits of incorporating audience participation into their programmes and websites, for example:

1.   Participation provides evidence that someone is listening.
2.   Participation serves the audience.

3.   Participation creates a sense of community.
4.   Participation provides new or unexpected content.

Let's consider each of these points in turn.

Participation provides evidence that someone is listening

Radio producers I have worked with find audience participation very rewarding on a personal level. While audience figures show how many people are using a service, listening to a programme or visiting a website, they are impersonal and cannot reveal how valuable the content is to the audience. Receiving comments, phone calls and emails, on the other hand, demonstrates that someone has been moved enough by your work to respond or take part.

Data beyond audience figures could conceivably be cited to make a case for continued funding of minority language services. For example, in his account of the success of the Frisian news site www.omropfryslan.nl, journalist Onno Falkena (2001: 76) refers not only to the 'growing number of visitors' to the site but also 'the stream of e-mails from all continents' as a means of assessing the website's impact.

Participation serves the audience

Although they are aware that only a minority of the listening audience will ever choose to take part in programmes, radio producers say they view participation as a way of better serving listeners, because it reflects the diversity of the target audience. To network radio producers, 'diversity' means ensuring programmes include voices from all the demographics and geographical areas (and hence, accents and dialects of English) that their programme is aimed at (BBC, 2011a). The concept of 'serving licence fee payers' is a major concern among BBC staff. Producers consider it only fair that everyone who contributes to the BBC's income should be – and feel – included within the BBC's output.

Minority language activists who claim entitlement to media provision on the basis of their rights as citizens (see, for example, Jones, 2001) may find they share similar ideologies with BBC producers in this respect.

Case study: The Big Toe Radio Show

From 2005 to 2007, I produced a daily children's programme called *The Big Toe Radio Show*. The show was aimed at 8–12-year children and was broadcast every afternoon on BBC Radio 7. Since the presenters were adults, it was especially important to find other ways of including children's voices in the programme, in order to reflect – and therefore serve – the target audience. For this reason, the show was broadcast live and incorporated lots of opportunities for children to participate in different ways, for example:

- *The Big Toe Team:* Three different children visited the studio each day to take part in the programme as the *'Big Toe* Team'. They chatted about themselves, helped interview the studio guests, played quizzes and introduced songs.
- *Phone-in games:* Every day one listener took part in a phone-in game such as *Farts and Parps* (a guessing game) or *Chicken Pig Horse Cow* (a memory game).
- *Hot Topic:* Every day the programme posed a question, such as 'If you could design your ideal bedroom, what would it look like, and why?' and listeners called or emailed in to give their answer. Children's answers provided lively content for the show and encouraged other children to take part.
- *Message-board:* We hosted a message-board so that listeners could interact online with the show and with each other. This method of participation was unpopular with the *Big Toe* listenership and considered largely unsuccessful.
- *Press Pack:* Each Saturday we broadcast 'reports' that had been written and submitted by children and pre-recorded over the phone. Children could submit reports about anything they found newsworthy, for example a book they had read, a new pet they had adopted or something they had studied at school.

Some of these forms of participation may be suitable for minority language media. The Welsh language news programme for children, *Ffeil*, which goes out on S4C, has already had success with a project similar to *Press Pack*, in which several hundred children sent in reports and the best went on to become reporters for the TV show.

On *Big Toe* we found that by welcoming various forms of participation simultaneously – written, spoken, long-form, short-form, pre-prepared and ad-libbed – we could include children of varying levels of linguistic ability and confidence. This approach may also work for minority language audiences, whose fluency and confidence may not be uniform across all language skills and all demographics.

Participation creates a sense of community

Some radio producers find that participation creates a feeling of community around a programme, which promotes listeners' loyalty and gives producers a clear image of the audience they are addressing. A sense of community is considered beneficial to the maintenance of endangered languages too (Cormack, 2007; but also cf. Eisenlohr, 2004).

An excellent example of successful community building around participatory radio content is *Wake Up to Wogan*, which went out on BBC Radio 2 from 1993 to 2009. Sir Terry Wogan's fans are known affectionately as TOGs (Terry's Old Geezers/Gals) and share a group identity based on, as the Radio 2 website puts it, 'that feeling of being old before your time' (BBC 2011b).

Participation provides new or unexpected content

The audience can provide radio producers with unexpected personal stories. Participation as a source of content may also be valuable to minority language media, especially where speakers of the language are thin on the ground.

Benedicto *et al.* (2001) describe how the Mayangna, an indigenous people of Honduras and Nicaragua, are included in the Nicaraguan media. They discuss a story that would not have been widely heard without the participation of a radio listener:

> (...) an elderly woman from a community called Brikput (...) heard a brief comment on the foundation of her community on the radio. Afterwards, during a field trip by Eloy Frank to the community, she talked to him to set the story right: her father had been the founder of the community and she was the only one left to remember the events. She told her story to Eloy Frank who taped and transcribed it. The story was later told in the radio and so, a part of the Mayangna oral tradition which was at risk of being lost was recovered and, again orally, re-transmitted to the new generations in the communities. (Benedicto *et al.*, 2001: 56)

As a linguist, I can see this as a little victory for language preservation and cultural maintenance. But looking at this from a radio producer's point of view, this is also an illustration of how audience participation can go further than generating a simple email, text or phone call. In this instance, the audience member provides core content for a programme.

Case study: Living with autism, Outlook, BBC World Service

Let me provide you with an example of how this kind of participation can be achieved in practice. In 2008 *Outlook*, a semi-topical human interest programme on the BBC World Service, received an email from a listener called Jonathan, who said he wanted to come on-air to talk about autism. We had a long phone conversation about his experience of being diagnosed with Asperger's Syndrome in his 30s. He said he had his own recording equipment and wanted to record something for us.

I thought his story sounded interesting so I talked him through what we wanted to get out of it:

- A written script in advance of recording that I could check and shorten if necessary.
- Good sound quality.
- Some background noise to give it 'texture' and differentiate it from the studio items in the programme (but no music, passing cars or anything difficult to edit).
- Some conversation with his children (and a signed parental consent form in the post).
- Audio files delivered separately and unedited so I could edit and mix them myself.

It was a lot to ask, but Jonathan followed the brief exactly. Thanks to the initiative he took in contacting us, we were able to broadcast a story we would never have known about otherwise. Jonathan's feature was a thoughtful, engaging and entertaining piece of radio, which in turn generated further contributions from other listeners who responded to his story.

I use this as an example of how, from a radio producer's viewpoint, UGC *ought* to work, but in my experience, it rarely does.

Challenges of Audience Participation

My experience with Jonathan was unusual in that he had a flair for telling a good story and he also took care to do exactly what I asked of him. Production is not always that straightforward, however, More often than not, participation presents challenges for radio producers, such as ensuring the quality of contributions and managing the logistics of recording listeners' voices. It can also be tricky to retain editorial control without rendering participation inauthentic or tokenistic. The 'authenticity' of audience participation is a complex topic that would merit further discussion.

The logistics and expense of broadcasting to a wide geographical area is recognized as a challenge not only to stations as far-reaching as the World Service but also to minority language services whose audiences are scattered. Pietikäinen (2008) points out the difficulties that Sami journalists experience in covering stories in remote places, as they do not have the time or resources to travel there themselves and cannot rely on the services of Sami-speaking freelance reporters in distant locations.

Case study: Food diaries, Outlook, BBC World Service

One of the most challenging pieces of participatory content I have worked on was *Outlook*'s 'food diaries'.

In 2008, *Outlook* wanted to reflect listeners' experiences of the global food crisis. Since most of the content scheduled for the programme at that time consisted of live studio interviews, the programme's editor wanted some user-generated content, in the form of 'audio diaries', to add some texture to the programme – new voices, new sounds, a feeling of being outside, of taking the listener away somewhere else for a few minutes. For that reason, we didn't want our listeners to send in emails or record an interview in a studio or over the phone; we wanted to hear them doing things, going about their business and talking about it at the same time.

The challenges we faced boiled down to the three issues identified above: quality (most of the listeners who contacted us did not have an interesting story to tell), logistics (a lack of local reporters) and authenticity (dilemmas relating to editing contributions by non-native speakers of English, whose knowledge of the language was limited).

Discussion

Producers' motivations and concerns

For language activists to make the most of the opportunities apparently presented by the current participatory media culture, it is important to understand the concerns and motivations of the staff that engage in the production of participatory content. I have presented brief case studies from my own professional experiences of incorporating audience participation in BBC network speech radio content. In these examples, the following major personal motivators for producers can be identified:

- Making really good content.
- Receiving recognition, especially from the audience.
- Having the creative freedom to try new ideas.

Day-to-day production concerns that arise in the examples above include.

- filling the allotted airtime;
- ensuring good sound quality;
- giving the programme enough 'texture' by using a variety of voices and sounds;
- serving licence fee payers by reflecting the diversity of the audience;
- trying to understand why content is successful or unsuccessful;
- balancing the authenticity of audience participation with the need to maintain editorial control and quality;
- attracting new listeners;
- logistical issues, for example recording audio in remote places.

Implications for endangered language media

Bearing in mind that the case studies presented above illustrate just some of the issues speech radio producers encounter, I propose the following recommendations for language activists and language communities who are planning to work with media to support language maintenance:

1. Not all radio producers are alike in their approach to *interactivity*. Some have sophisticated *multi-platform* skills, others have little experience of working with new media. *Communities should consider carefully whether it is more appropriate to partner with a broadcaster with a close eye on emerging media trends and technologies, or a broadcaster whose use of participation is more traditional,* bearing in mind the risks of becoming the 'junior partner' as presented in the introductory essay by Browne and Uribe-Jongbloed.

2. At all stages, *the needs of the linguistic community must be taken into account.* As Cunliffe (2007: 133) points out, the discussion of the potential of online media 'must be grounded in the realities of access and use'. For instance, even if they are fluent speakers of the minority language, some audience members may not be confident at writing the language. If this is the case, a radio phone-in may be more effective at encouraging participation than, say, an online message board. *Communities should consider whether the aim is to encourage audiences to talk, or to increase their confidence in writing.*

3. As other authors have suggested (e.g. Cotter, 2001; see also Browne and Uribe-Jongbloed introduction to this volume), *communities should consider their policy on the 'correctness' and fluency of the minority language permitted on-air.* Demanding a high level of competence can exclude participants and be off-putting to audiences. On the other hand, tolerating non-fluent or mixed language can jeopardize the quality of

the content which is a major source of motivation for producers and valued by members of the language community.

4. *Keep a copy of all your audience feedback.* Do not underestimate its value in motivating production staff and potentially providing evidence of 'value' to funders.

Conclusions

Although this chapter is built on the assumption that audience participation in media may encourage minority language speakers to use their language more, very little is known about what the real opportunities are for minority languages in the contemporary media landscape and how to exploit them. What I hope this chapter illustrates is that, by taking each other's aims, motivations and concerns into account, minority language communities and media practitioners can find common ground on which to explore the potential for audience participation in language revitalization contexts.

References

BBC (2011a) The BBC and diversity, accessed 8 June 2011. http://www.bbc.co.uk/diversity/.

BBC (2011b) What is a TOG? Accessed 8 June 2011. http://www.bbc.co.uk/radio2/shows/wake-up-to-wogan/what-is-a-tog/.

Benedicto, E., Frank, E., Pulinario, S. and Avelino, S. (2001) Indigenous presence in the Nicaraguan media: The Mayanga. In C. Moseley, N. Ostler and H. Ouzzate (eds) *Endangered Languages and the Media* (pp. 55–58). Bath: Foundation for Endangered Languages.

Cormack, M. (2007) The media and language maintenance. In M. Cormack and N. Hourigan (eds) *Minority Language Media: Concepts, Critiques, and Case Studies* (pp. 52–68). Clevedon: Multilingual Matters.

Cotter, C. (2001) Continuity and vitality: Expanding domains through Irish-language radio. In L. Hinton and K.L. Hale (eds) *The Green Book of Language Revitalization in Practice* (pp. 301–311). San Diego: Academic Press.

Cotter, C. (2010) *News Talk: Investigating the Language of Journalism.* Cambridge: Cambridge University Press.

Crystal, D. (2000) *Language Death.* Cambridge: Cambridge University Press.

Crystal, D. (2003) *A Dictionary of Linguistics and Phonetics* (5th edition). Malden, MA: Blackwell.

Cunliffe, D. (2007) Minority languages in the internet: New threats, new opportunities. In M. Cormack and N. Hourigan (eds) *Minority Language Media: Concepts, Critiques, and Case Studies* (pp. 133–150). Clevedon: Multilingual Matters.

Deuze, M. (2006) Ethnic media, community media and participatory culture. *Journalism* 7 (3), 262–280. doi: 10.1177/1464884906065512.

Eisenlohr, P. (2004) Language revitalization and new technologies: Cultures of electronic mediation and the refiguring of communities. *Annual Review of Anthropology* 33 (1), 21–45.

Falkena, O. (2001) Frisian all over the World: The unique experience of one year. In C. Moseley, N. Ostler and H. Ouzzate (eds) *Endangered Languages and the Media* (pp. 76–79). Bath: Foundation for Endangered Languages.

Jones, G. (2001) The state and the global marketplace in the provision of minority media services. In C. Moseley, N. Ostler and H. Ouzzate (eds) *Endangered Languages and the Media* (pp. 11–15). Bath: Foundation for Endangered Languages.

Pietikäinen, S. (2008) Broadcasting indigenous voices. *European Journal of Communication* 23 (2), 173–191. doi: 10.1177/0267323108089221.

Part 3

Media Convergence and Creative Industries

12 Towards a Template for a Linguistic Policy for Minority Language Broadcasters

Eithne O'Connell

Introduction

Back in 1991, the respected sociolinguist Joshua Fishman (1991: 395) cautioned against pinning too many hopes on the media when it comes to ensuring the survival of minority languages, suggesting that the domains of home, community, education or work were more important. A decade later, he was still sounding a note of caution and describing as a fetish the attitude of some minority language activists towards mass media (Fishman, 2001: 482). His initial warning was challenged a year later by an edited volume of essays where it was argued enthusiastically that ethnic minority media was 'making a substantial contribution to the continued survival of minority languages' (Riggins, 1992: 283). Amongst the many benefits listed by Riggins as accruing from minority language media were the improved language skills amongst speakers, the dissemination of new terminology, the presentation of positive linguistic role models for young people and an enhancement of the image/visibility of the language and its speakers (1992: 283). These are certainly important benefits of minority language broadcasting and being the most obvious and visible, they are also the most frequently discussed. However, if we think of broadcasting as an industry involving many different stakeholders and if we consider how its various media professionals use the minority language in many contexts other than just within the narrow confines of making of programmes, we can see how minority language broadcasting has the scope to make a much greater and broader-based contribution to the future of the language than envisaged in the examples listed by Riggins (see, for instance, O'Connell et al., 2008).

Convergence: The Dissolution of the Media Domain Paradigm

Whatever about the situation some 20 years ago, there seems to be little point nowadays in continuing to argue about whether or not the other domains of home, community, education and work are more important than media. For one thing, minority language media can no longer be viewed as separate from these domains. Rather, in this dawning age of multi-platform broadcasting, in which radio, television, mobile phone, computer and other technologies are converging, it is more realistic to view the media in sociolinguistic terms not only as a domain existing in its own right but increasingly also as one which enjoys a growing presence in each of the other domains mentioned above and one which can link them all in new and complex ways. At this early stage in the process of convergence, we can only guess at the full range of challenges and possibilities that will arise for the media, in general, and minority language, in particular. But what we can already see is that we will have to adapt to more than just new technologies. Communication processes are changing too. The ways in which we interact socially and professionally not only as individuals but also as members of audiences and contributors of programme content are changing and our traditional understanding of the media, media professionals, audiences, genres and content. will change as well. As media content and consumer behaviour become much more dynamic and participatory, commercial and advertising models will also have to be adjusted accordingly. The implications all this will have for minority language media will unfold as part of a gradual process of evolution and adaptation. Perhaps minority language broadcasters will benefit in the new dispensation. Indeed, the proliferation of digital channels and the likely attendant loss of content quality due to cost cutting, while presenting even more competition for cash-strapped minority language programming, may offer new possibilities for attracting larger transnational audiences to the specificity of much minority language output.

The transnational appeal of minority language media may not be immediately obvious but over the past decade some 2 million members of the Galician-speaking diaspora in South America have been able to watch Televisión de Galicia thanks to satellite, thereby swelling audience numbers to a previously unimaginable extent (Guyot, 2004: 24). While Irish, as a much smaller minority language, does not have the same potential transnational audience, TG4's web presence does now also give it a global reach beyond the new virtual linguistic community it has forged in recent years within the island of Ireland. These examples show the potential of new technology to reach minority language speakers scattered across the globe. In the case of Irish, access facilitated by new technologies also offers opportunities to attract new audience members, for example, from (a) Irish speakers living in northern Ireland or overseas, (b) the nearest and linguistically closest Celtic language neighbours, namely Scottish Gaelic/*Gàidhlig* speakers, (c) speakers of other minority languages and (d) individuals from around the world interested in the content offered and/or in learning or improving their Irish skills. Descendants of Irish emigrants throughout the world who want to engage with the language of their ancestors as well as students in the various university departments in the United States of America, Russia, Poland, the United Kingdom, Germany, Canada, Australia and China, where Irish can be studied, will be able to enjoy easier access to the language and its speakers thanks to increased multi-platform delivery. Recent efforts on the part of an Irish computer scientist, Kevin Scannell, at the University of St. Louis in the United States, point to some of the new and exciting ways in which minority languages and the media are developing. His website (http://borel.slu.edu/nlp.html) features a site that trawls Twitter to find everyone tweeting in an indigenous or minority language, a web crawler for building minority language corpora automatically and various corpora in a number of minority languages, including Irish and Welsh, Aymara and Zulu. Websites like this point the way to the future, but it remains difficult to foretell what ongoing convergence will bring. Nonetheless, we can prepare ourselves a little by looking critically at the experiences of the past and by trying to learn from them, so as to develop innovative and effective ways to use all aspects of the evolving broadcasting industry to support minority language communities into the future, regardless of whether those communities are traditional and regional/national or virtual and global. Indeed those distinctions will come to mean very little as Irish speakers located as far from each other as Boston, Borneo and Béal an Daingin tweet their thoughts into the ether allowing them to be read by anyone under the sun provided they are on Twitter and have the linguistic knowledge to understand them.

I have commented above and elsewhere on the fact that for all the insistence on the need for minority languages to have dedicated media in order for them to survive and prosper, writings on minority language media do not usually focus on the language and there has not been much close scrutiny of the various, specific contexts in which a minority language is actually used by media professionals (O'Connell, 2007: 214; something remarked upon in Browne and Uribe-Jongbloed's research agenda, and mentioned in Cormack's conclusions as well). Using some sample questions based on observations relating to the changing Irish broadcasting situation, I hope to show that the linguistic focus in minority language broadcasting tends to be on programme content. Meanwhile, the potential impacts of all the other linguistic interactions which are integral to the overall broadcasting project or organization may be ignored or at least underestimated in terms of importance. While not wanting to suggest that any struggling minority language media organization should be bound by a narrow policy straitjacket, there may be merit in broadcasters drafting guidelines relating to *all* aspects of minority language use/output in their workplace, rather than just thinking of programme content. The first step would be for media professionals to review every aspect of their work, possibly in cooperation with language planners and sociolinguists, with a view to developing awareness as to the implications of their linguistic practice, not only for audiences but also for their colleagues and business partners, and the wider minority language community in which they are located. The review could capture current practice, identify strengths and weaknesses and inform consideration of the future language-related possibilities offered by multi-platform delivery. The aim would be to develop best linguistic practice in the broadcasting sphere and allow minority media professionals to exchange ideas and insights with minority language broadcasters elsewhere, possibly with a view to closer collaboration. It is in this context that some issues, which could be usefully addressed in a formal or informal linguistic policy template for minority language broadcasting, are discussed in the next section.

Irish Broadcasting

In Ireland, the evidence to date suggests that while minority language broadcasters understand implicitly that their work is part of a broader cultural and linguistic agenda, they have not traditionally seen themselves as necessarily having a specific contribution to make to language planning goals. There can be no doubt that the development of Irish language media was seen from the outset by the State as part of a broader policy to preserve the language in those areas where it was still the daily mode of communication (i.e. the Gaeltacht) and revive it elsewhere. Shortly after the foundation of the Irish Free State in 1922, the first tentative steps in Irish language broadcasting were taken by 2RN (1926), a Dublin-based radio station with limited coverage and later in the 1930s by Radio Éireann, which had a more national reach (Watson, 2003). The national radio station, expanded in 1961 to incorporate television and become RTÉ, Raidió Teilifís Éireann, and RTÉ has since then continued to broadcast a subset of its programmes in Irish on both platforms. In 1972, a dedicated Irish language radio station aimed primarily at native speakers of the Gaeltacht, Raidió na Gaeltachta, was established. An Irish language television station intended to have a broader national appeal was founded in 1996 and named Teilifís na Gaeilge, or TnaG, and this in turn was re-branded in 1999 as TG4. By 2011, state support for Irish language broadcasting was by no means still solely confined to the Republic of Ireland. In 1982, BBC Radio Ulster started to broadcast in Irish and BBC Northern Ireland is also an established broadcaster in Irish, now offering multi-platform facilities to help people wanting to learn the language.

Speaking a decade ago at a seminar on broadcasting in Irish and Breton, Cathal Póirtéir, a senior Irish language radio producer, commented that in the course of his entire career in RTÉ, he did not think he had ever seen a language planning document. Moreover, despite the presence of what he described as a benevolent Director General and sympathetic Director of Television, Irish language television programmes seemed at that time to him to be produced on an *ad hoc* basis and apart from operating Raidió na Gaeltachta, there did not seem to be a clear policy within the organization in relation to the Irish language (Kelly-Holmes, 2001: 52).

The lack of a formal language planning policy in relation to Irish broadcasting, as identified by Póirtéir, may come as a surprise, given that Irish language broadcasting, like most minority language broadcasting ventures elsewhere, has always been supported and funded by the State. Where a government decides to spend significant sums of money from state coffers annually on such support, one might expect the funding to be linked to some kind of general political, social and educational rationale. The current website for TG4 describes the television station as de facto 'the most positive and high profile government policy for the Irish language for the past fifty years' (TG4, 2011). Whether or not this was the founding intention or is, in fact, the current reality, it is interesting to note that statements made by those centrally involved in TG4, prior to it becoming independent of RTÉ in 2007, suggest a gap between in-house staff and audiences in relation to expectations as to what the broadcaster's main purpose actually was. An early employee of the station, Cillian Fennell, stated unequivocally in 2001 that 'the television station is not a language revival movement' (Kelly-Holmes, 2001: 54).

Celebrating the first 10 years of the station in 2006, Cathal Goan, the first Ceannasaí or Head of TnaG/TG4, suggested that over the first 10 years different groups had expected the station to be innovative, serve Irish speakers, appeal to the national audience and be attractive to those who did not know the language. All these views framed the station in terms of a language service, but in his personal opinion, TG4 had always been and was still at that time primarily a television service rather than a language one (Goan, 2008: 175). On one level, that was fair enough since broadcasters are broadcasters and their first duty is to make and broadcast programmes. Yet even within the organization, the broadcasters may not necessarily form a homogeneous group or adhere to precisely the same corporate understanding of their mission. It is possible, rather, within the same station that management, programme makers and other staff may have differing perspectives or at least different priorities. Then there are the agendas and expectations of the other interested parties or stakeholders: language activists, the wider minority language community, minority language learners, external production companies, audiovisual translators who provide dubbing or subtitling services, language planners, teachers, viewers who do not understand the language at all, etc. In an ideal world, the needs and expectations of each of these constituencies would be considered and integrated to some extent into both the broadcaster's mission statement and the full range of linguistic practices in operation within the organization. In an effort to sketch out how this might be attempted, it is possible to identify at least five distinct headings within broadcasting under which linguistic perspectives and/or practices could be usefully investigated: corporate mission, in-house communications, broadcasting language, translation and commercial dealings.

Use of Minority Language in Broadcasting

Those responsible for drafting and implementing the mission statement, for example, may have attitudes and approaches to the use of the minority language that differ either subtly or significantly from studio technicians, clerical staff, presenters, translators and buyers. Any attempt to be prescriptive, given the differing parameters within which various minority language broadcasters operate, would be ineffective, if not impossible here. Instead, some key issues relating to linguistic practice in the five areas will simply be explored by means of some sample questions. The inspiration for these questions comes necessarily from the Irish situation and it is clear that a number of different questions may be more relevant for other minority languages.

Sample questions about language use in minority language broadcasting:

1. *Corporate mission:*
    What is the mission/corporate understanding or purpose of the broadcasting station?

Is the corporate vision a top-down externally imposed view, based on legislation or statutes and imposed on the organization?

Which stakeholders participated in the drafting of the mission?

Has the mission been formulated by management and/or other staff, for example as a five year plan?

Has the station's mission been developed bottom-up on the basis of feedback from all the employees and/or the wider minority language community?

Can the current vision be readily adapted in response to feedback and changing circumstances, for example convergence?

How are the professional media broadcasting expectations balanced against linguistic/language planning expectations?

2. *In-house and external communication:*

Is the minority language the daily language of in-house written and oral communication?

Are all employees fluent speakers of the minority language? If not, is there any contractual obligation on them to develop some or a high level of linguistic competence?

Is there a policy of helping employees, regardless of language competence, to improve their oral and written linguistic skills?

In which language(s) does the station conduct its external communications?

3. *Broadcasting:*

Are language issues addressed differently, depending on programme genre, audience etc.? For example, are there special linguistic guidelines for children's programmes or advertisements?

Standard versus dialects:

To what extent is the standard form of the minority language as opposed to dialects used in programmes?

Is there any conscious attempt to balance the representation of different dialects or is one favoured over others?

Has a particular dialect come to prominence by default or design across the broadcasting spectrum or in a particular programme genre?

If so, what consequences might this have in the short to medium term?

Registers:

Does the minority language have a developed set of spoken and written linguistic registers?

Does the programming schedule present opportunities for the use/development of a full range of registers?

Are presenters encouraged to use predominately formal/informal registers?
Are they encouraged to speak in their own dialect?

Terminology:
Is terminological support provided to in-house staff/commissioned programme makers?
Is there an in-house terminologist?
Is there an in-house online term bank?
Is there a formal link to/co-operation with a national or other minority language term bank? If so, is the flow of terminology one-way or bidirectional?
Can the public access the term bank? Can they propose terms or only access existing ones?

Editorial policy:
Do programme presenters and participants receive direction or feedback from editorial staff relating to such linguistic issues as terminology, grammar, pronunciation, etc.?
Is there a broadcasting style or pronunciation guide?
Programme participants:
Is consideration given to balance between native speakers, fluent speakers and learners used on individual programmes and throughout the complete schedule (depending on programme genre, this may relate to presenters, interviewees, audience, actors, etc.)?

4. *Translation:*
Does the station buy programmes made in other languages? If so, does the station or an external company translate them before broadcast?
Does the station provide guidelines as to translation principles and procedures?
If the station buys original foreign language AV material, what percentage is in (a) the neighbouring dominant language, (b) other major languages and (c) other minority languages?
What is the attitude of the broadcaster to a commissioned programme based on a foreign language script translated into the minority language, as opposed to one based on an original script in the minority language?
What percentage of overall programme output originates in another language and is then dubbed or subtitled into the minority language?
Have the advantages and disadvantages of broadcasting minority language subtitles been weighed against each other?

Is the decision to purchase dubbed or subtitled material linked primarily to cost issues?

Are minority language programmes broadcast with subtitles in (a) the minority language, (b) the neighbouring dominant language and (c) both?

Are minority language subtitles closed, that is must be deliberately selected by viewer or open, that is the viewer has no choice?

Are subtitles in other languages (e.g. English in Ireland) closed, i.e. must be selected by viewer or open, i.e. the viewer has no choice but to view them?

5. *Commercial dealings:*

Does the station make its own programmes?

What percentage of its programmes does it purchase?

Does the station commission some or all of its programmes from independent production companies?

Does the broadcaster conduct some, most or all its external commissioning business through the minority language?

Does the station give preference when buying AV material to programmes made by companies which conduct their business entirely/ in part through the minority language?

Does the station give preference to programmes made by companies located within an area where the minority language is spoken, for example in Ireland, are tenders from independent *Gaeltacht* AV production companies given preference, if all other factors are equal?

Are advertisements carried and if so, is there a requirement that all (or a certain percentage) of them be in the minority language?

If not, are advertisements in the minority language offered a discounted rate?

While accepting that in any particular minority language broadcasting scenario, the range of issues and therefore the types of questions that can be usefully posed will vary, these sample questions have been listed in order to illustrate just some of the many different ways in which minority language media professionals are necessarily engaged with linguistic choices on a daily basis. It is clear that in most real-life scenarios a number of the issues underlying the questions would have to be addressed in order for the broadcasting organization to function efficiently. However, quite a few issues might not only not be addressed but also not even be registered as important by some media professionals, even though their relevance would be understood by language planners, translators, educators, etc. It is fairly clear that broadcasting decisions based on a language policy will have certain results or contribute to certain outcomes. But it is sometimes not understood that other decisions also of a linguistic nature, taken with little reflection on an *ad hoc* basis, will just as certainly have implications in the short, medium or long term for the very minority language community which provides the broadcaster with its very *raison d'être*. The issues at stake for minority languages are many and complex and so a small sample of examples of possible implications of certain decisions will have to suffice to illustrate some of the factors worth consideration.

The first issue of the *broadcasting mission* is probably the one least likely to have escaped encapsulation in some kind of policy statement. However, the often tricky relationship between the minority language speakers and the dominant neighbouring language community can result in minority language broadcasters being given a very general, non-committal brief. While this can allow great freedom, it can also make the interpretation of broadcaster's role highly dependent on particular individuals at any given time. This may lead to inconsistencies of direction and output over time and can hamper the integration of the media into wider language planning goals. An example is the case of RTÉ which was understood, at least prior to the founding of TnaG/TG4, to have a special responsibility in relation to Irish language broadcasting but the precise nature of the responsibility was never clarified or quantified. This made it difficult for Irish language activists to make anything other than subjective criticisms relating to the extent of RTÉ's Irish output. Another example of differing corporate and audience positions is identified by Ó hIfearnáin (2008: 195), who points out that campaigners for TnaG/TG4 expected programming based on their own language and values but, in fact, the broadcasters remoulded 'the self-image of speakers of all competences and challenged the prescriptive expectations of linguistic correctness by legitimising the appropriateness of informal and mixed language in specific and, in some cases, non-specific contexts'.

The second issue identified is that of *in-house practice* and is closely linked to the broadcaster's mission. Those who hold the view that TG4 is first and foremost a television station will probably adopt a pragmatic stance on the extent to which the minority language should be the language of daily communication for all employees. For example, if a really good technician with weak Irish is available, professional skills might outweigh linguistic skills as a condition of employment in the eyes of the employer. On the other hand, those who espouse the view that TG4 is primarily a key instrument of a broader language planning agenda will be acutely aware of the limited number of domains in which most Irish speakers can use their first language. They will therefore attach greater importance to a vision of the station as one of a relatively small number of work environments where minority language speakers can use their first language. Their view is based on a concern that the presence of just one person may be enough to force a group of minority language speakers to switch code, thereby changing the entire linguistic ambience in the workplace, possibly for a generation or more. In situations where intergeneration transmission of a minority language is no longer guaranteed, and domains where the language is generally spoken are shrinking, minority language workplaces have particular importance, given the amount of time spent at work.

The third issue concerns *the kind of language used* in programmes and advertisements. The question of how to use what language in which context is something that even media professionals working in a world language like English often have to address, whether they take their cue from *The Economist*'s style guide or the BBC's Pronunciation Research Advisory Unit. Indeed, in 2010 the EC launched a clear writing campaign for its staff, such were the problems that citizens encountered when reading EC documentation.

When the written form of Irish was standardized, the Munster dialect had a strong presence. Now that TG4 has its headquarters in Connemara, which is in the province of Connacht, there is a perception in some quarters that the Connacht dialect is in the ascendant. Certainly, when it comes to the dubbing of children's programmes, the largest Irish language player, Telegael, is located just down the road from TG4 and has easier and cheaper access to actors from the Connemara Gaeltacht than from other more distant locations. Ó Mianáin (2008: 186) showed that in a random sample of children's series on TG4 which he conducted in 2006, 12 were predominantly in Connacht Irish, 3 in the Ulster dialect and 2 had an even distribution of dialects.

If, for argument sake, the availability of Connemara Irish speakers to work as dubbing actors were to result by default in their dialect becoming the most widely spoken in children's programmes, children around the country could come to perceive Connemara Irish to be the most prestigious dialect. The implications of such a perception both for the development of a standard spoken form and for the speakers of the other two dialects in general would be significant. As Ó hIfearnáin has observed,

> TG4 is part of Ireland's linguistic landscape but it also creates a linguistic landscape of its own, on screen, within the ambiguous diglossic context of the Irish speech community (...) It is a participant, generator and legitimiser of linguistic norms'. It will be interesting for students of sociolinguistics to look back after fifty years and study precisely which

new linguistic norms the station generated and how. But it is likely that such norms will have been established by chance rather than in response to specific language planning needs identified at the time of the station's foundation or thereafter. (Ó hIfearnáin, 2008: 195)

The creation and dissemination of standardized terminology has always presented a very real problem for minority languages, both in terms of cost, time and acceptance by ordinary speakers. But the successful propagation of terms is vital if minority languages are to hold their own. However, thanks to the development of online term banks and the scope offered by convergence for increased participation of ordinary citizens in terminology formulation, broadcasters could play a major role in this area. Providing terminologists have editorial control, minority language broadcasters using crowdsourcing models could invite users to draw on their own linguistic and specialist subject knowledge to research and suggest terms and give feedback on current usage, including acceptability of new terminology. A key element in terminological crowdsourcing would be a direct link online between the broadcaster and the minority language's official terminology standardizing body so as to avoid duplication of effort and ensure consistency of terminological use.

The fourth issue relates to the *use of translated material* in minority language broadcasting, be it scripts translated into the minority language or the dubbing and subtitling of material. The implications of the extensive use of subtitled and dubbed material for minority language broadcasting has been addressed in detail elsewhere (O'Connell, 2007; O'Connell & Walsh, 2008), but it is worth summarizing a few key points here. First, as Øverås (1998) has shown, translated text is not just the source text rendered in the target language. Rather, translations are characterized by a number of distinctive features which include a lot of cohesive explicitness and very few lexical repetitions, colloquialisms or metaphors. These features also appear in original texts but when their distribution is studied in both original and translated texts, they would appear to constitute 'parameters within which to identify a text as a translation' (Øverås, 1998: 586).

If translations are marked texts, a broadcaster relying heavily on translated texts is exposing speakers to an atypical form of language. Minority language broadcasters tend to dub disproportionately large amounts of children's programming into their language to keep costs down while maintaining high production values. But there seems to be little awareness that wide-scale dubbing (or subtitling for that matter) may have implications for language maintenance in minority language environments.

Furthermore, many minority language broadcasters use open subtitles in the neighbouring dominant language regardless of the evidence that this can have a detrimental effect on minority language speakers' experience by making a monolingual programme a bilingual one (O'Connell, 2007).

The fifth issue concerns how the broadcaster operates externally in relation to the *linguistic practices of their business partners*. Critical to the survival of a minority language is the creation of employment opportunities in the area where the language is spoken. Ideally such employment also offers the chance to work in the minority language. In the 1970s in Ireland, some companies moving to Gaeltacht areas brought with them both expert staff and new technologies. The newcomers generally did not know Irish and this resulted in the adoption of English technical terms by Irish-speaking employees, even in cases where appropriate Irish terms were in existence. Mac an Iomaire (1983) has shown how that early stage of industrialization had a positive effect on employment opportunities in Irish-speaking areas but simultaneously had the negative effect of encouraging language shift from Irish to English in the workplace. A quarter of a century later, Mac Murchú (2008: 210–213) has described the Irish language employment, offered by his independent production company Nemeton located in An Rinn/Ring, one of the smallest *Gaeltacht* areas. Twenty-five full-time and up to fifty part-time Irish speakers provide up to 200 hours of television, much of this for TG4, and this has brought great benefits to the surrounding community. As Mac Murchú puts it, the media professionals

> have had a positive effect on the prominence of the language locally ... in comparison to ten years ago, things have improved greatly (...) you have a better chance of hearing a conversation in Irish in the local shops, bars or other public places (...) Not only did we get an Irish-language channel for our children, but we got this huge secondary benefit which has impacted on the whole community. (Mac Murchú, 2008: 213)

Conclusions and Discussion

In conclusion, the Irish sociolinguist, Ní Laoire, suggests that although

> there is little evidence of a direct causal, measurable link between media and language styles in a speech community, it is nevertheless true that all elements of the media form part of the linguistic mix that is a speech community and can be accepted as reflecting current language use to some degree. (Ní Laoire, 2008: 191)

Moreover, she argues that 'the media may influence the speed and spread of changes in language use through their role in picking up and reflecting changes in progress' (Ní Laoire, 2008: 191). With reference to the effects of Irish language radio broadcasting on style and usage since the 1972 foundation of Raidió na Gaeltachta, she identifies 'increased intelligibility between regional dialects, increased and developed capacity for style shift towards levelled and standardised varieties, and an increase and development in use of specialised registers and specialist vocabulary' (Ní Laoire, 2008: 191) and she wonders whether the effects of TG4 will be comparable. One option is to wait a generation and then trace the linguistic changes that have occurred. The other option, in line with considerations outlined here, is for media professionals involved in minority language broadcasting to recognize the media as a key element in broader language policy. By focusing attention on the language element of minority language broadcasting and reflecting critically on current linguistic practice in all sectors of the industry, policies can be developed to maximize the contribution of broadcasting to the future of the minority language.

References

Fishman, J.A. (1991) *Reversing Language Shift: Theoretical and Empirical Foundations of Assistance to Threatened Languages*. Clevedon: Multilingual Matters.

Fishman, J.A. (2001) From theory to practice (and vice versa): Review, reconsideration, and reiteration. In J.A. Fishman (ed.) *Can Threatened Languages be Saved? Reversing Language Shift Revisited: A 21st Century Perspective* (pp. 451–482). Clevedon: Multilingual Matters.

Goan, C. (2008) The early days and the future. In E. O'Connell, J. Walsh and G. Denvir (eds) *TG4 @ 10: Deich mbliana de TG4/Ten years of TG4* (pp. 175–176). Conamara: Cló Iar-Chonnachta.

Guyot, J. (2004) Languages of minorities and the media: Research issues. *Mercator Media Forum* 7 (1), 13-28.

Kelly-Holmes, H. (ed.) (2001) *Minority Language Broadcasting: Breton and Irish*. Clevedon: Multilingual Matters.

Mac an Iomaire, P. (1983) Tionchar na tionsclaíochta ar Ghaeilge Chonamara Theas. *Teangeolas* 16, 9–18.

Mac Murchú, I. (2008) AV production, Irish language and community. In E. O'Connell, J. Walsh and G. Denvir (eds) *TG4 @ 10: Deich mbliana de TG4/Ten Years of TG4* (pp. 210–213). Conamara: Cló Iar-Chonnachta.

Ní Laoire, S. (2008) TG4, the Irish language and Irish-language speech. In E. O'Connell, J. Walsh and G. Denvir (eds) *TG4 @ 10: Deich mbliana de TG4/Ten years of TG4* (pp. 191–194). Conamara: Cló Iar-Chonnachta.

O'Connell, E. (2007) Translation and minority language media – Potential and problems: An Irish perspective. In M. Cormack and N. Hourigan (eds) *Minority Language Media: Concepts, Critiques and Case Studies* (pp. 229–247). Clevedon: Multilingual Matters.

O'Connell, E. and Walsh, J. (2008) Fotheidealú agus dubáil: Aistriúchán agus teilifís Ghaeilge. In C. Dillon and R. Ní Fhrighil (eds) *Aistriú Éireann: Gnéithe de chultúr an aistriúcháin liteartha in Éirinn* (pp. 97–107). Belfast: Queens University Press/Cló Ollscoil na Banríona.

O'Connell, E., Walsh, J. and Denvir, G. (eds) (2008) *TG4 @ 10: Deich mbliana de TG4/Ten Years of TG4*. Indreabhán, Co. na Gaillimhe: Cló Iar-Chonnachta.

Ó hIfearnáin, T. (2008) The linguistic landscape and the performance of language on TG4. In E. O'Connell, J. Walsh and G. Denvir (eds) *TG4 @ 10: Deich mbliana de TG4/Ten Years of TG4* (pp. 195–197). Conamara: Cló Iar-Chonnachta.

Ó Mianáin, P. (2008) Voicing the future: The language of TG4's children's programmes. In E. O'Connell, J. Walsh and G. Denvir (eds) *TG4 @ 10: Deich mbliana de TG4/Ten Years of TG4* (pp. 185–187). Conamara: Cló Iar-Chonnachta.

Øverås, L. (1998) In search of the third code: An investigation of norms in literacy translation. *META* 43 (4), 571–588.

Riggins, S.H. (1992) The promise and limits of ethnic minority media. In S.H. Riggins (ed.) *Ethnic Minority Media: An International Perspective* (pp. 276–288). Newbury Park: Sage.

TG4 (2011) Background, accessed 26 May 2011. http://www.tg4.ie/en/corporate/background.html.

Watson, I. (2003) *Broadcasting in Irish: Minority Language, Radio, Television and Identity*. Dublin & Portland, OR: Four Courts.

13 Legislating the Language of Cinema: Developments in Catalonia

Júlia Cordonet and David Forniès

Introduction

Films in Catalan cinemas are almost exclusively exhibited in Spanish. Catalan is seldom the language of the films exhibited: in 2007, out of 859,803 screenings, only 26,382 were in Catalan, accounting for 3.07% of all films showed (Idescat, 2010), although it should be borne in mind that this percentage includes all films produced, dubbed or subtitled in Catalan.

Confronted with this uneven situation of the Catalan language, the Catalan Government prepared a bill on cinema distribution in 2009 and presented it to legislation immediately afterwards, leading to its approval by the Catalan Government in 2010. The bill demanded for 50% of all screenings to be shown in Catalan. However, in order for the bill to enter into force as a law, it required Parliament to give the final approval. The bill had the support of four out of the six political parties in Parliament, and it also had the backing of various associations that promote the Catalan language. Opposing the law were distribution and exhibition companies, which were firmly against it, arguing that such an increase in Catalan screenings would lead to lower viewership. Despite this difficult scenario, the Law on Cinema was finally approved in July, 2010 (Ley 20/2010, de 7 de julio, del cine., 2010).

However, it is hard to know how this situation will develop. Around the same time, in June, Sentence 31/2010 of the Constitutional Tribunal of Spain declared overturned the preference for Catalan in the public administration and media. Also, several sentences from the Supreme Tribunal and the Superior Justice Tribunal have reduced the effect of linguistic legislation in favour of Catalan in education and civil administration.

Facts about the Catalan Language

The Catalan language is spoken by over 7.7 million speakers and 10.8 million people claim to be able to understand it (according to official census information, 2001–2004, Institut d'Estadística de Catalunya, Institut d'Estudis Catalans, Institut Balear d'Estadística, Institut Valencià d'Estadística and Govern d'Andorra). Catalan has more users than nine EU official languages (i.e. Danish, Estonian, Finnish, Irish, Latvian, Lithuanian, Maltese, Slovak and Slovene).

Catalan is used across four states:

It is spoken in *Spain*, where it enjoys co-official status, alongside Spanish, in the regions of Catalonia, the Valencian Country, and the Balearic Islands. It is also spoken in the Franja (inside Aragón) where it has a limited recognition, and in El Carxe (inside Murcia), where it has no recognition.

In *France*, in the region of Northern Catalonia, it is not official, although it has a very limited recognition by the Department of the Eastern Pyrenees.

In the small state of *Andorra*, Catalan is the only official language.

It is also spoken in *Italy*, in the city of L'Alguer (Alghero), where it is not official, although it enjoys limited recognition by both the Parliament of Italy (since 1999) and the Parliament of Sardinia (since 1997), as well as by the city council.

According to the 2001 census, Catalan is spoken by 4.6 million people in Catalonia, while 5.9 million people understand the language. The population of Catalonia is 7.5 million. Catalan is a 'usual language' for 47.6% of the Catalan population, while it is an 'initial language' to a further 35.4%, according to the 2008 Survey on Linguistic Uses. Around 12% of the Catalan citizens do not have Catalan as their family language/mother tongue, but they learn the language (mainly at school) and use it actively. This is not an unusual situation, where minority languages are concerned.

A similar trend is also noticeable in Andorra where the 2009 official survey (Centre de Recerca Sociològica, 2009) evidenced that 29% of Andorran residents claim that Catalan is their mother tongue, while 38% mention Catalan is their 'own' tongue. This implies that 9% of Andorran residents consider Catalan as their language despite having an altogether different mother tongue.

Cinema and Language in Spain

Before engaging in the discussion about the Catalan cinema legislation, it must be pointed out that films are usually dubbed for cinema exhibition in Spain. Contrary to what happens in many countries in Europe, subtitled films in original version are by no means the default version that people would expect at a screening. Indeed, there are quite a few cinemas that specialize in subtitled versions, but mainstream cinemas always show dubbed versions of foreign films. Dubbing is mainly provided in Spanish, as we explain below.

General legal framework for cinema and language in Spain

In 2007, the Parliament of Spain passed Law 55/2007 on Cinema (Ley 55/2007, de 28 de diciembre, del Cine, 2007). This law establishes the general framework for cinema production, distribution and exhibition in Spain. The law allows distributors to screen films from any country, as long as they are screened, whether dubbed or subtitled, in one of the official languages of Spain (Art. 14). It also provides financial assistance to films produced in any of the official languages of Spain (Art. 24), and it establishes a specific fund for films in official languages other than Spanish (Art. 36).

In line with previous laws (i.e. Law 3/1980 on the Regulation of Screen Quotas and Film Distribution and Law 17/1994 on Protection and Fostering of Cinematography), Law 55/2007 on Cinema establishes a yearly 25% quota for the exhibition of European films (Art. 18). Those films had to be dubbed or subtitled into any of the official languages of Spain. None of these laws has required films to be distributed in Catalan version.

What do current norms say in Catalonia?

Apart from Law 55/2007, the situation of Catalan in cinemas is mainly regulated by two norms:

1. Law 1/1998 on Linguistic Policy (Llei 1/1998 de 7 de gener, de política lingüística, 1998) enacted by the Parliament of Catalonia. Its article 28 states that the Catalan Government should foster film production in Catalan, including dubbing and subtitling foreign films into Catalan. It also says that the Government may pass regulations to introduce compulsory linguistic quotas for screenings.
2. Law 22/2005 on Audiovisual Communication of Catalonia (Llei 22/2005, de 29 de desembre, de la comunicació audiovisual de Catalunya, 2006)

passed by the Parliament of Catalonia. Under Title VIII, Chapter II, the law says that the Government of Catalonia should foster the development of the cinematographic industry of Catalonia, although it does not specify in which language this is to be done.

In addition to these regulations, there is another provision: Decree 267/1999 on the administrative regime of the cinematographic and audiovisual sector (Decret 267/1999, de 28 de setembre, sobre règim administratiu de la cinematografia i l'audiovisual, 1999) passed by the Government of Catalonia. However, this decree does not include any reference to the language in which a film is to be screened.

Regulations on Language in Cinema in Other Catalan-Speaking Territories of Spain

The *Valencian Country* adopted the Law on the Audiovisual Sector in 2006 (Llei 1/2006, de 19 d'abril, de la Generalitat, del sector audiovisual, 2006). Article 1 of the law states that one of its goals is 'in particular, to support the audiovisual works in Valencian' ('Valencian' being the name officially given to the Catalan language in the Valencian Country). Article 8 foresees a system of public financial assistance to 'promote and foster the audiovisual sector and the Valencian audiovisual and cinematographic works'. The law specifies (Art. 10) what are 'Valencian audiovisual and cinematographic works'; in relation to language, it says that 'Valencian audiovisual works shall be made for their original version preferentially in Valencian'.

Thus, the law does not require films to be produced in Catalan. Note that the text only says 'preferentially' – without defining how this 'preference' is to be granted or ensured – and even fails to include 'cinematographic works' in this part of the provision. Furthermore, the law does not set any linguistic quota in cinema exhibitions. It only demands a quota for TV broadcasters to show 'Valencian audiovisual and cinematographic works'. But since those works do not need to be produced in Catalan, it essentially has no binding obligation towards the use the language.

Hence, the 2006 law has failed the implementing principles contained in at least one previous act, the 1998 Law on the Creation of the Academy of the Valencian Language, whose preamble vowed for a 'systematic policy of promotion of the use of the Valencian language in [...] the cultural industry: books, newspapers and magazines, theatre, cinema, and in general in the audiovisual sector' (Llei 7/1998, de 16 de setembre, de la Generalitat Valenciana, de creació de l'acadèmia valenciana de la llengua, 1998).

In the *Balearic Islands*, the 1986 Law on Linguistic Normalization states (Art. 31.1) that 'the Government of the Autonomous Community shall foster production and exhibition of films that are made, dubbed or subtitled in Catalan [...]', providing some level of commitment to Catalan in the cinema (Ley 3/1986, de 19 de abril, de normalización lingüística, 1986).

In the *Franja* and *El Carxe*, there are no specific legal texts aimed at providing any form of protection or support to Catalan in cinema production or exhibition.

Regulations on Language in Cinema in Other Catalan-Speaking Territories Outside Spain

The *Principality of Andorra* has a limited number of regulations as regards to language in cinemas. Essentially, this is regulated in the 1999 Law on Official Language Use Planning (Llei d'ordenació de l'ús de la llengua oficial, 1999; for an English version of this text, see http://www.ciemen.cat/mercator/butlletins/39-06.htm), which states (Art. 15) that 'advertisements and posters concerning cinema, theatre, shows or any other cultural manifestation must be written in Catalan, without any prejudice to titles or denominations in other languages'. More specifically, Art. 28 states that 'with the purpose to help and spread the official language, public administrations must foster [...] the exhibition, sale or renting, in any audiovisual media, of films and documentaries in a Catalan version or subtitled in Catalan, which will be given priority with respect to those copies in other languages'. Thus, this does not include quotas and does not require any cinema to schedule films in Catalan language.

In *Northern Catalonia* and *L'Alguer* there are no specific legal texts which provide any protection or support to Catalan in cinema production or exhibition.

Audience and Exhibition Situation of Catalan in Cinemas

The new Law on Cinema of Catalonia is a result of the situation of the language in this particular area of cultural interest. Since the transition to democracy (1975–1977), Catalan language has been conquering linguistic domains and public areas. Efforts have been made in order to increase the presence of the language in the media (public Catalan TV and radio). Incentives have been made available to the translation of websites and television programmes into Catalan. Grants and public funds have been directed to the cultural industries in order to create, publish and produce media in Catalan. Even if not all these efforts have been equally fruitful, the pace has enabled, slowly but surely, to increase the presence of the language in all domains of society. There has been, in the cultural arena, one noticeable exception: cinema. For some reason, despite the amount of money spent in dubbing films, they were not shown in cinema halls, save for a few exceptions. The data on screenings for Catalonia presents a clear picture: in 2007 only 3% of the showings were in Catalan, quite a reduced number, as already pointed out.

Data from the different public reports issued by the Barometer of Communication and Culture (http://www.fundacc.org/) show the situation of the Catalan language in cinemas for 2007 in the Valencian Country, Balearic Islands, Catalonia and these three territories together, and it also includes the same information in the Balearic Islands and Catalonia for 2008 and 2009.

In 2007, when asked about the language of the last film people had seen in the cinema, in the whole territories studied a mere 2.4% responded it was in Valencian/Catalan. In Catalonia it was where more people answered affirmatively to having seen the last film in Catalan, where it peaked at 4% of the whole universe of respondents. On the other end of the spectrum, in the Balearic Islands only 0.8% replied affirmatively, and in the Valencian Country it was even lower, hitting the bottom at 0.1%. In the last two territories, the percentage of people who had seen the last film in languages other than Catalan or Spanish was higher than that of the people who had seen the last film in Catalan (1.4% and 0.4%, respectively).

The data for 2008 and 2009 included in the Barometer of Communication and Culture show that the percentage of Catalan in the cinemas has decreased in 2009 and it also shows that Spanish is the majority language of the Cinemas both in Catalonia and in the Balearic Islands. This is the situation the new Act on Cinema is aiming to address in Catalonia.

Many of the producers and owners of cinema halls and multiplexes in Catalonia have showed their opposition to the measures regarding language that the new Law on Cinema of Catalonia is going to implement. They have actively displayed their animosity mainly towards the expected demand of 50% of the copies of the films to be exhibited either dubbed or subtitled in Catalan, as purported in Article 18.1 (Ley 20/2010, de 7 de julio, del cine., 2010). Their main argument to support their opposition to these measures is that there is no demand for Catalan cinema and that this would lead to huge economic losses for the sector.

The Pro-Language Platform (http://www.plataforma-llengua.cat/) has looked at these arguments in its 'Study on Practices and Legislation around Language in the Cinema in Some European Countries, Quebec and Catalonia' (Plataforma per la llengua, 2010). The report presents data of the study on the offer and demand of screenings in Catalonia. According to this study, the audience of Catalan cinema increased by 17.2% between 2006 and 2007; more films were offered in Catalan in the cinemas in 2007 than in 2006 (146 titles versus 107 in 2006). During that same period the viewership of cinemas, in general, decreased 6% in Catalonia and 7.7% in the whole of Spain. Providing further data, this study effectively proves that demand for Catalan cinema was not decreasing, as was the general trend in Spain and Europe through that period (2006–2007), but instead the demand for Catalan cinema was directly linked to its offer: when more titles in Catalan were made available, audience for them increased. Demand is evidently constrained by availability.

Regarding the box-office takings in Catalan cinema, the study shows that they are very similar to the takings of cinema projection in other languages: the screenings in Catalan are equally profitable than those in other languages.

The New Law on Cinema: Main Points

The law has recently been enacted and its main points are now binding. This is a positive development, although its implementation would need to be assessed before it can be deemed a success.

In its preamble, the law claims that

Catalan is widely spoken and understood by the majority of the population of Catalonia.

Catalan has a relevant place in books, theatre, music, newspapers and magazines.

In spite of this, Catalan has a very low rate in cinema showings and this undermines the citizens' right to watch a movie in Catalan or through Catalan subtitles.

In order to overcome this situation, the law states the following[1]:

Article 18. When a film is first exhibited in Catalonia, either dubbed or subtitled, with more than one copy of the work, distribution companies have the obligation to distribute fifty per cent of all analogue copies in a Catalan language version. (…) When the transfer technology is digital, all distributed copies should have Catalan linguistic access incorporated into them. In the screening of these works, exhibitor companies have the obligation to screen 50% of all projections of the work in Catalan language version following criteria related to population, territory, scheduling, and ticketing, which must be compiled annually and undertaken according to regulations. This obligation must be respected in the total number of exhibited projections both for dubbed copies and also for those projections exhibited in a subtitled version. Exhibitors and distributors should also guarantee the balance between Catalan and Castilian [Spanish] in advertising for those films covered by this article.

Article 24.1. The Catalan Institute of Cultural Industries must establish a Cooperation Program of Cinema Screens of Catalonia of voluntary membership, with the aim of creating a Cooperation Network of Cinema Screens of Catalonia, whose main goal must be disseminating Catalan and European cinema and fostering cinematographic culture in Catalonia.

Article 24.2. The Cooperation Network of Screens must be constituted by all those cinemas, public or private, that voluntarily join it [...].

Article 25.1. The Cooperation Network of Screens aims at the preferential screening of cinematographic feature films and short films, along the following conditions:

(a). Having been produced in Catalonia, preferably in Catalan original version.

Article 25.2. Cinematographic works screened by the Cooperation Network of Screens, if not in original in either Catalan or Castilian [Spanish], must be screened subtitled in Catalan.

Conclusion: A Law to Put Catalan on an Equal Footing in Cinemas

There is legal basis, even from the Spanish Law on cinema, to take initiatives aiming to foster the screening of films in Catalan, whether dubbed or subtitled. The former absence of Catalan in cinemas led to a situation through which, much too often, watching a film in Catalan constituted an open act of militancy: few of the cinemas in Barcelona and its outskirts – where the majority of the population of Catalonia is concentrated – made films in Catalan available. In many towns in the Catalan territory, it was even impossible to find a single cinema where films in Catalan were shown. This situation undermined the right of Catalan speakers to watch movies in their language, a language that the basic law of Catalonia (the Statute) defines as the 'own language' of the country.

Consequently, the Law on Cinema was conceived and enacted to try to change this situation and adapt cinema exhibition to that ideal, bearing in mind that the use of Catalan in other cultural industries has been much wider in scope and reach. It has been considered a successful laboratory of diversity (Petit et al., 2010) along the lines of the Convention on the Protection and Promotion of the Diversity of Cultural Expressions (UNESCO, 2005).

What we have evidenced is that there is room to substantially increase the screenings in Catalan, because there is a real market and a real demand for them. A further study of the impact of this law, in the coming years, would serve to prove the point that it was lack of availability, rather than lack of demand, what kept Catalan away from the cinema screens.

Note

1. This translation has been produced by Mercator Legislation and it is not an official version of the original Catalan text.

References

Centre de Recerca Sociològica (2009) Coneixements i usos lingüístics de la població d'Andorra 2009, accessed 16 May 2011. http://www.catala.ad/images/stories/Coneixements09.pdf.

Decret 267/1999, de 28 de setembre, sobre règim administratiu de la cinematografia i l'audiovisual. (1999) Accessed 16 May 2011. http://www.upf.edu/sintesi/1999/d267.htm.

Idescat (2010) Estadística de l'audiovisual a Catalunya 2009. Barcelona: Institut d'Estadística de Catalunya, Generalitat de Catalunya. Accessed 16 May 2011. http://www.idescat.cat/cat/idescat/publicacions/cataleg/pdfdocs/eac09.pdf.

Ley 3/1986, de 19 de abril, de normalización lingüística. (1986) Accessed 16 May 2011. http://noticias.juridicas.com/base_datos/CCAA/ib-l3-1986.t3.html.

Ley 20/2010, de 7 de julio, del cine. (2010) Accessed 16 May 2010. http://www.boe.es/boe/dias/2010/08/07/pdfs/BOE-A-2010-12709.pdf.

Ley 55/2007, de 28 de diciembre, del Cine. (2007) Accessed 16 May 2011. http://noticias.juridicas.com/base_datos/Admin/l55-2007.html.

Llei 1/1998 de 7 de gener, de política lingüística. (1998) Accessed 16 May 2011. http://www20.gencat.cat/docs/Llengcat/Documents/Legislacio/Llei%20de%20politica%20linguistica/Arxius/lpl_llei.pdf.

Llei 1/2006, de 19 d'abril, de la Generalitat, del sector audiovisual. (2006) Accessed 16 May 2011. http://www.docv.gva.es/datos/2006/04/21/pdf/doc/2006_4604.pdf.

Llei 7/1998, de 16 de setembre, de la Generalitat Valenciana, de creació de l'acadèmia valenciana de la llengua. (1998) Accessed 16 May 2011. http://www.docv.gva.es/datos/1998/09/21/pdf/doc/1998_7973.pdf.

Llei 22/2005, de 29 de desembre, de la comunicació audiovisual de Catalunya. (2006) Accessed 16 May 2011. http://www.gencat.cat/diari/4543/05363034.htm.

Llei d'ordenació de l'ús de la llengua oficial. (1999) Accessed 16 May 2011. http://www.ciemen.cat/mercator/butlletins/39-06.htm.

Petit, M., Baltà Portolés, J., Gómez Bustos, L. and Reguero, N. (2010) An international laboratory for diversity: The Catalan law of cinema. In A. Sekhar and A. Steinkamp (eds) *Mapping Cultural Diversity: Good Practices from Around the Globe* (pp. 22–25). Rheinbreitbach, Germany: German Commission for UNESCO/Asia-Europe Foundation. Retrieved from http://www.unesco.de/fileadmin/medien/Dokumente/Kultur/U40/Mapping_Cultural_Diversity_FINAL.pdf.

Plataforma per la llengua (2010) *Estudi sobre les pràctiques i legislacions entorn de la llengua al cinema en diversos països europeus, Quebec i Catalunya.* Barcelona: Plataforma per la Llengua. Accessed 16 May 2011. http://www.plataforma-llengua.cat/media/assets/1538/Estudi_cinema_des09.pdf.

UNESCO (2005) Convention on the protection and promotion of the diversity of cultural expressions, accessed 18 May 2011. http://unesdoc.unesco.org/images/0014/001429/142919e.pdf.

14 The Contribution of BBC ALBA to Gaelic: A Social and Economic Review

Douglas Chalmers, Mike Danson, Alison Lang and Lindsay Milligan

Introduction

After it was launched in September 2008, BBC ALBA stands out as a significant milestone for Gaelic language and culture; it is the first dedicated Gaelic-medium television channel in history. The channel is a BBC-licensed service that is operated as a partnership between the BBC and the MG ALBA. It combines three media (television, radio and internet), an annual content budget of £14 million and targets a weekly viewership of 250,000 persons. This means that the channel is expected to be attracting more viewers to Gaelic television than there are people who understand the language in Scotland, since only 78,402 people aged above 3 years were reported to understand Gaelic in the 2001 census (GROS, 2005). In achieving this goal, the channel functions on a budget that is significantly lower than those for minoritised languages in Wales (£104 million for S4C in 2010) and Ireland (€55 million for TG4). Nevertheless, since its launch BBC ALBA has gone from strength to strength and achieves an average weekly viewing reach of 220,000. In this chapter, we will discuss the channel's position and contribution to the contemporary use of Gaelic in Scotland, beginning with a brief discussion of the policy framework out of which the channel arises, the kinds of economic impacts it is making, and finally discussing its social importance. The media have previously been critiqued in terms of their importance to the reversing of language shift for minoritised languages (see Fishman, 1991), but more recent criticism suggests that the advent of Web 2.0 means that media provision that is able to connect to its audience through multiple platforms (e.g. BBC ALBA) may, in fact, be a strong contributor to a language's present and future linguistic vitality (see the contributions of Cormack and Jones to this volume). While the chapter will ultimately applaud the channel's contribution to Gaelic development in Scotland, especially around its economic impact (Chalmers & Danson, 2009), it will pose questions about the potential limits of media in terms of their ability to foster the acquisition and usage of minoritised languages.

This contribution to the debate on the role of BBC ALBA first provides the policy context in which the channel operates. Drawing on our previous research, the economic impact is introduced before the different elements of its social contribution are discussed, with regard to status and behavioural impacts especially. Future developments and constraints are then explored before the conclusions are derived.

Policy Framework

The policy framework in which BBC ALBA has been developed and is maintained begins in 1990, with the Broadcasting Act 1990 (c. 42). This Act established a fund dedicated to Gaelic television, administered by MG ALBA (the operating name of the Gaelic Media Service), and since this time there have been two broadcasters – STV and the BBC – that have aired the Gaelic programming funded by MG ALBA in addition to their own funded Gaelic content. It is worthwhile to note, however, that the BBC's engagement with Gaelic predates this Act by many years, having committed itself to the language since 1923 (although the broadcasting of Gaelic on the BBC was confined to radio).

In the early years of Gaelic television, potential viewers contended with irregular and inconvenient programming schedules (Seirbheis nam Meadhanan Gàidhlig, 2006). Gaelic programming was sporadic, sometimes scheduled in poor time slots and was not sustained equally throughout the year. However, this has changed greatly since the BBC and MG ALBA agreed in principle in 2005 to work in partnership to establish the channel, leading to the innovative collaboration agreement in 2007 that enabled the creation of BBC ALBA a year later. No longer dependent on finding time slots in other channels' schedules, BBC ALBA can make available a broader range of content through its regular schedule providing Gaelic content every evening, including primetime.

Alongside the Broadcasting Act 1990 (c. 42) (and subsequently the Broadcasting Act 1996 [c. 55] and Communications Act 2003 [c. 21], which amended the powers of MG ALBA and made other provisions in relation to Gaelic broadcasting), BBC ALBA is also a provision that fulfils the UK's ratification of the European Charter for Regional or Minority Languages with respect to Gaelic in Scotland. The provision is particularly relevant to Article 11, Paragraphs 1 a (ii), 'to encourage and/or facilitate the creation of at least one radio station and one television channel in the regional or minority languages' and 1 c (ii) 'to encourage and/or facilitate the broadcasting of television programmes in the regional or minority languages on a regular basis' (Council of Europe, 1992).

Before BBC ALBA had been established, the intention to move forward with plans to create this kind of dedicated Gaelic television service had been articulated by the Gaelic language planning organization, Bòrd na Gàidhlig (BnaG), in their National Plan for Gaelic 2007–2012 (BnaG, 2007) and, more recently, has been referenced in their An Ginealach Ùr na Gàidhlig (BnaG, 2010). In the former of these two documents, the Bòrd describe how

> [t]he new Gaelic Digital Service [BBC ALBA] … is anticipated to have a positive impact at many levels including increasing artistic and technical skills, extending economic opportunities, stimulating parents' interest in Gaelic education, appealing to and serving adult learners and strengthening Gaelic usage in extremely important media. It holds significant potential to assist with the development of positive attitudes to the acquisition and transmission of Gaelic. (BnaG, 2007: 11)

Having placed such importance on the provision of a dedicated Gaelic television channel (and associated radio and internet), the Bòrd also made the creation of such a channel a key development priority in the National Plan (BnaG, 2007: 25). After BBC ALBA had been established, and when planning for the 'new generation' of Gaelic users, the Bòrd also named BBC ALBA as a strategic partner for targeting adult learners and for guiding these learners to fluency (BnaG, 2010: 3, 10, 11).

This is the policy framework in which the channel operates. It is one in which BBC ALBA is not only a source of entertainment in the Gaelic language but also one in which it is expected to have strong economic, social and linguistic contributions to make throughout Scotland. Considering the broad range of benefits the channel is expected to bring about within this policy framework, the remainder of this chapter will consider early indicators of these effects.

Economic Impact

As already mentioned, in 2007 Bòrd na Gàidhlig described that BBC ALBA would have the ability to 'extend economic opportunities' in Gaelic

(BnaG, 2007: 11). It is this impact, the effect of the channel in terms of economy and job creation, that will be reviewed.

Previous research has attested to the importance of the Gaelic creative and cultural industries (CCI) to the economy in Scotland (Chalmers & Danson, 2009). Over 8000 full-time equivalent (FTE) jobs in Scotland can be accounted to this industry, which includes radio and television. In Glasgow alone, CCI expenditure particularly in the Gaelic sector is estimated at £4 million creating about 200 FTEs, with the media alone accounting for £2.5 million and 120 and 140 FTE, mostly graduate, jobs (cf. Chalmers & Danson, 2009).

Thus, within this cultural and creative industry, the Gaelic labour market is strong. This is a market that has been defined as one in 'which knowledge of the Gaelic language is a condition of employment' (Campbell *et al.*, 2009). Evidence of the vitality of the Gaelic labour market within the broader Scottish media industry comes most recently in the form of a study that was conducted on job advertisements that used the criterion of 'Gaelic essential'. This study demonstrated that, of the 595 relevant FTE positions advertised, 110 were in the media (see Table 14.1). While there were comparatively more advertisements using this criterion posted by local authorities (280 advertisements) and for positions in further and higher education (118 advertisements), it is encouraging, given the propensity to employ highly skilled staff and as a contribution to widening the diversity of the job opportunities, that 18% of all Gaelic essential posts advertised within this period were in the media. Ultimately, this suggests that the sector in which BBC ALBA operates is growing and helping to create positions in which people can put their Gaelic skills to use (see Table 14.1).

We also know that individuals who have the ability to speak, read and write Gaelic are employed in associate professional and professional

Table 14.1 FTE and PTE job advertisements by sector (Chalmers & Danson, 2010)

	FTE	PTE
Arts and music	14 (2%)	2 (2%)
Culture and heritage	12 (2%)	3 (3%)
Development	33 (6%)	10 (10%)
FEI/HEI	118 (20%)	6 (6%)
Local authority	280 (46%)	70 (70%)
Media	110 (18%)	6 (6%)
Publishing	16 (3%)	3 (3%)
Other	12 (2%)	10 (10%)

occupations (including the media) in a proportion greater than that of the rest of Scotland. The most recent census of 2001 indicates that 17.4% (2436 individuals) of Gaelic users (with the ability to speak, read and write the language) were employed within a professional occupation and that 17.8% (2483) of these people were in an associate professional position. Among these associate professionals, 18% (447 individuals) reported to be employed in culture, media and sport. This is proportionately greater than for Scotland as a whole, which suggests that 'Gaelic essential' designated jobs are highly concentrated within the 'Gaelic Creative Class'. These and other indicators seem to suggest that those who are employed within Gaelic media enjoy high-ranking occupations and that the skill sets of these individuals are particularly strong in comparison to the wider Scottish population. The 'talent index', a measure that helps to identify qualifications, is comparatively high for those who are employed in Gaelic-essential posts in relation to Scotland as a whole: 68% of those in Gaelic-essential posts are ranked at Group 4+ (having at least a first degree), but only 19.5% of those within Scotland fit this category.

Reviewing the figures for the economic impact of Gaelic media in Scotland, the available data suggest that this industry, of which BBC ALBA is a part, is making a positive contribution to Scotland's economy in general (Chalmers & Danson, 2009). Gaelic media employs highly skilled individuals and allow Gaelic users to enjoy and apply their associate professional and professional status and training. While these facts alone should be considered to be positive, as a corollary, media provision, like BBC ALBA, also has the added benefit of creating cultural products through the medium of Gaelic with which others throughout the country can engage; in addition, it contributes to the retention of the Gaelic-speaking creative class within Scotland although not within the Gàidhealtachd. It is the potential effects of this engagement that we will discuss in the next section.

Social Contributions

Television in a minoritised language is often regarded as having social benefit beyond sheer entertainment. It has been described as helping to '[e]ducate, entertain, inform, celebrate, [and] challenge' language users (Hegarty, 2003: 36), and to provide 'a forum and a tool to enhance and celebrate (...) language and culture' (David, 2004: 6). In New Zealand, for example, the *Māori Language Strategy* suggests that television 'informs, educates, and entertains a broad viewing audience, and, in doing so, enriches New Zealand's society, culture, and heritage' (New Zealand Government, 2003: 11). Similarly, the contribution BBC ALBA intends to make to Scotland includes non-economic and social contributions. Recurring among the many stipulated hopes for this television are three primary objectives: that television might aid in the process of reversing language shift (RLS) through (a) improving the language's status, (b) increasing language learning and (c) increasing language usage. On the basis of previous research, the remainder of this chapter will briefly consider the likelihood of BBC ALBA making contributions in the areas of status and language behaviour (including learning and usage).

Status impact

BBC ALBA aspires to 'normalize' Gaelic in Scottish society (Lang, 2010). It hopes to foster more positive attitudes toward Gaelic, among both Gaelic speakers and non-speakers. In order to ensure that the largest possible audience can access the channel and its associated web space and radio provision, programming has adopted an inclusive style by carefully using subtitles, by emphasizing visual elements where possible and by attempting to provide entertainment that cannot be accessed in the dominant English media (e.g. by airing sports, matches and music events that cannot be seen elsewhere).

There is strong qualitative evidence that media provision, like BBC ALBA, can make a positive contribution to the perception of status for a minoritised language. Howell (1992) has argued that provisions, akin to BBC ALBA, are important to help children in particular feel that their minoritised language has prestige value. Television programming is thought to encourage the formation of cultural identities by showing its audience what a particular cultural identity group looks, sounds and acts like. In fact, some researchers have gone so far as to claim that 'mass media forms [like television] constitute ... [a] primary cultural resource' (Mastronardi, 2003: 83). Although the concept of cultural identity is contentious, because each person may associate different traits with this identity, it is logical that when accessing BBC ALBA Gaelic users are affirming their sense of 'Gaelicness': 'The mere act of making a viewing choice may enhance one's sense of belonging in a group and be important to overall self-concept' (Harwood, 1999: 129). The presence of a provision like BBC ALBA should, therefore, give a sense of community to minority language users by affirming that there is an identity group to which they belong. As MacLennan (2003: 72) explains of Gaelic in Scotland, viewing minority language television 'helps us to see ourselves as people that belong to this society rather than as strangers in a strange land'. Not only does this programming show its viewers an example of people who are part of the cultural identity group but also the decision to view this television becomes a way to declare one's sense of belonging.

In a large-scale 10-year longitudinal study of the demand for Gaelic arts (Sproull & Chalmers, 1998), the authors concluded that amongst the Gaelic arts, Gaelic television (in the period before BBC Alba) appeared to have the greatest impact on attitudinal perceptions, including the *desirability of Gaelic being used in other areas of public life, such as business and schools* (Sproull & Chalmers, 1998: 37, 40); *the relevance of Gaelic to local economic development; the employment and careers of young people* (26–27, 44, 46); *respondents' willingness to choose Gaelic Medium Education for their children* (41–44); *and their desire to live and work within their local community* (40). The study found that Gaelic television, compared to any other Gaelic artistic media, such as live events or radio, was the most influential arts medium, having a positive influence amongst both fluent/near-fluent speakers and those with limited ability in the language. Importantly, these conclusions were drawn just before the welcome increase in Gaelic broadcasting brought about by the creation of the new channel.

In addition to this kind of contribution to status, BBC ALBA helps to affirm the *contemporary relevance and presence* of Gaelic in Scotland to both users and non-users alike. In this latter regard, the use of Gaelic in media helps fight against misconceptions of the language as being one that is unfit for contemporary Scottish life. These kinds of attitudes toward Gaelic are still very prevalent. Research, conducted in 2003 by Market Research UK (MRUK) in collaboration with the BBC and Bòrd na Gàidhlig Alba (the precursor to the existing Bòrd na Gàidhlig), confirms this as, of 1020 people interviewed in a national survey, 28% agreed and 15% strongly agreed that Gaelic is not of value in contemporary society (Market Research United Kingdom, 2003). One of the most important contributions BBC ALBA, therefore, has to make for Gaelic development is to help the wider Scottish public recognize the contemporary use of the language.

Behavioural impacts

There are two kinds of behavioural impacts that BBC ALBA may be able to make on Gaelic in Scotland: learning and usage. With regard to learning, which is part of the channel's remit, it is hoped that, through engagement with Gaelic programming, people may increase their fluency in the language. With regard to usage, it is hoped that engaging with Gaelic media will not only constitute a form of language use but also encourage language use in other domains. Each of these behavioural impacts will be considered briefly here.

The contention that minoritised language television can help individuals to learn the language seems to be widely held (e.g. Chazan, 2003; Dalby, 2003; Tosi, 2003). The programmes shown on stations like BBC ALBA afford viewers the opportunity to engage with a wide variety of accents and to provide video and audio clues in unison (Salaberry, 2001), which is thought to be beneficial to language acquisition and, of course, studies on the effect of television on language acquisition are numerous. However, the samples used in research studies, and the target audience of television programming, can often complicate the extent to which we can say that there is evidence for the effectiveness of television at improving language learning.

Studies based on first language skills and the impact of television often use infant and child participants and have found no significant evidence demonstrating that home viewing facilitates the improvement of language abilities (Patterson, 2002; Rice et al., 1990; Scarborough & Dobrich, 1994).

The initial results of studies examining how television affects second language skills are exceedingly positive, supporting the contention that television can be used to improve language use. In an experiment carried out in the United States of America, for example, it was found that Spanish language soap operas had a constructive impact on second-year undergraduate Spanish language students' abilities with listening comprehension, confidence when speaking and ability to provide detail in narration (Weyers, 1999). Unfortunately, the environment in which study participants viewed second language television was artificial; in this study participants viewed television programming in a school classroom under the supervision of an instructor rather than at home. The fact that these students viewed Spanish language soap operas in a classroom setting, where they were provided with plot synopses in advance of viewing and coursework after viewing the programmes, means that there were supports provided to these participants in order to facilitate comprehension and learning. Although we cannot expect comparable supports (i.e. synopses and follow-up questions) to be available in the home environment, it is important to note that BBC ALBA does provide support for learning through its website, and so interested and motivated learners can use programming to help hone their language skills, provided they have a reasonably large extant vocabulary in this other language (Secules et al., 1992).

The second behavioural impact that may be achieved through BBC ALBA is the increased usage of Gaelic. The theoretical paradigm used often when discussing the way in which television consumption affects this kind of behaviour is Social Cognitive Theory (SCT in Bandura, 1986). This theory is adopted to suggest that the content of television programming has a either direct impact upon or a cause–effect relationship with its audience's behaviour (Lull, 2000). It should be noted that SCT is often critiqued as a foundation for media impact research for inadequately acknowledging audience autonomy or its ability to derive an unforeseen or unintended message from television programming.

While Bandura and many others who work with SCT are able to demonstrate that television can help influence behaviour by modelling, it should be acknowledged that Bandura and colleagues construct television series to evoke particular results by modelling desirable behaviours. Bandura has four principles underpinning these television series (see Dittman, 2004): (a) to model transitions from 'bad' to 'good' behaviour, (b) to contrast 'good' and 'bad' role models showing 'good' and 'bad' consequences, respectively, (c) to develop audiences' emotional investment in characters with the aim of sustaining viewing and (d) to provide resources to help support behaviour change in the targeted areas (e.g. providing a helpline phone number). What this ultimately suggests is that we cannot presume that a television provision like BBC ALBA will make a strong contribution in terms of increasing the use of Gaelic unless the programming is created with the intention of eliciting certain effects (e.g. modelling the behaviour of using Gaelic in widening domains, of switching from English to Gaelic and showing negative consequences for characters who persist in using the dominant English language). It may not be deemed appropriate or desirable to sacrifice the creative and artistic integrity of Gaelic programming in order to consciously seek to modify behavioural practices, but it should be acknowledged that when television is considered in order to have the best chance of modifying behaviour these are the kinds of techniques that are used to help achieve behaviour change.

To sum up these points, while BBC ALBA may have a beneficial impact on language abilities for some people who engage with the programming, it is less certain if viewing will be able to change people's habitual language behaviours. Nevertheless, since engaging with BBC ALBA does constitute a form of language use itself, the channel should be regarded as being beneficial in these areas and able to make some behavioural impact.

Future Developments

The future of BBC ALBA is promising, and the recent decision by the BBC Trust to authorize the carriage of the channel on Digital Terrestrial Television (marketed as Freeview and at present the digital television platform with the highest audience uptake in the United Kingdom) has continued to add to this positive perspective. From July 2011 this allows a greater number of people to access the channel, which until then could be accessed only by those with digital satellite. There also are indications that after a period of negotiation, the channel may finally appear on Digital Cable, again with the intent of widening potential viewership.

Key to the channel's future development, however, remains the development of content and funding strategies,   responding to the examples of S4C and TG4, to create programming in genres underrepresented in the BBC ALBA schedules and in the Scottish production industry, particularly drama and children's content, in addition to an enhanced offering in those genres already identified with particular viewing demographics (e.g. news and entertainment aimed at Gaelic speakers, and sport, music and factual programming aimed at both Gaelic speakers and non-speakers).

In considering this development, and so the priorities for investment and resource allocation within the BBC, as demonstrated above the medium of television is particularly potent in generating wider economic impacts through the market for goods and services associated with specific programmes. These social and economic, as well as language-specific, benefits of BBC ALBA need to be factored into these debates and discussions. So, consistent with the conclusions of previous research on Gaelic arts and culture in Skye and Lochalsh (Chalmers, 2003) and Glasgow (Chalmers & Danson, 2009), the identification of synergies with other forms of usage and learning, and of economic impacts, for example sales of products, highlights the importance of BBC ALBA to Scotland.

Conclusions

As a medium of influence, media provision is able to reach minoritised language communities that are 'geographically dispersed' and, if it is able to alter aspects of economy, status and behaviour, could therefore also be a powerful resource for RLS (Martí et al., 2005: 182). This brief review of BBC ALBA, Scotland's Gaelic language television channel (with provision also being made on internet and radio) has demonstrated the important role the channel has to play on the economic development of Gaelic and its status in Scotland. BBC ALBA is an important source of employment for the growing Gaelic Creative Class, and has the added benefit of helping to create and disseminate high-quality products that can be enjoyed by many. Less certain is the contribution BBC ALBA will make to the learning and use of Gaelic in Scotland; however, there are some positive indicators that such contributions can be made. As BBC ALBA moves into the second decade of the 21st century, it will be critical that the channel explores and develops programming content and that it continues to explore the range of interactive options offered by Web 2.0. Finance will also be a key issue for the future, as the channel at present operates on a shoestring budget, despite its proven importance and contributions. The analyses presented here suggest that, if these challenges can be addressed, then the BBC ALBA channel offers to be a valuable instrument in reversing language shift.

References

Bandura, A. (1986) *Social Foundations of Thought and Action: A Social Cognitive Theory*. Englewood Cliffs: Prentice-Hall.

BnaG (2007) National plan for Gaelic 2007–2012. Inverness: Bòrd na Gàidhlig. Accessed 17 May 2011. http://www.bord-na-gaidhlig.org.uk/National-Plan/National%20Plan%20for%20Gaelic.pdf.

BnaG (2010) Ginealach Ùr na Gàidhlig: An action plan to increase the numbers of Gaelic speakers. Inverness: Bòrd na Gàidhlig. http://www.gaidhlig.org.uk/Downloads/Ginealach_Ur_na_Gaidhlig_B.pdf.

Campbell, I., Chalmers, D., Danson, M. and MacLeod, M. (2009) *Measuring the Gaelic Labour Market: Current and Future Potential* (Final Report, Stage 1). Inverness: Highlands and Islands Enterprise and Skills Development Scotland.

Council of Europe (1992) European Charter for Regional and Minority Languages. Strasbourg: Council of Europe.

Chalmers, D. (2003) *The Economic Impact of Gaelic Arts and Culture*. Glasgow: Glasgow Caledonian University.

Chalmers, D. and Danson, M. (2009) *An Economic Impact Study of Gaelic Arts and Culture in Glasgow*. Glasgow: City of Glasgow Council.

Chazan, M. (2003) Language and learning: Intervention and the child at home. In A. Davies (ed.) *Language and Learning in the Home and School* (pp. 67–77). London: Heinemann Educational.

Dalby, A. (2003) *Language in Danger*. London: Penguin.

David, J. (2004) Aboriginal language broadcasting in Canada: An overview and recommendations to the task force on aboriginal languages and cultures. Accessed 15 March 2011. http://www.aptn.ca/images/stories/corporatepdfs/aboriginal_language_and_broadcasting_report_final_nov_26_04.pdf.

Dittman, M. (2004) Changing behavior through TV heroes. *Monitor* 35 (9), 70.

Fishman, J.A. (1991) *Reversing Language Shift: Theoretical and Empirical Foundations of Assistance to Threatened Languages*. Clevedon: Multilingual Matters.

GROS (2005) *Scotland's Census 2001: Gaelic Report*. Edinburgh: General Register Office, Scotland.

Harwood, J. (1999) Age identification, social identity gratifications, and television viewing. *Journal of Broadcasting & Electronic Media* 43 (1), 123–136.

Hegarty, K. (2003) BBC Northern Ireland and Irish. In J. Kirk and D. Ó Baoill (eds) *Towards Our Goals in Broadcasting, the Press, the Performing Arts and the Economy: Minority Languages in Northern Ireland, the Republic of Ireland, and Scotland* (pp. 36–39). Belfast: Clo Ollscoil na Banriona.

Howell, W.R. (1992) Minority language broadcasting and the continuation of Celtic culture in Wales and Ireland. In S.H. Riggins (ed.) *Ethnic Minority Media: An International Perspective* (pp. 217–242). London: Sage.

Lang, A. (2010) BBC Alba: The impact of the new Gaelic television channel. Paper presented at the Media Convergence and Linguistic Diversity, Aberystwyth, Wales.

Lull, J. (2000) *Media, Communication, Culture: A Global Approach* (2nd edition). Cambridge: Polity Press.

MacLennan, I. (2003) BBC craoladh nan Gaidheal: Co sinn? In J. Kirk and D.Ó Baoill (eds) *Towards Our Goals in Broadcasting, the Press, the Performing Arts and the Economy: Minority Languages in Northern Ireland, the Republic of Ireland, and Scotland* (pp. 67–

72). Belfast: Cló OlMarket Research United Kingdom (2003) *Attitudes to the Gaelic Language: BBC*. Inverness: Bòrd na Gàidhlig Alba.

Martí, F., Ortega, P., Idiazabal, I., Barreña, A., Juaristi, P., Junyent, C. and Amorrortu, E. (2005) *Words and Worlds: World Languages Review*. Clevedon: Multilingual Matters.

Mastronardi, M. (2003) Adolescence and media. *Journal of Language and Social Psychology* 22 (1), 83–93. doi: 10.1177/0261927x02250059.

New Zealand Government (2003) Māori Television Act. Accessed 16 May 2011. http://legislation.govt.nz/act/public/2003/0021/latest/096be8ed80609b75.pdf.

Patterson, J.L. (2002) Relationships of expressive vocabulary to frequency of reading and television experience among bilingual toddlers. *Applied Psycholinguistics* 23 (04), 493–508. doi: doi:10.1017/S0142716402004010.

Rice, M.L., Huston, A.C., Truglio, R. and Wright, J.C. (1990) Words from 'Sesame Street': Learning vocabulary while viewing. *Developmental Psychology* 26 (3), 421–428. doi: 10.1037/0012-1649.26.3.421.

Salaberry, M.R. (2001) The use of technology for second language learning and teaching: A retrospective. *The Modern Language Journal* 85 (1), 39–56.

Scarborough, H.S. and Dobrich, W. (1994) On the efficacy of reading to preschoolers. *Developmental Review* 14 (3), 245–302. doi: 10.1006/drev.1994.1010.

Secules, T., Herron, C. and Tomasello, M. (1992) The effect of video context on foreign language learning. *The Modern Language Journal* 76 (4), 480–490.

Seirbheis nam Meadhanan Gàidhlig (2006) Annual report and statement of accounts for 2004/2005. Stornoway: Seirbheis Nam Meadhanan Gàidhlig.

Sproull, A. and Chalmers, D. (1998) *The Demand for Gaelic Artistic and Cultural Products and Services: Patterns and Impacts*. Glasgow: Glasgow Caledonian University.

Tosi, A. (2003) Between the mother's dialect and English. In A. Davies (ed.) *Language and Learning in Home and School*. London: Heinemann Educational.

Weyers, J.R. (1999) The effect of authentic video on communicative competence. *The Modern Language Journal* 83 (3), 339–349.

15 Multilingual Practice of the EITB Group and its TV Provision for Teenagers

Amaia Pavón and Aitor Zuberogoitia

Introduction

This chapter explores the early years of the Basque public broadcasting group EITB and the main aims that were defined in the law which led to its creation, paying special attention to the different interpretations given to that law and the development of EITB into a multilingual media conglomerate.

Furthermore, it studies EITB's TV Basque language provision for teenagers and develops a methodological proposal for the study of bilingual teenagers' habits of consumption in the era of digital convergence. It presents the results of a pilot study on the methodology, to assess the tool for further, more extensive research on media consumption.

The information that results from this exploration tries to provide answers to the following questions:

- How many Basque media outlets do teenagers use?
- What are their motivations to use those media?

EITB's Early Years and its Linguistic Approach

Apart from some sporadic broadcast in the 1960s, the Basque language arrived on TV screens in the 1970s. It aired for the first time in the Northern Basque Country in 1971, thanks to Maite Barnetxe's Basque language reports on French public TV. It was quite a few years later that it made its first appearance on Spanish public TV, in the special broadcast for the Basque Autonomous Community, and reached Navarre in the 1980s (Alkorta & Zuberogoitia, 2009; Arbelbide, 2002; Basterretxea, 1997; Ubeda, 2008).

All Basque language programming was broadcast in a discontinuous and sporadic way. The real *Big Bang* of Basque in television came with the arrival of Euskal Irrati Telebista (EITB), the Basque Public Broadcasting Group. Its creation process was quite complex: it must be remembered that the fall of Franco's regime and the 1981 *coup d'état* attempt in Spain took place within a very short period of time. Thus, the Basque Government felt forced to create new structures and institutions as quickly as possible, with the uncertainty of not knowing how long they would last.

They worked quickly, and occasionally withholding information from the central government in Madrid to speed up the process, as Ramon Labaien, former Culture Minister of the Basque Autonomous Government, admitted some years later (Labaien in Azurmendi, 2004). The following fact is illustrative of the pace of the process: the Basque Government designated the group's board of directors at the beginning of April 1982, more than 1 month earlier than the law which prompted the creation of EITB had been approved by the Basque Parliament (20 May 1982).

Later, in August the same year, a team of 42 people was sent to Germany to receive the necessary training in the Hamburg Studios and, directly afterwards, they began broadcasting, on 31 December 1982 (shortly after S4C in Wales). There were almost no journalists trained to work in Basque. There was no experience of television, except for a couple of programmes that had been aired on Spanish public TV, broadcast from 1975 onwards, and the aforementioned reports prepared by Maite Barnetxe on French public TV since 1971. It was a real adventure.

Considering the pressure under which Basque television started, it is worth looking back at the 20 May law to review its main statements. According to this law, these are the four main goals of EITB:

- To guarantee the right of Basque citizens to information and political participation.
- To support the Basque education system.
- To promote and extend Basque culture.
- To promote and extend the Basque language.

The law was interpreted in different ways: while the former Culture Minister Ramon Labaien claims that ETB (Basque Public TV) was originally thought of as a monolingual broadcaster solely in Basque (see, for example, Azurmendi, 2004), others (Zupiria, in Alkorta & Zuberogoitia, 2009: 130; Amatiño, in Diez Unzueta & Otermin, 2006: 50; Torrealdai, 1985) argue that it was conceived as a bilingual media from the outset. In any case, it started broadcasting content in both languages, using subtitles in Spanish or Basque (depending on the language broadcast) for some programmes. There was an important turning point in 1986 with the unexpected launch of its second channel, ETB2, broadcasting only in Spanish. It took place following the controversy caused by the previous bilingual arrangement (cf. Torrealdai, 1985).

Some public media were created after the 1982 law, and nowadays the EITB Group operates through four public limited companies owned wholly by EITB: Euskal Telebista SA (television), Eusko Irratia SA and Radio Vitoria SA (radio) and EITBNET SA (internet) (see Diez Unzueta & Otermin, 2006 for a more detailed account of EITB's structure).

From a sociolinguistic point of view, EITB is a multilingual group: some of its media work through Basque (TV channels: ETB1 and ETB3; radio stations: Euskadi Irratia and Gaztea), some others are Spanish (TV: ETB2 and Canal Vasco; radio: Radio Euskadi), some others are bilingual, Basque and Spanish (TV: ETBsat; radio: EITB Musika) and finally there is its multilingual web presence (www.eitb.com, in Basque, Spanish, English and French).

Media, Teenagers and the Basque Language

Before talking about EITB's media provision and young people, we should emphasize two important aspects in the process of digitization of television and audiovisual content.

First, we cannot fail to mention the YouTube phenomenon as a successful tool in the audiovisual field on the internet. YouTube is nowadays one of the many general-content platforms, but it has prompted a revolution in audiovisual media. These kinds of platforms and the way they deliver audiovisual content have led to thinking about a new model for television, on-demand television, where users have the power to choose what, how, when and where they want to consume audiovisual products.

Second, we have witnessed in 2010 the digitization of the television signal in the Southern Basque Country. This has obliged public and private channels to make major infrastructure investments in order to be able to broadcast via digital terrestrial television. Apart from that, television, as traditionally understood, has been forced to move to the internet, and we have seen how the platforms of these networks have evolved exponentially over the past years. So much so that the websites of traditional broadcasters have, in fact, become indispensable complementary spaces among other functions to, as noted above, offer video on-demand and promote interaction with the user.

It is within this context that we should discuss the teen audience. Because these *digital natives* are heavy users of the new audiovisual technologies, they are the ones who have best adapted to the process and new era of the medium.

Concurrently, we should not fail to mention the various environmental studies, and psychology and communication theories that confirm the influence of the environment in the perception of reality and modes of behaviour. Based on these assumptions, Morduchowicz (2009) believes that the media are fundamental in teenagers' processes of identity construction:

For most young people, popular culture – taken to mean audiovisual and media culture in general in this book – is the place from where they provide meaning to their identity. Within it, teenagers shape their individual and collective identities, and learn to speak about themselves in relation to others.

Young people, whose identities are drawn at the crossings of written text, electronic images, and popular culture, live a different cultural experience, new ways to perceive, feel and see. Shopping centres, cafés, television, music recitals and new technologies alter the perception young people have of reality and the way they conceive the world to be. If the identities of young people are defined not only in the book they read but also, fundamentally, in the television programmes they watch, in the multimedia text through which they navigate, in the music they listen to and the films they choose to watch, it would thus become necessary to analyse the way in which young people engage with cultural goods.

Para la mayoría de los jóvenes, la cultura popular – entendida en este libro como la cultura audiovisual y mediática en general- es hoy el lugar desde el cual dan sentido a su identidad. Los adolescentes modelan en ella sus identidades individuales y colectivas y aprenden a hablar de sí mismos en relación con los otros.

Los jóvenes, cuyas identidades se trazan en la intersección del texto escrito, la imagen electrónica y la cultura popular, viven una experiencia cultural distinta, nuevas maneras de percibir, de sentir de escuchar y de ver. Los centros comerciales, los cafés, la televisión, los recitales de música y las nuevas tecnologías modifican la percepción que los jóvenes tienen de la realidad y el modo en que conciben el mundo. Si las identidades de los jóvenes se definen no sólo en el libro que leen sino, y fundamentalmente, en los programas de televisión que miran, en el texto multimedia por el que navegan, en la música que escuchan y en la película que eligen, será necesario entonces analizar la manera en que los jóvenes se relacionan con los bienes culturales. (Morduchowicz, 2009: 9)

We should also bear in mind that adolescence is a key age in the construction of a person's identity and the role of media in that process is also remarkable (Buckingham, 2002; Casas, 2000; Livingstone, 2002; Montgomery, 2007; Morduchowicz, 2009). All these reasons confirm the importance of research on usage and media consumption patterns of this specific target audience, which is, conversely, especially important for minority language communities.

Josu Amezaga, a sociologist and professor at the EHU-UPV, has advocated in favour of promoting an effective language policy for the younger audience in the era of digitization:

> (...) What we see [here] is that the number of Basque-speakers is very high amongst young people, and if we add the 'quasi-Basque speakers' – that is, people capable of understanding the Basque language – we are talking in some cases about more than 90%. So, you have a large number of Basque speakers, and that group is, in my opinion, the most important one from a linguistic policy perspective. Why? Because that is [the place] where the main imbalance between knowledge and usage takes place. So, I think if the main task for the education system is to increase knowledge of the language. Impacting on motivation is, in my opinion, the biggest challenge for the media. (Amezaga, 2009)

The data is illustrative enough: there is a population of 82% of Basque speakers or *almost Basque speakers* amongst young people (referring to the data of 2006 of the Autonomous Community provided by the Eustat, Basque Institute of Statistics) (Eustat, 2006b), but their daily use of Basque hardly reached 20% in 2006.

EITB and the Offer in Basque for Teenagers of the Digital Era

We have to set EITB within the context of the *digital era*. It is obvious that in this new audiovisual paradigm there is a need to rethink the meaning of television as a general public service. Joselu Blanco, head of EITB programming, presents the future of generalist TV as follows:

> In TV channels, especially those with a public remit, we must decide what kind of public we want to address because we don't have sufficient resources to reach out to everyone. The role of public television is not static in this changing scenario. And so, in our case, we are compared to our competitors who have at least ten times more power than us to

produce things. And yet we have maintained our position up there, and now we hope to keep it.

We were fewer channels, so the social profitability of public television was much higher. Over the years it will be much smaller and it will generate a debate in society, and well, we'll see where we stand. The States themselves will have to choose what they want from public television. (Blanco, 2010)

Without a doubt, the outlook for public media is uncertain. What will happen, in this context, with the four points of the 1982 law presented above? Moreover, looking into the present rather than into the past, how does EITB respond to these four points nowadays as regards its teenage audiences?

We have already mentioned the radio station Gaztea ('Young' in Basque), which is a very interesting case in point. It was created in 1990 as a double-remit radio station aimed at teenagers and young people in general. It had originally broadcast in Basque for the region of Gipuzkoa and in Spanish for the regions of Bizkaia and Araba. However, the Spanish language remit was not as successful as expected, and by 1995 the EITB board decided to close it down and keep only the Basque language broadcast. The latter continues broadcasting today and has around 127,000 listeners according to the 2010 audience figures (see, for instance, Gaztea, 2010).

The case of EITB's TV channels is quite different. Regarding TV available in Basque within the group, there are many programmes directed at children and fewer at teenagers.

We can mention the website www.eitb.com/gaztea as a specific product in Basque aimed at this age group. A section of the website, called *Gaztea Telebistan,* redirects the user to ETB3's webpage. According to Blanco, ETB3 is making a significant commitment to reach young audiences in Basque. However, he has stressed that this is not a significant target group taking into account the full spectrum of the actual audience: 'However much you see it as significant, if you extrapolate it to the one hundred per cent of the population it is not an important group' (Blanco, 2010).

Along with offering *Gaztea,* Blanco mentioned certain other programmes suitable for this age group, but produced for a wider target audience: '... Paradoxically *Goenkale* [a soap opera] remains a product that they still watch, also *Wazemank* [a comedy show] (...)' (Blanco, 2010). It must be noted, though, that ETB does not produce any specific product aimed at young audiences. What is the reason for that? Blanco provides the following explanation:

What is certain is that young people of that age [group] increasingly consume less television through what we have hitherto known as TV: terrestrial, satellite ... They spend less time on television, compared to other methods of consuming audiovisual information such as through the Internet. As well as that, we should consider that, regarding the population as a whole, they are a group that has little importance; we can say, in conclusion, that generalist television channels do not go out of their way to generate products for them. (Blanco, 2010)

Developing a Methodological Proposal

With these ideas in mind, we aim to develop a methodological proposal for the study of bilingual teenagers' habits of consumption in the era of digital convergence (see also Pavón, 2010). We conducted a pilot study in order to test the methodology and detect possible threats to its validity. It is worth noting that the qualitative and quantitative methods were combined to gather the data.

The research methodology consists of three main parts closely interrelated. First, a series of interviews with heads of programming at ETB provide useful information about ETB's programming criteria and about the new media environment for the audiovisual media on the internet. Then, following the interviews, and using the information they provided, design and implementation of a survey was carried out, in order to obtain quantitative data about teenagers' media consumption. Finally, a focus group session was done to qualify and enrich the information provided by the surveys.

In the first stage, we have carried out three in-depth interviews. Two interviews have been directed at defining the concept of television over the internet. For this, we interviewed Ruben Sanchez, creator of the web TV *LostinTV* and director of the programme *NickdutNik* (a programme about the Net and ICTs) for ETB3, and Hibai Castro and Adur Larrea, creators of the web TV *Ibaizabaltb.com* (it offers Basque-only content). We also interviewed Joselu Blanco, Programme Director of ETB, in order to gather information about TV production in Basque aimed at this target audience.

Conversely, we designed a survey taking five aspects into account:

(1)   *Sociolinguistic profile of the adolescents.* We have taken into account the model proposed by Moring (2007) to design this block of the questionnaire. We ensured that the questions allowed for us to

ascertain the language biography of the participants and a profile of their language use.

(2)   *Technological equipment of the adolescents.* We wanted to gather information about the accessibility of teenagers to audiovisual technology, such as access to laptop computers, internet connection, video cameras or mobile phones equipped with suitable technology for video reproduction. This block was based on the questionnaire used by the University of Melbourne's Educating the Net Generation project (available at www.netgen.unimelb.edu.au).

(3)   *Modes of consumption of conventional television.* Based on other research on the consumption of conventional television (Basterretxea *et al.*, 2007; Medrano Samaniego *et al.*, 2007), we wondered how do young people view conventional television, and what and how much of it do they watch.

(4)   *Modes of consumption* in the new era of internet television, focusing attention on the following three main areas:

a.   Websites of conventional television broadcasters.

b.   General platforms that show content produced by other people or by media companies: YouTube, Vimeo, etc. We wanted to investigate the use made of these platforms, the viewing of videos and downloads and uploads they perform.

c.   Websites with their own video content. Students have been asked to mention the sites they access for video content consumption.

(5)   *Patterns of consumption of television through mobile phones.* In this brief section, we have tried to investigate to what extent do young people today watch video via their mobile device.

After designing the questionnaire, we selected our study group from one of the schools in the Ikastola Arizmendi, in the High Deba Valley, a region with a high percentage of Basque speakers. The selected centre, Almen in Mondragon, was chosen because of its proximity to the school (2 km from the faculty) and because it was an appropriate study group in terms of number of students.

The survey was completed by 207 of the 208 selected students, all in the 1st–4th year of DBH (Secondary Education).

Finally, a focus group was formed with 10 students in order to obtain qualitative data. It was divided into two parts:

(1)   First, we asked them about the questionnaire itself, to find out whether there were incorrect or incomprehensible statements or questions, and also to get a feeling of their perception of the survey.
(2)   They then talked about the reasons of their consumption patterns.

Gathered Information

The analysis presents correlations between the pupil's appreciation (based on the surveys and the focus group) of EITB production and the criteria of the Basque public TV (according to Blanco's quotations from the interview), to see if they actually match one another.

On the other hand, some additional correlations are presented, based on what the experts (Sánchez, Castro and Larrea) said in the interviews about the redefinition of the concept of television over the internet and what teenagers' told about their new ways of consumption in the surveys and in the focus group. Thus, these are the main findings:

(1)   The interviewed teenagers seemed to confirm Blanco's statements. We can summarize their commonalities in two ways:

(i)   Blanco claimed that genre fiction is the favourite amongst teenagers. He also adds that the reality show *El conquistador del fin del mundo* is the most successful programme within this audience age group. Analysing the results of the programmes most watched by the 207 respondents, we have the following:

A.   *El conquistador del fin del mundo* [reality show] (42%)
B.   *Los protegidos* [teenagers' drama] (22.7%)
C.   *Los Simpson* [cartoons] (19.8%)
D.   *El Internado* [teenagers' drama] (15.9%)
E.   *Física o química* [teenagers' drama] (15.4%)

It is worth noting that the other four programmes (B, C, D and E) are broadcast by the Spanish private channel Antena 3, the TV network which has received the highest audience rating in this research. It should also be mentioned that all participants commented on the importance of peers when watching this type of content. All of them mentioned that they regularly talk with their friends about the programmes they watch.

(ii)   Blanco stated that a TV programme requires the following features to be successful amongst teenagers:

> The truth is that successful products for young people need young people themselves to be the main actors, as in TV series like *Física o química* or *El internado*; [in] reality shows like *Fama*, [in] talent shows ... These are the most successful. Teenagers live on the edge, everything is exciting for them. And they certainly do not want lessons, they think that older people do not understand their world. (Blanco, 2010)

The young people interviewed stressed these same issues, when justifying the reasons for watching certain programmes: 'I liked the tests that the contestants have to pass, because they are very exciting', said one of the girls in the focus group, talking about *El conquistador del fin del mundo*. 'I like it because it shows things that happen to people the same age as us', remarked another girl when describing the TV series *Física o Química*.

(2)   As Blanco himself remarked, teenagers are not the main target group of EITB's Basque language TV channels. This point is clearly reflected in the TV programmes most watched by the study group. With regard to Basque content, three programmes were mentioned, but with a reduced viewership:

- *Kirolez Kirol* [sports programme] mentioned by 3.3% of the students.
- *Goenkale* [soap opera]: 2.8%.
- *Wazemank* [comedy show]: 0.48%.

Three programmes were shown to the focus group participants, taking into account the information requested by Blanco: the aforementioned *Goenkale* and *Wazemank*, and *Mihiluze* (a game show based on Basque language). All the participants claimed to know *Goenkale*, and commented that they had been fans of this series at some point in their life (it began broadcasting in 1994), but for various reasons none of them continues to watch the series nowadays (some of their comments were, for instance, 'my relatives still watch it but I prefer going to my room to go on Tuenti [Spanish social networking site, popular with teenagers]'; 'I consider it boring nowadays, it's not exciting at all, it's very repetitive').

With regard to the other two programmes, no one claimed they watched either of them, to the extent that several participants were unaware of the existence of the programmes. When asked about the reasons not to watch those programmes, all asserted that there are 'better things to do' than watch these programmes (browsing Tuenti, for example).

Taking into account the sociolinguistic profile of the 207 respondents (71% have Basque as their mother tongue and 73% reported using more Basque than Spanish with their friends), it is remarkable to see that their consumption of audiovisual products in Basque in conventional television is very limited.

The same applies to internet video: while 80% of respondents said that they always or almost always watch the videos in Spanish, in Basque this proportion is lower than 26%, with 22% of them claiming they always, or almost always, watch them in English.

Our study confirms that these teenagers' consumption of audiovisual production in Basque is minimal.

(3)   The teenagers' consumption of television over the internet is still low. YouTube is the preferred platform, but after listening to the students in the focus group and examining their answers in the questionnaires, we conclude that the social networking site 'Tuenti' is the one they use the most. Very few other sites are mentioned by the adolescents but, amongst them, sport and music websites were the most notable (especially that of *Marca,* a Spanish sports magazine).

(4)   Despite having suitable technology to allow for audiovisual content to be watched through their mobile phones (58% of participants claimed they could do so), most of them claimed never to use their mobile phones for this purpose (88.4%).

Conclusions

This research is the first step towards a more ample analysis of the Basque adolescents' audiovisual consumption in the digital era, taking as a starting point the history of the biggest Basque media group (EITB) and its multilingual provision. Previous research on the subject (Basterretxea *et al.,* 2007; Medrano Samaniego *et al.,* 2007) was carried out in the analogue context, before the digitization of TV broadcasting and the implosion of the audiovisual on the internet. The methods previously used were analysed and reformulated. A new methodology was developed, adapted to the study of the digital environment and took into account new elements such as the *technological equipment used by adolescents, and their modes and patterns of consumption. Through this pilot study, this new methodology has shown its validity to provide answers to our research questions.*

Regarding the findings of the methodology, we have reached the conclusion that we should not be investigating the audiovisual content on the internet as an isolated phenomenon (see Cormack's concluding chapter for a lengthier debate on this issue). Being a multimedia platform, we must take into account other uses and applications of the network (such as social networking sites), since video consumption is closely linked to them.

The study presented here was carried out in a valley region (High Deba) with very specific sociolinguistic features: 63.8% of Basque speakers and 16.9% of quasi-Basque speakers in 2006 (Eustat, 2006a). Because of this specificity, it cannot be extrapolated to be representative for the entire Basque Country. More research is required in other areas of the Basque Country with different sociolinguistic features in order to obtain a much more accurate diagnosis.

Our aim is to carry out that broader research. The information obtained will serve to examine these aspects: how many media do teenagers use in Basque? What are their main motivations to use those media? Is the Basque audiovisual content adapted to teenagers' preferences and new ways of consumption? This information will be very useful when it comes to influencing teenagers' audiovisual viewing habits and to strengthen a communication and media infrastructure based on Basque language, in order to guarantee its presence and visibility in the public sphere.

References

Alkorta, L. and Zuberogoitia, A. (2009) *Masa-komunikaziotik Informazioaren Gizartera: Euskararen bideetan barrena.* Bilbo: UEU.

Amezaga, J. (2009) *Euskara digitalizazioaren garaian: Zein hizkuntza hitz egiten du komunikazio gizarteak?* Summer Course 2009. EHU-UPV. San Sebastian.

Arbelbide, X. (2002) *Maite Barnetxe (1941–1986).* Bidegileak bilduma, Gasteiz: Eusko Jaurlaritzaren Argitalpen Zerbitzu Nagusia.

Azurmendi, N. (2004) *Ramon Labaien: Euskal telebista, hutsean sortua.* Andoain: Andoaingo Udala.

Basterretxea, J.I. (1997) Telebistak 25 urte Hego Euskal Herrian. *Jakin* 98, 11–20.

Basterretxea, J.I., Idoyaga, P., Ramírez de la Piscina, T. and Zarandona, E. (2007) *Alfabetizazio berriak: Euskal Herriko neska-mutilak eta komunikabideak.* Gasteiz: Eusko Jaularitzaren Argitalpen Zerbitzu Nagusia.

Blanco, J. (2010, 26 March) [Personal interview].

Buckingham, D. (2002) *Crecer en la era de los medios electrónicos.* Madrid: Morata.

Casas, F. (2000) La adolescencia: Retos para la investigación y la sociedad de cara al siglo XXI. *Anuario de Psicología* 21 (2), 5–14.

Diez Unzueta, J.R. and Otermin, J.M. (2006) *EITB 1982–2007: Hegaldi-kronika.* Donostia: EITB.

Eustat (2006a) 2 urteko eta gehiagoko biztanleria, lurralde-eremuaren eta euskara-maila orokorraren arabera, accessed 10 May 2010. http://eu.eustat.es/ci_ci/elementos/ele0000400/ti_2_urteko_eta_gehiagoko_biztanleria_lurralde-eremuaren_eta_euskara-maila_orokorraren_arabera_2006/tbl0000488_e.html.

Eustat (2006b) 2001–2006 artean euskaldunen kopuruan ia 118.000 lagun gehiago ditugu, accessed 10 May 2011. http://www.eustat.es/elem/ele0004700/not0004712_e.html.

Gaztea (2010) Inoizko audientzia onenak izan ditugu: Mila esker! Accessed 17 February 2011.   http://www.eitb.com/gaztea/osoa/569360/inoizko-audientzia-onenak-izan-ditugu-mila-esker/.

Livingstone, S.M. (2002) *Young People and New Media*. London: SAGE.

Medrano Samaniego, C., Palacios, S. and Barandiaran, A.A. (2007) Los hábitos y preferencias televisivas en jóvenes y adolescentes: Un estudio realizado en el País Vasco. *Revista Latina de Comunicación Social 62*. Accessed 17 February 2011. http://www.ull.es/publicaciones/latina/200702Medrano_S_yotros.htm.

Montgomery, K.C. (2007) *Generation Digital: Politics, Commerce, and Childhood in the Age of the Internet*. Cambridge, MA: MIT.

Morduchowicz, R. (2009) *Los jóvenes y las pantallas: Nuevas formas de sociabilidad*. Barcelona: Gedisa.

Moring, T. (2007) Bilingualism, identity and the media in inter- and intra-cultural comparisons. Research Plan. Swedish School of Social Science & University of Helsinki, Helsinki.

Pavón, A. (2010) Nerabean eta ikus-entzunezko edukien kontsumoa digitalizazio garaian: Leintz bailarako gazteen kasua. Unpublished research to obtain certificate of research proficiency. Mondragon University. Mondragon.

Torrealdai, J.M. (1985) *Euskal Telebista eta euskara*. Donostia: Elkar.

Ubeda, J.A. (2008) *Jose Mari Iriondo: Euskal kulturaren komunikatzaile*. Andoain: Andoaingo Udala.

16 Tell a Song/Waiata Mai/Abair Amhrán: Singing Out

Ruth Lysaght

Bíonn dhá insint ar scéal agus dhá leagan déag ar amhrán
(There are two sides to every story, and twelve versions of every song)
– Irish seanfhocal (proverb)

Introduction

This chapter compares two television series about traditional singing from opposite sides of the globe on the national indigenous television stations Whakaata Māori (Māori Television Service, New Zealand) and TG4 (Teilifís na Gaeilge, Irish language television, Ireland). Part of the responsibility of both stations is to encourage the culture associated with their respective indigenous languages, of which song is an integral feature. Māori Television and TG4 broadcast a genre apparently unique to indigenous minority language television – a traditional singing series which forgoes common televisual framing devices in favour of a less formal presentation of 'live' performance, and assumes some cultural knowledge on the part of the audience. *Mōteatea* (MT) and *Abair Amhrán* (TG4) use televisual conventions and forms to engage with an older oral culture and to draw the audience into the 'space' where the song is being transmitted. The programmes invoke a sense of place and community on screen in an attempt to convey the original context and integrity of the song. Central to this is the re-familiarization of the indigenous language, or the recognition of the language as real and present in the lives of the viewers. *Abair Amhrán* and *Mōteatea* demonstrate some of the ways in which a television station may interact with a continuous tradition of live performance, providing a broader platform for traditional singers and new composers and introducing a new audience to each song using visuals and contextual explanations.

Continuity of Tradition

There is a continuous musical culture in both the Irish language and te reo Māori, despite change and attempts to break the tradition through the years of cultural imperialism. *Béaloideas*, the oral tradition in Ireland, initially worked through druidic and bardic schools, and frequent public performances. Poets were respected, often forming part of a chief's retinue and asked to compose praises or *aortha* (satires) about the enemies of their patron. Others travelled the country, testing the hospitality of various chiefs. As with *tōhunga*, the *filí* (poets, seers) or bards spent several years learning stories and poetry from the elders. Sensory deprivation and mnemonic devices enabled them to remember genealogies and important stories verbatim. These people were the living archives of their tribe, and those of a high level were also composers of new material. There is also a strong oral tradition in te ao Māori, where knowledge and customs were passed on from one generation to the next by means of waiata, haka, whaikō rero, pepeha and other forms (Kāretu, 1992: 28). Values and the social code were woven into stories and transmitted through myth and legend (Sadler, 2007).[1] Sharples (2007) figures mōteatea as a link to this past 'he taura ki te Ao Kohatu' (a line going back to the Stone Age). Their purpose is to transmit cultural treasure:

> ... *kei te mōteatea ōna tini āhuatanga e akiaki ana i te hinengaro o te tangata kia mau, kia tuku, kia hī ake anō i te mātauranga i tukua ihotia hei te wā e hiahiatia ana*
> Mōteatea has many purposes. It intends to encourage the continuation of oral tradition and knowledge retention so that generations after may seek this knowledge when they desire (translation by Tupe whānau). (Mōrehu, 2006)

This is similar to the Irish context, even in contemporary times, as Lillis Ó Laoire explains:

> A highly developed appreciation of music and song often forms an integral part of this world view and, indeed ... the performance of songs and dances (...) celebrated community and created a continuity between the living and the dead, between those absent and those present. (Ó Laoire, 2000: 41–42)

However, today the songs are known well only in certain regions, as the essential method of passing them on involves face-to-face teaching or frequent exposure to good performers. Only in areas where the language and culture are strong can this process occur naturally, and such areas are few. The purpose of each song in the *sean nós* [Irish] and *mōteatea* [Māori] traditions is to transmit a story and to pass on a memory.

Sean nós (old style) is unaccompanied traditional singing in the Irish language. Often, the best songs do not spell out their message, so that the audience has to think about the meaning of the song, to concentrate on the words and atmosphere. Often, the deeper meaning of a song may emerge in the listener's mind after the actual performance. *Mōteatea* is a type of classical Māori chant. Mervyn McLean categorizes it apart from haka and karakia, which he defines as stylized speech (McLean, 1996: 235), because of its melody. The form and style of *mōteatea* has evolved over time, especially since they came in contact with European culture (Royal, 1997, 2009). Charles Royal sets out the functions of mōteatea as many, ranging

> from consoling the heart of an afflicted lover, to informing people of a calamity. They incite a people to warfare and even curse them. Mō teatea relate genealogy and can initiate a youngster into the curriculum of the whare wānanga. (Royal, 1997: 6)

In this way, *mōteatea* are clearly carriers of cultural treasure. In both the Irish and the Māori traditions, the lyrics are more important than the air, and in each, there are certain ways of emphasizing important words (Māori performers do it with movement, and Irish singers with melismatic ornamentation or pauses).

Abair Amhrán and Mōteatea

The programmes *Abair Amhrán* and *Mōteatea* speak to an audience who have some knowledge of the songs, but who might not know all the words or meanings. They also showcase the talent and virtuosity of those singers who perform the songs on-screen – although in the case of both programmes, the song is more important than the singer. The purpose of the programmes is to carry on story and song, translating them not only into a new media but also into a new societal context.

How does a Tradition of Performance Translate to Television?

Although the performances of the songs in *Abair Amhrán* and *Mōteatea* are rehearsed, they are 'almost as live', and the singing of the songs does constitute a communication of information. The performance appears to be 'live' not only on the level of performance, in the singer's awareness of the camera, but also on an affective level, in the singer's felt relation to the song. Obvious differences occur between live performance and the recording of songs for a television programme. In natural performance, the songs emerge organically from the gathering. For television, the songs are chosen in advance by the production company (in consultation with chosen singers), and the format of presentation is approved by the broadcaster and the funding body. Unlike traditional performance of *mōteatea* or *sean nós*, on television, the setting is more or less staged, and elements of teaching and performance are mixed. Traditionally, teaching was done either separately (to a group of youngsters) or allowed to happen implicitly (learners would listen and gradually pick up the words and meaning from live performance), and the performance of songs was generally for sheer enjoyment and sharing particular stories with the assembled audience. In order to approximate the atmosphere of these live sessions on television, the producers use televisual techniques to draw in a distant audience.

Three important elements transmitted by the song are translated in various ways to television. These are a sense of place, a sense of community and relationship with language.

Place

The opening sequence of *Mōteatea* links people and place through music. On the faces of several people are projected topographical graphics, contours or rippling water, as a background to the lyrics. With a low pulsing beat, the lyrics sustain a mood of calmness. Between the old and peaceful faces is shadow. The camera appears to be a static witness to the movement from face to darkness to new face. Dark eyes are, as in icons, the focal point of the shot, even as the faces seem to slide slowly out of frame. This conveys a sense of the intangible, as curved lines glide over skin and remain unbroken until the next face. The movement of the images evokes a sense of how ephemeral human existence can be, while the continuous lyrics denote the power of song to carry values on from one person to the next. The people create the song, but the song is greater than any individual.

Abair Amhrán is set mostly outdoors, amongst important features of the Irish landscape, and usually the place we see on screen is linked to the singer (indeed the location was mainly decided 'on the road' (McCarthy, 2009)) or to the content of the song, as in 'Cailleach an Airgid', if not both. This means that the viewer is able to 'see' the whole country and hear the songs associated with different parts. Never does a map appear to show the relative location of the places, but often shots of signposts will indicate where the song is set. An Irish audience is otherwise expected to recognize the area.

Mōteatea, in contrast, is shot overwhelmingly in studio, and singers from all over the country converge in the Newmarket HQ of Māori Television to record their song. In a black-box studio, a singer or group of singers, often wearing black, stand barefoot or in stockinged feet on a wooden floor. The absence of shoes implies a marae (meeting house)-type setting. This atmosphere implies an audience ready to listen and feel part of the performance, and creates a link with the 'space' of Māori culture. The studio provides a neutral venue for multiple iwi (Māori social units or community groups), and indeed evokes a more positive spiritual 'no place': Te Kore, the origin of all creativity. The connection to geographical place is evoked through the words of the singer who explains the song. Their iwi (tribe) – which appears as a strapline on screen – often gives a clue to location for a culturally literate audience. The appropriateness of setting and song is vital to a culturally consonant performance. The composer Rob Ruha's explanation of his song 'E rere rā te mātihetihe' shows how it is rooted in place, in this case, the farm Matakao in Wharekahika, where he used to love lying on the long grasses (pātiti). At the beginning of this mōteatea, we see an exterior shot, before returning to the studio, where the uncle mourns the loss of his nephew in the song.

People: Relationship

> *He aha te mea nui o te ao? He tangata, he tangata, he tangata.*
> *(What is the most important thing in the world? It is people.)*
> – Māori whakataukī (proverb)

Both *Mōteatea* and *Abair Amhrán* represent different generations, because this is vital to any understanding of how these songs work. They must be alive between different age groups. In *Abair Amhrán*, families or teachers and students sing together – a living example of how to effect intergenerational transmission. The viewers at home also benefit from witnessing – if not participating – in the process. Probably the most contentious decision in the production of *Abair Amhrán* was the way many songs were 'interrupted' by switching from one singer to another. If the intention of the producer was to show a continuity of tradition across different ages and areas, some of the 'purists did not like the style of breaking up songs with chat and getting different performers singing the same songs' (McCarthy, 2009), because they saw it as disrespectful to the personal interpretations of the individual singers.

Generations are mentioned again and again in *Mōteatea*, sometimes in the context of composition and how the song was handed down, and sometimes in the context of reception and how the purpose of the song is to educate and encourage future generations. In *Mōteatea,* performance is explicitly foregrounded as important. Different gestures and p kana (facial expressions of wairua being released) convey further layers of meaning to the singing. When a group perform, their actions are not always in unison, as the performers have interpretative room to respond to the lyrics in their own way. As Tau (2001: 69) notes, 'one's body movements ... represent forms of thought in a language that exceeds the rest'.

An important feature of the singing tradition in both cultures is that it is live, and that the audience is generally close (physically and relationally) to the performer. The audience may also become performer – the roles are not rigid. In *Abair Amhrán*, the audience is 'translated' to screen by means of friends or family members of the singer, who act as 'stand-ins' for the viewer. As in *Mōteatea*, the viewers are linked to what they see and hear first by the songs themselves and second by their knowledge of the story. For people who are unfamiliar with the song, they first must experience it – the performance, the ihi, the wehi, the spirit. Marcia Browne (2005), following Hunkin, remarks that ihihangaranga (weaving of spiritual power through feeling a sonar vibration of the waiata) is a phenomenon experienced through the performance of good singers, whereby the wairua or spiritual power of the song is communicated to the listeners (Browne, 2005: 27). This 'x-factor' (Browne, 2005: 27, 42), makes a connection beyond words: 'It's as if the reo is a vehicle or "conductor" of the wairua, and the singer the catalyst' (Rangihau, 2004, quoted in Browne, 2005: 27). A similar deep response obtains in the Irish context, as expressed by Dick Roche:

> It's part of what we are. When I hear a song in Irish, to my shame, I don't understand   it ... but when I hear that song, it resonates. It makes me want to – cry is the wrong word – but it does make me feel emotional. (Roche, on Ireland AM, 2009)

As the listeners experience the song, they may then accumulate some knowledge (through thinking themselves, or through explicit instruction by the singer or composer) and listen again, making a stronger connection to the meaning of the song. *Mōteatea* repeats the songs, interspersing them with explanation, whereas in *Abair Amhrán* each song is performed only once, some prior knowledge is assumed. In this way, the television broadcast of traditional singing assists viewers in the process of reacquainting themselves with a half-known/half-forgotten language. Unlike 'normalization', which implies a wider use of the language in various social settings, perhaps with attendant standardization; 'reconnection' means that people and communities are getting to know their own dialect and beginning to feel comfortable with the idea of using it themselves. I see the term 'reconnection' as useful, because it doesn't insist on the actual use of or ability in the language, but rather on the quality of relationship the person has with it. Obviously, this relationship will be deeper if there is some ability to use the language, but this is not a prerequisite.

Conveying the meaning of the songs

The difference in presentation of the context and meaning of the songs in *Mōteatea* and *Abair Amhrán* reflects the ethos of their respective broadcasters. Where Māori Television aims to convey a sense of an organized knowledge and tradition long neglected in the New Zealand public arena, TG4 is concerned to avoid connotations of the schoolroom, preferring to emphasize the entertainment aspect of the service. These differing approaches reflect attitudes to the indigenous language and its image, and result from the sociopolitical and historical context of New Zealand and Ireland. The camera in *Abair Amhrán* is presented as incidental, whereas in *Mōteatea* it takes on a formal framing role. In both programmes, the singers may speak about their song, before or after a performance. In *Mōteatea*, most performances are introduced in this way, and some also repeat particular verses after the explanation has been given, which gives the audience a chance to reconsider the meaning of the song in the light of what they have learned. Neither programme uses a presenter as intermediary between the songs/singers and the audience, resulting in a relatively direct connection.

However, for viewers who lack the requisite cultural knowledge, the experience has the potential to be confusing or dislocating. It is not that such people necessarily demand bite-sized, pre-digested and repetitive television – but rather that some elements of the programmes' content can appear opaque to the non-insider. It is usual in the minority language media context that different audiences will have different levels of understanding. The more 'expert' viewers from the minority language culture experience a particular pleasure, as it is rare that their cultural knowledge is reflected on national television screens. The solution for viewers who, although interested, are less familiar with the material is to accept as inevitable some degree of being culturally at sea at least in the initial stages, and to engage with the aspects of the programme which are more 'open' to them, such as the music itself. There is a value to things not being immediately 'easy access'; indeed part of the sense of the oral tradition inheres in the process of reflecting on and relating to the song.

Language

In *Mōteatea*, the lyrics of the songs appear on screen as the group performs in unison, enabling a viewer to join in at home. The lyrics in te reo begin as white font on a violet-to-black background, which becomes transparent to reveal the singers. This visual 'pas de deux' makes the singers and lyrics appear to converge into one – layers of whakapapa (layers, strata, often used to refer to genealogical links and interconnections). There is direct explanation of a song's context or significance to camera, which means that although the lyrics are not translated, a non-Māori speaker may still appreciate the gist of the content.

Abair Amhrán does not show the lyrics of the songs visually, but occasionally a singer will comment on the meaning of a particular line. Unlike *Mōteatea*, in *Abair Amhrán* the viewer thus has no possibility of singing along unless he or she already knows the song. However, the air of the songs and the constantly moving visuals breathe life into what for some might otherwise be an inaccessible cultural artefact. The viewer can appreciate the other features of the song (melody, performance, accompanying images and juxtapositions) without knowing the literal meaning of the words. This is also an important part of the oral tradition – sometimes meaning emerges later. It is important to note that, despite glosses and explanations, the meaning of the song is still not fully explicit. This is not because of a wish to conceal, or a failure to reveal, on the part of the singers or the programme makers – but rather due to the character of the tradition. Only part of the meaning of the song can be conveyed (whether by television or in live performance), because part of the interpretative work lies with the listener. The song must be taken inside and be re-sung by another person, who in the experience of that performance can discover the story or greater significance.

Conclusions

Both programmes convey a sense of layers of meaning on and beyond the screen in their treatment of the songs, singers and setting. The absence of a presenter leaves the content open to more dynamic interpretation on the part of the viewer. In the beginning, these songs were solely about place or people (emotion and information). Now, on television in the post-colonial era, they are also about language. They are a way of passing on the craft and the words to the next generation. In an episode of *Abair Amhrán*, Pádraigín Ní Uallacháin says that the best way to pass on a song is for children to pick it up naturally rather than to 'learn' it formally. These programmes therefore see television taking on the role of *seanachaí* (storyteller) or *tohunga* (expert). In presenting traditional songs on screen, the Māori *Mōteatea* and Irish *Abair Amhrán* draw on the power of a continuous oral tradition to create a new relationship between people and their language and culture. The 'creative potential' (Royal, 2009) of the minoritised culture is here presented and re-imagined on its own terms. Tradition is reinvented as the song moves from live performance to the 'as live' medium of television. The spirit of the language is the current which runs through singer and song, an electrifying relationship between traditional and contemporary identity.

Note

1. Māori traditional knowledge continues to be transmitted mostly orally. For this reason, readers will find quotations and references to lectures and talks rather than to printed documents from some Māori sources.

References

Browne, M. (2005) Wairua and the relationship it has with learning te reo Māori within Te Ataarangi. M.A., Massey University, Massey.

Ireland AM (2009, 17 March) [Television]. Ireland: TV3.

Kāretu, T. (1992) Language and protocol in the Marae. In M. King (ed.) *Te Ao hurihuri: Aspects of Moritanga* (pp. 29–42). Auckland: Reed.

McCarthy, T. (2009, 20 October) [Forefront Productions – personal email].

McLean, M. (1996) *Maori Music*. Auckland: Auckland University Press.

Mōrehu, N. (2006) Mōteatea: pātaka whakairinga kōrero. *MAI Review/*, 1.

Ó Laoire, L. (2000) Metaphors we live by: Some examples from Donegal Irish. *Western Folklore 59*(1), 33–48.

Royal, T.A.C. (1997) *Mōteatea and the transmission of history.* Ōtaki Historical Society. http://www.orotokare.org.nz/assets/moteateaandhistory.pdf.

Royal, T.A.C. (2009) Te Kaimanga: Towards a new vision for Matauranga Māori. Paper presented at the Manuao Lecture Series, Wellington.

Sadler, H. (2007) Lecture on Mātauranga Māori. University of Auckland.

Sharples, P. (2007, 20 July) Ngā Mōteatea Launch; Waipapa Marae – Press release: The Maori Party, 'Scoop' Independent News. Accessed 17 May 2011. http://www.scoop.co.nz/stories/CU0707/S00208.htm.

Tau, T.M. (2001) Mātauranga Māori as an Epistemology. In A. Sharp, P.G. McHugh and W.H. Oliver (eds) *Histories, Power and Loss: Uses of the Past – a New Zealand Commentary* (pp. 61–74). Wellington: Bridget Williams Books.

17 Languages: Obstacles and Brand Values in the Age of Media Convergence

Bea Narbaiza, Josu Amezaga, Edorta Arana and Patxi Azpillaga

Introduction

Minority languages in Europe have been progressively acquiring a position in the mass media. Initially, this started in the print media, with the exception of daily newspapers; later, they had a foothold in radio and, finally, in television (see Browne and Uribe-Jongbloed's introduction to this collection). When, after considerable effort, these languages came to occupy space and time on television, a more expensive and more complex medium, we find ourselves at a moment of change. This moment of change is characterized by three factors: first, the multiplication and transnationalization of the provision of media content; second, at the same time, we witness a significant decrease in the presence of minority languages in the media in quantitative terms; and third, the moment of change is also characterized by the multiplicity of meanings acquired by communication – people who were traditionally only receivers have also become producers and distributors of content.

There are, under these circumstances, at least two groups of actors involved in the production of content. On the one hand, the traditional media – public and private, big and small – existing players in the analogue world who are concerned with adapting themselves efficiently to the possibilities opened up by new technologies and consumption patterns. On the other hand, there is a new group of players, the majority of them young, who are unknowingly shaping new models of content production and consumption in an individualized, independent and almost unexpected way.

In this chapter, we analyse the present situation of these media, their capacities and assets, and their structural strategies and programming. Our information comes from interviews held with members of the management teams of eight European media companies: EITB (the Basque Country), CCMA (Catalonia), S4C (Wales), BBC ALBA (Scotland), TG4 (Ireland), Omrop Fryslân (Friesland) and STV (Finland) (see also Amezaga *et al.*, 2010).

From Modernity to Post-Modernity

Normalization, revitalization or preservation makes up the terminology that traditionally appears when the terms mass media and minority languages are in conjunction with one another. We have always set out from the assumption that the mass media, together with the education system, are basic and indispensable tools in those processes of normalization, revitalization or preservation. Consequently, the presence of those languages in the mass media becomes a goal in itself.

Media in minority languages started with print media (though not daily newspapers), moving often concurrently to radio and finally to television, in the singular and the most prestigious of the media. Television is the medium that classifies 'us' and 'them'; the medium that constructs and shows reality; the medium for which all the political campaigns everywhere in the world are designed, through which messages are sent, from the most public to the most intimate.

Owing to its technical complexity, its cost and, above all, owing to the modern conception of television as a public service, access to that medium requires the involvement – occasionally simply the permission with all that this implies – of public institutions: another of the keys to normalization, revitalization or preservation. It has even been asserted that televisions in minority languages are, in fact, mechanisms of linguistic policy (Moriarty, 2007).

From the onset, television in Europe has had a public service character, which has enabled different states to regulate – either directly or through bodies appointed by them – aspects related both to the content of broadcast and to the structure of broadcasting, including the use of the radio-electronic spectrum, its conditions and its limitations.

In fact, as Kevin Robins (1998) points out, the history of both radio and television is in many ways the development of legal and regulatory systems that attempt to impede the transnational tendency of these media. The latter are central to the development of societies and national communities within Europe, and are involved in producing and reproducing the national imaginary. In spite of the fact that national territorial borders, together with the national systems of broadcasting, might seem to be, inherent to the nature of radio and television, this is clearly not the case. In fact, broadcasting systems were instituted in a way that would correspond to the social, political and legal systems so that each nation state could regulate these media, as well as any other that might emerge, in national terms, legitimated by the public service character conferred upon them.

It was in that context of public service – on many occasions in the name of public service itself and the territorial state limits it implied – that many of the minority language televisions with their own broadcasts were developed. In fact, the European Charter for Regional or Minority Languages (Council of Europe, 1992), which has been frequently employed for establishing the number of languages and their speakers and which we shall use again to see the access of those languages to television, defines minority or regional languages in *territorial* terms, as opposed to facing other immigrant languages, as noted below:

Article 1: Definitions: For the purposes of this Charter:
(a)   'regional or minority languages' means languages that are:
- traditionally used within a given territory of a State by nationals of that State who form a group numerically smaller than the rest of the State's population; and
- different from the official language(s) of that State; it does not include either dialects of the official language(s) of the State or the languages of migrants;
(b)   'territory in which the regional or minority language is used' means the geographical area in which the said language is the mode of expression of a number of people justifying the adoption of the various protective and promotional measures provided for in this Charter;
(c)   'non-territorial languages' means languages used by nationals of the State which differ from the language or languages used by the rest of the State's population but which, although traditionally used within the territory of the State, cannot be identified with a particular area thereof.

Even while maintaining a public service character for terrestrial transmissions, the most liberal positions, those most favourable to market laws and least favourable to state intervention, have in the name of diversity permitted access by private companies to terrestrial television and will liberalize the use of satellite and cable. As a result of liberalization, the paradox arises that content which is not available on terrestrial television can be consumed by payment via cable or satellite.

The development of these technologies and their liberalization start a process whose principal characterization is transnationalization and in which digital terrestrial television is no more than a link.

It is important to emphasize that at the start of transnationalization the companies providing content, and therefore the principal actors of the process, are of course the big media groups, in particular those based in the United States and Japan, and also the public and private companies that developed over the years as a result of the public service responsibilities bestowed upon them in the age of terrestrial broadcasting.

The process of transnationalization will have a levelling effect on the public and private broadcasting corporations and the big media groups, making them 'content producers'. In this first phase, however, the production centres, as well as content, continue to follow territorial criteria of a national or intra-national scope where televisions in minority languages are concerned, as well as the classical unidirectional schema of communication.

The aim will be to reach the greatest number of individuals, who decide to install one of the many available receivers, independent of the place where they are located: another of the characteristics of post-modernity. It has since been observed that place of origin is one of the key collective factors in that supposedly individual choice. This has emerged in many studies (including Sinclair, 1996) on the use made of television by different diaspora, and its effect on them from the linguistic and cultural points of view. This is also the case in the minority language communities recognized as such in the Council of Europe's (1992) 'European Charter for Regional or Minority Languages', ratified in 1992 and still in force although repeatedly questioned from several perspectives.

Television Channels and Television Content in Minority Languages in the European Union: A Possible Categorization

Access to television in these languages involves a highly varied casuistry, given the heterogeneity of the minority linguistic communities. Some of them are articulated around languages that are minority languages in one territory but official in another, that is in the so-called 'kin states' (such is the case of many communities originating from displaced populations, a phenomenon that is more common in Central and Eastern Europe than in Western Europe). Others, however, are languages that are present on a single territory and without a state that considers them official. The former are found in many cases in frontier territories or territories close to their kin states, which has on occasion facilitated access to mass media in their own language. In recent decades, besides, the development of satellite television (and more recently television on internet) has led to the availability of television provision – to varying degrees – in these languages within the reach of speaker populations. On the other hand, in other cases we find linguistic minorities that have instigated their own television broadcasts, on occasion arising from, or specifically directed to their own community. There is a very wide range among the latter, from those with several channels that broadcast 24 hours a day in the specific language to those which have only minutes per week of television programmes. Finally, we find minority language communities that have not yet reached television as a medium.

In Table 17.1, we can see the different regional minority languages (RML) classified according to their possibility of access to television. It can be observed from the table that 10 linguistic minorities, which represent a third of the speakers of RML, have a considerable presence in television (more than 1000 hours a year). Another nine minorities (with approximately 10% of the speakers) have access to television provision that is appreciably lower, in some cases only a few minutes a week. The following 58 minorities have access, at least by satellite, to television broadcasts in their language but which originate from kin states; this represents a little below a third of the population of 55 million mentioned above. Finally, there are 23 communities that do not have any television service available in their own languages, which, in terms of the population affected, represents the remaining quarter. It is worth underlining the fact that all the minorities that have a kin state have access to one or more television broadcasts in their language.

Minority Language Media or Media in Minority Languages?

This categorization highlights the contrasting differences of access that different linguistic communities have with respect to television provision. However, we have found in interviews held with members of the management teams of eight European media companies (EITB – the Basque Country; CCMA – Catalonia; S4C – Wales; BBC Alba – Scotland; TG4 – Ireland; Omrop Fryslân and STV-Suomi) that there are many similarities among those televisions included in the same category, which mark out a common trajectory in many respects.

The majority of television services that broadcast over 1000 hours annually started broadcasting in the 1980s as general information channels. Nearly all of them are public corporations and even if private they are funded with public money as they have a public service broadcasting remit.

The language, its normalization, revitalization or preservation, is the constitutive element of all these television services. In the context of the Spanish state, the mass media and their linguistic normalization function

Table 17.1 Television in regional minority languages in Europe

Regional minority linguistic communities with their own broadcasts	More than 1000 hours of broadcasts annually: Catalan (Spain and France), Galician (Spain), Basque (Spain and France), Welsh (United Kingdom), Frisian (the Netherlands), Luxembourgish (Luxembourg), Swedish (Finland), Irish (Ireland), Scottish Gaelic (United Kingdom), Italian (Slovenia)
	Less than 1000 hours of broadcasts annually: Friulian (Italy), Finnish (Sweden), Breton (France), Corsican (France), Ladin (Italy), Occitan (France), Sorbian (Germany), Saami (Sweden), Saami (Finland)
Regional minority linguistic communities without their own broadcasts but with access to television in their language via satellite	German (Belgium, Czech Republic, Denmark, France, Hungary, Italy, Poland, Romania and Slovakia), Turkish (Bulgaria Greece and Romania), Russian (Estonia, Latvia, Lithuania and Bulgaria), Romanian (Hungary), Ukrainian (Latvia, Poland and Romania), Bulgarian (Greece), Portuguese (Spain), Polish (Czech Republic, Latvia and Lithuania), Serbian (Hungary and Romania), Greek (Italy), Dutch (France), Hungarian (Austria, Romania, Slovakia and Slovenia), Czech (Austria), Macedonian (Bulgaria and Greece), Slovak (Austria, Czech Republic and Hungary), Catalan (Italy), Luxembourgish (France), Albanian (Greece and Italy), Slovenian (Austria, Italy and Hungary), Croatian (Austria, Hungary and Italy), Slovenia), Armenian (Bulgaria), Belorussian (Latvia and Poland), Danish (Germany), Irish (United Kingdom), Lithuanian (Poland)
Regional minority linguistic communities without access to television broadcasts in their language	Low Saxon (the Netherlands), Sardinian (Italy), Walachian (Greece), Romani (Slovakia), Kashubian (Poland), Romani (Hungary, Romania, Bulgaria, Czech Republic and Slovenia), Corsican (Italy), Asturian (Spain), Francoprovençal (France and Italy), Occitan (Italy and Spain), Ruthenian/Lemkish (Poland), Faroe (Denmark), Tatar (Romania and Bulgaria), Mirandese (Portugal), Saterlandic (Germany), Cornish (United Kingdom)

correspond to more ambitious political projects in which language is central, while in other situations they tend to be part of a response to the defence of the rights of bilingual communities. All are languages present in a single continuous territory, though this is somewhat more complicated in the Catalan case, and in the case of Swedish in Finland, where, moreover, it is an official language throughout the state.

All the people interviewed agreed that the mass media they manage have played a fundamental role in achieving this fundamental objective, to which they attribute its full significance. The role of television was perceived by the professionals' interviews to be extremely important in the processes of normalization, revitalization and preservation and they were of the view that there was an unquestionable contribution by their respective media organizations to grammar and syntax, as well as in the elaboration and application of new concepts and vocabulary in all fields (news, sports, entertainment, etc.) and in all registers (formal and informal). This aspect, which is closely related to the corpus of the language, leads to two other facets of normalization that are relevant to the spread of knowledge of the language and the relation between languages and the users of those languages. The managers interviewed emphasized that users of those languages today have more linguistic tools at their disposal to apply in any register than ever before.

The last aspect concerns the relationship that exists between three specific elements within the communities: first, those persons who do not know the minority language; second, the language itself; and third, the function that television must fulfil with respect to that population – which is often the majority – insofar as it is financed with public funds.

The solutions have involved bilingual televisions with a generalized use of subtitles in the official majority language of the territory where they are located; these subtitles are optional or overprinted on the broadcasts of content in minority languages, as in the case of televisions in Scotland, Wales and Ireland. In the case of languages where there is a common root for both the majority and the minority languages, although the commitment is exclusively to the minority language, interventions in the majority language are not dubbed or subtitled, as in the case of the Catalan television. Exclusive use of the languages for the different channels is the solution chosen by Basque television, which has exclusive channels in one language and the other. Digital television, as in the case of Swedish television in Finland, provides the option of selecting audio in the desired language, in sports broadcasts, for example.

Thus, the aim of reaching the highest possible number of spectators is achieved in a certain way. It is not a question of making products for a few; in this respect, the minority language can be understood as representing an obstacle when trying to reach the largest possible audience.

For this reason, specialization of content has been sought in the media of the minority language. Sports content and content aimed at children and youths have received preferential treatment and the results have been evaluated positively.

Specialization together with exclusiveness is the key to the future. It is a question of making products that moreover must serve all the media. These managers thus remind us that the companies they direct are not only television channels but also corporations that include internet and, with the exception of S4C in Wales, radio as well.

The internet multiplies not only the media, the channels, but also the actors of communication. With 'mass self-communication', according to Castells (2009), communication ceases to be unidirectional, acquiring numerous directions and converting individuals into subjects of communication.

Although the continuation of mass media in the minority language is not an issue in this context of the apparent levelling, which is understood to be one of the competition, the interviews with some of the minority language television managers pointed to the suggestion that language normalization has ceased to be the main objective of the television service. These media organizations see themselves as producers of audiovisual content, rather than being social instruments for language normalization, revitalization or preservation. In short, content becomes the substantive part of the process, language becomes an adjective or a descriptor, and is, in fact, an exclusive adjective for each of these media organizations, as they are the only provider of television in their language, and therefore is one of their major brand values.

It is worth asking in this context whether or not this perception of those who direct minority language televisions is a new phenomenon; whether it can be extended to all media in the same degree; and, if this is the case, the type of criteria it responds to, as well as the repercussions that might derive from their application.

References

Amezaga, J., Arana, E., Azpillaga, P. and Narbaiza, B. (2010) *Ethnic Minority Television in Europe: Commonalities and Differences between Regional Minority Languages and Immigrant Minority Languages*. Poitiers: MHSH.

Castells, M. (2009) *Communication Power*. Oxford: Oxford University Press.

Council of Europe (1992) European Charter for Regional and Minority Languages. Strasbourg: Council of Europe.

Moriarty, M. (2007) Minority language television as an effective mechanism of language policy: A comparative study of the Irish and Basque sociolinguistic contexts. PhD thesis, University of Limerick, Limerick.

Robins, K. (1998) Spaces of global media, accessed 23 March 2011. http://www.transcomm.ox.ac.uk/working%20papers/WPTC-98-06%20Robins.pdf.

Sinclair, J. (1996) *New Patterns in Global Television: Peripheral Vision*. Oxford: Oxford University Press.

List of People Interviewed

Gestrin, M. (2009)	FST's Director. Stockholm, 4 December.
Gibson, Rh. (2007)	S4C's Director of Commissioning. Aberystwyth, 3 November.
Manteca, C. (2009)	Antenna and Programming Director at TV3. Barcelona, 16 June.
Murray, M.M. (2009)	Head of Gaelic Digital Service, BBC Scotland. Glasgow, 23 January.
O Gallchoir, P. (2009)	TG4's Director General. Dublin, 1 October.
Tolsma, R. (2010)	OMROP's Editor in Chief. Leeuwarden/Ljouwert, 13 January.
Zupiria, B. (2009)	Head of ETB. Bilbao, 31 March.

Concluding Remarks: Towards an Understanding of Media Impact on Minority Language Use

Mike Cormack

Minority language media (MLM) studies is developing fast, as the essays in this book make it clear. No longer is it an obscure corner of media studies, limited to looking at a few of the better known linguistic minorities. Alongside a greatly widened range of languages, new media in all their forms (especially the so-called 'social media') have moved to be the central focus. This does, however, raise a basic question – why are we doing this work? The answer must be that MLM studies has a fundamentally different orientation from mainstream media studies or, for that matter, from studies of media use by other minorities, such as ethnic groups. It is concerned with how media can be used to help languages. If it drifts away from this focus, then it becomes simply a part of mainstream media studies that happens to look at minority languages and loses any claim to be a distinctive and coherent area of study. But if the *raison d'être* is language, the question arises as to how media – and more specifically, new media – can be used to help languages. Whatever reasons or causes we might give for media developments in general – commercial, technological or social – helping a language is not likely to be one of them. The technologically and commercially driven development of new digital media simply emphasizes this point. However much minority languages may use new media, such media were not developed with these languages in mind. Indeed, it could be convincingly argued that the main thrust of new media, as far as language is concerned, is to consolidate the power of the globally dominant languages.

The importance of new media to minority languages has, of course, been recognized by many, not least by the writers in this book. In her conclusion to *Minority Language Media* in 2007, Niamh Hourigan raised a number of issues for future research to which new media were central – the rise of global English on the internet, the digital divide as it is manifested in minority languages and the movement towards globalization (Hourigan,

2007). In their chapter in this book, Donald Browne and Enrique Uribe-Jongbloed have outlined a research agenda for MLM studies in which new media are the central focus. Over and above these more general essays, the studies in this book, such as those looking at uses of Facebook, go a long way in answering the need for study of the uses of new media in relation to minority languages.

However, all this makes it appropriate to take a step back and to reconsider the basic question of how new media might help minority language use. In earlier essays, I have considered this issue from the point of view of more traditional media (Cormack, 2007) and in relation to one minority language (Cormack, 2010). Here, the focus is on the general issue in relation to new media. Media research typically does various things. It can recount media history, it can examine policy, it can analyse media texts and it can look at the audience's uses of, and reactions to, the media. However, those of us involved in minority languages want it to do something else – to help a language and also, probably, a culture.

This issue can be put more precisely as being the lack of a full understanding of how media can be of use in language maintenance. Many assumptions are routinely made about the ways in which media of all kinds can help the situation of a minority language. Media give status to a language, they can link up and unify different segments of the language community, they can focus political development, they add to the minority language culture, they can provide a context for economic development and, indeed, contribute directly to it. Over and above these practical points, media provision in a minority language answers human rights claims and helps in the important work of preserving as much of human language and culture as possible. All of these points have been frequently made (including by this author) and there is no doubt of their general importance. What they do not tell us much about, other than in a very indirect way, is how development and use of the media by minority language communities actually helps language maintenance, how it might encourage people to speak a specific language when the dominant social, economic and political structures (not to speak of the media themselves) all work in favour of a different language.

Of course, many useful and informative studies have been made of particular minority language situations (as the essays in this book clearly show). There have, however, been fewer attempts to consider MLM as a whole, as an area about which we might be able to generalize. What we see is a concentration on specifics, and a corresponding lack of full discussions of broader issues, in particular the issue of the media's role in language maintenance. It is not going too far to say that at the heart of MLM studies is an absence; an absence which seriously affects the contribution that work in this field of study can make to the actual situations in which minority language communities find themselves. That language decline can still take place in communities which have been provided with a range (even if limited) of electronic media emphasizes the point. This absence can be more clearly seen by considering issues related to new media and to language planning.

The Challenge of New Media

The nature of new media, and of the social interactions they involve, means a major change from traditional approaches to the media. There is no definitive text in many new media products. Websites can be accessed by the user in many different ways, they can be continually changing, and there is no single linear structure which users are likely to follow. The database becomes the paradigm for many new media forms (Manovich, 2001) in which the media text experienced by any given user becomes one of the many possible manifestations of elements of the database's content. As Glyn Williams has made it clear, this has implications not only for the end-uses but also for the organization of media production itself (Williams, 2007).

In addition to the lack of a clear-cut media text, there is no easily identifiable audience situation. When the same content can be accessed on television, on a desk-top computer, on a mobile phone or on a DVD, not only it becomes extremely difficult to think of how the audience might be understood but also, more importantly, it can become significantly misleading to even use such a term as 'audience' with its implication, however weak these days, of a body of people with some kind of shared experience and some kind of average response or range of responses. There can be little sense of a coherent audience in the future. But with a fragmented audience, it is not at all clear how can audience impact be measured.

Perhaps, some new term is needed to get us away from the whole notion of audience research. There was always something artificial about talking of 'the audience', always the danger of talking of one object, rather than seeing the multitude of behaviours which go into what is called 'audience reaction'. The research imperative to be able to make concrete generalizations was always in danger of overriding the acknowledgment that we are dealing with many individuals, not one or even a few groupings.

Not only are new media changing our ideas of the audience but also they seem to be changing our idea of what a community is. The popularity of the idea of a 'virtual community' is the most obvious sign of this, but even without going to the extreme of talking about communities which are only defined electronically, it is clear that the term 'community' does no longer have the strong territorial foundation which it once had. Think of such uses as 'the classical music community', 'the research community' and 'the Catholic community'. With communities of interest and communities of occupation, we are moving away from the traditional sense of a territorially defined community. In bilingual communities, it becomes even more difficult to pin down who is, and who is not, part of the language community. Consider these categories of minority language speakers: native speakers living within a territory that is predominantly minority language speaking, native speakers living outside that territory but still using the language regularly, irregular users of the language, fluent non-native speakers living within the territory, fluent non-native speakers living outside the territory, learners within the core language territory and learners living outwith the territory (a category with potentially a global range).

New media permit us to include all of these within a broadened notion of the language community, without turning that community into a purely virtual one (as others have suggested, the notion of a networked community is perhaps a more useful term here). But how, then, can new media be most suitably used to help this community, apart from in the most basic sense of bringing it into being? It is not at all clear, especially since the greater the emphasis on new media, the greater is likely to be the push towards a less territorially based notion of the community (see Mac Uidhilin's contribution to this collection, for example).

The last point to make about new media is that they are not 'policeable' in the way that old media were. Content cannot be controlled in the way that was at least possible with old media. The fragmentation at every level (production, text and audience) is enough to demonstrate this. Whereas traditional media content for minority languages was based on what media producers thought would be appropriate (whether in terms of simply maximizing audiences or in terms of educating it), new media move away from this model and, of course, the sheer amount of content makes policing impossible.

The issue of controllability of new media raises questions of linguistic standards (as noted by Browne and Uribe-Jongbloed in their research agenda in their chapter). Language use in such media outlets as Facebook, Twitter, emails and text messages is frequently different from traditional language use. The same standards do not apply. If 'correct' grammar and spelling are seen as being an important part of language development, then such a policy will be doomed in social media. Not only that, a mixture of languages is likely to be a feature of the language of bilinguals in social media. In fact, mixing of languages is already recognized as a common feature in bilingual situations. The difference with new media is that patterns which were once more common just as spoken forms, rather than written ones, are likely now to appear in texts.

From one linguistic point of view, of course, new media are a definite improvement over old media. They encourage the active involvement of the user much more explicitly than did traditional media. If the user is creating content, whether at the level of a website or just at the level of email and text-messaging, they are in a very different linguistic situation from that of the traditional viewer of films and television. This should be better for language use, including language learning. The problem for minority language activists is how this can be tied into language maintenance efforts.

If this emphasis on new media is thought to ignore 'digital divide' issues, that is social differentiation on the basis of access to new media, the distinction between the digital 'have' and 'have not', then it should be noted that even people who are not using computers will be using digital versions of old media (such as multichannel television) and the overall social trends will depend on majority use of media. This does, however, raise the possibility that in some minority language situations, language maintenance becomes the preserve of the professional middle classes (a situation not unknown, even without the impact of new media), as the digital divide puts even more economic pressure on the less well-off to abandon the minority language.

Language Planning

All these elements are brought into focus by considering the issue of language planning. Language plans have often been seen as critical for minority languages and they crystallize the problem of what the media can do in given situations.

A traditional view of the media's role in language developments can be seen to be expressed in the work of Joshua Fishman. In his Graded Intergenerational Disruption Scale, Fishman mentioned the media only as an institution at the two fullest levels in his scale (Fishman, 1991: 87–109) and traditionally some language planners have followed this, seeing media as part of the ultimate picture of language support, but not as being so relevant to language revival at its more basic levels in the home and in the local community. Even in 'old media' terms, it has always been possible to argue that this was too restrictive a view of media. Fishman seems to have had in mind media organizations which could exist only at a specific degree of community development and whose output intervened at these specific levels. But, in fact, media are now all-pervasive (and have been for many years), interacting with language users at all levels of language development, from the family home to international communication. With new media this becomes even more obviously the case. (See also Elin Haf Gruffydd Jones's chapter in this volume for a new reading of Fishman's views.)

An example of recent language planning, and one which, by implication, takes a similar view to Fishman, is the National Plan for Gaelic in Scotland (produced by Bòrd na Gàidhlig in 2007). Here the implied view of the media is as a technology for particular use at the broad community level. This is true even of new media. The Plan suggests that a digital service will 'unite the scattered Gaelic communities, and it will promote the positive benefits of Gaelic ... and positively encourage language use and acquisition' (how it will do these latter tasks is not explained). It will 'create significant employment opportunities, increasing artistic and technical skills, stimulating parents' interest in Gaelic education, appealing to and serving adult learners, and strengthening Gaelic usage in extremely important media' (BnaG, 2007: 46). This is a broad view of media as part of the general background of a linguistic community, helping in various ways, but hardly central. When it comes to research topics, there is only one suggestion in the plan – a media audit to identify gaps in media coverage. (In fairness to Bòrd na Gàidhlig, they have been involved in a rather different media research topic, and one which meshes much more closely with new media – the possibilities of the use of Gaelic in computer games.)

There is, of course, a very good reason why media have often not had a role to play in language plans. Media organizations are usually beyond the influence of language planners. There is little point in developing a policy for minority language media use if the media organizations involved are unlikely to take notice of it and cannot be forced to consider it. Even though their economic situation is usually different from majority language media, the imperative to maximize the audience is still there. Some exceptions are found to this, for example in Catalonia and the Basque Country where language planning is built into the structures of regional government and where the central funding for broadcasting comes from those governments (see, for example, Corominas Piulats, 2007).

The general problem is that language planning has usually been seen as a 'top-down' activity. The institutional organizer develops a plan and this is then imposed, one way or another, on the population. New media, on the other hand, consist (partly, but importantly) of 'bottom-up' activity, with initiatives being developed by the users themselves. It is not at all clear how traditional language planning efforts could be employed in new media in any meaningful way when even the appearance of any kind of prescriptivism is likely to give rise to resistance.

This raises an even broader question: what could language planning mean in the digital future? When digital media pervade most of the society and when user participation becomes all-important, how could any language plan be effectively put into action? Digital media affect all four of the traditional aspects of language planning – status planning, corpus planning, language use and language acquisition. However (as already noted), digital media are not policeable for language. At the very least, this suggests that language planning for minority languages needs to be completely re-thought if it is not to lose contact with the activities of language users.

Tom Moring's notion of 'functional completeness' (Moring, 2007, and his essay in this book) is useful at this point as a way of focusing on the changes in media provision in minority languages. He describes functional completeness as meaning 'that speakers of the language, if they so choose, can live their life in and through the language without having to resort to other languages, at least within the confines of everyday matters in their community' (Moring, 2007: 18). The application of this idea to traditional media is clear. But it is less clear how it might be applied to new media, especially social media, given their indiscriminate nature, the vagueness of what we might call the media product (as was concluded by Pavón and Zuberogoitia in their chapter) and the permeation of new media by dominant languages, particularly English. Many minority language speakers in Europe, for example, would probably expect access to English language websites as part of any kind of functional completeness, regardless of their own language preferences. Moring's notion of the 'strict preference condition' (Moring, 2007: 28) points to the centrality of language choice in minority language media issues. As he puts it, 'to what extent will the Minority Language speaker use media in the Minority Language, and to what extent will he/she prefer to lean on the majority language outlets in conformity with the majority? ... is there a strict preference for the Minority Language and can that preference be met?' This focuses the question very well, but its application in the digital future is not so clear.

Towards a Framework of Understanding

All of this raises issues for the conduct of MLM research. What kinds of research are needed for the digital future? What do we actually want to know about minority languages in the media? As already noted, Browne and

Uribe-Jongbloed have usefully outlined an ambitious research agenda earlier in this book. In addition to that list (although to some extent overlapping with some of its issues), I wish to push for the importance of gaining a clearer idea of how MLM impact on actual language use. Without this, MLM research will continually be playing 'catch-up' – reporting on what has already happened. What is needed is an account of media–language interaction which emphasizes the use of language consequent to media use. Just noting and describing media use is not enough if we want to have an impact on language maintenance.

What would such an account contain? It would certainly turn away from textual analysis. The difficulty of this type of research will be clear from the uncertainty as to what the new media text might be. It would also turn away from notions of the collective audience experience. There simply will be no very obvious entity of that kind. It will also avoid any kind of straightforward linear model of media impact. It will, however, concentrate on actual media use, on the linguistic consequences of such use and so also on context, that is, the context in which the media interaction takes place (Ó Laoire has put emphasis on this point, see Ó Laoire, 2001). Such an account should be capable of covering all media, of covering all user situations and of giving us confidence that we can achieve a better understanding of media use in minority languages. As a step towards such an account, we can start by considering the framework that is needed.

One way to approach such a framework would be to consider the most salient variables in media use in a minority language situation. Consider first the varieties of language effect. Immediate language use may change due to media use, or longer-term language use. Attitudes to the language may change (which of course would be expected to have longer-term consequences). In addition, language changes may concern the amount of language use or the type of language use (in relation to dialect, grammar, vocabulary, etc.). Another set of variables concerns types of media use. At the most minimal, this may be merely 'reading' the text. On the other hand, it may include responding to the text, or a fuller participation in it, or even, of course, originating the text. Clearly, these variables are of central importance when considering language use. The third set of variables concerns the context of media consumption. This context, in particular in relation to other language users, can be of major importance. Media consumption may be solitary, it may be in the form of a dialogue with another media user or it may be as part of a group. And of course the group may be speakers of the minority language or speakers of another language.

Another variable, and perhaps the most difficult to pin down, concerns linguistic identity. John Edwards has suggested that this is possibly the most important element when choice of language is made (Edwards, 1985). But if this is so, it suggests that how the media text interacts with such identity will be important. In this case, we would need to develop some measure of such identity, however vague it might be, in order to trace its role in the media–language interaction. An excellent step in this direction is the chapter by Vincze and Moring in this book. One final point worth noting is the question of how the decision to use the media is made. The difference here is between someone happening to see a media product simply 'because it's on', and so with no active choice of their own, and someone consciously choosing to use media.

Out of these different factors, a likely conflux would seem to be the intersection of the attitudes of the media user, how active their participation in media use is, and the consequent development of their linguistic behaviour (this latter, of course, coming from continuing media use, rather than just one example). At the very least, it may become possible to identify patterns of media use which are related to linguistic behaviour. However, this media use – particularly with the young people who are the future for any minority language community – is likely to cover a wide range of new media, and rather than patterns of specific media and specific content, we are likely to arrive at more abstract accounts of media use.

At this point, it is worth considering what sociolinguistics has to offer media studies. There has been less direct overlap than might have been expected between that discipline and the media studies context in which much study of MLM has developed. The most frequently used concept from sociolinguistics in MLM studies has probably been the notion of ethnolinguistic vitality (as can be seen in some of the essays in this book). However, perhaps what is needed is a more thorough-going ethnography of language use in relation to the media. Notions of speech communities and code-switching would also seem to be potentially of great use. Sociolinguists' attention to the actual practices of language communities is something which can be of direct benefit to MLM studies. If those involved in media studies more generally have in the past criticized other disciplines for not taking the media seriously enough, then the traffic is not all one-way. Studies of the media in which questions of language are involved need to listen to what other disciplines – particularly sociolinguistics – have to say.

All this suggests a mode of research which would be attentive not only to the many variables involved but also to the sociolinguistic context. The reasons why people choose specific types of media and specific types of media context can obviously be complex. The reasons why people are encouraged – or discouraged – to use a particular language following from media interactions are also likely to be complex. However, without tackling this head-on, MLM studies may miss the chance to directly help minority languages.

Conclusions

If we want to use the media to help language development, we need to understand the processes by which people interact with language in the media, but in a general way which will cover any media interaction. Simply studying what is happening or has happened, while important, is not enough. Immediate reactions do not tell us much, and broad language trends are too long-term to be useful (we cannot wait until the next census results). Such an approach might even be able to rescue a role for the media in language planning.

There is of course an economic side to all of this. As long as MLM are dependent on public funding, there is going to be a need to show what benefits they are having for the languages concerned. This means that the clearer we can be about the processes by which media help in the maintenance of a language community, the better. It may be, of course, that much of the digital world will be outside the realms of subsidized media. However, it is likely that radio and television will continue to play a central role in the future, even though the ways we use them may change, and in that case public funding will continue to be required.

References

BnaG (2007) The National Plan for Gaelic/Plana nàiseanta na Gàidhlig. Inverness: Bòrd na Gàidhlig.

Cormack, M. (2007) The media and language maintenance. In M. Cormack and N. Hourigan (eds) *Minority Language Media: Concepts, Critiques, and Case Studies* (pp. 52–68). Clevedon: Multilingual Matters.

Cormack, M. (2010) Gaelic in the new digital landscape. In G. Munro and I. Mac an Tàilleir (eds) *Gaelic Communities Today* (pp. 127–137). Edinburgh: Dunedin Academic.

Corominas Piulats, M. (2007) Media policy and language policy in Catalonia. In M. Cormack and N. Hourigan (eds) *Minority Language Media: Concepts, Critiques, and Case Studies* (pp. 168–187). Clevedon: Multilingual Matters.

Edwards, J. (1985) *Language, Society and Identity*. Oxford: Blackwell.

Fishman, J.A. (1991) *Reversing Language Shift: Theoretical and Empirical Foundations of Assistance to Threatened Languages*. Clevedon: Multilingual Matters.

Hourigan, N. (2007) Minority language media studies: Key themes for future scholarship. In M. Cormack and N. Hourigan (eds) *Minority Language Media: Concepts, Critiques, and Case Studies* (pp. 248–265). Clevedon: Multilingual Matters.

Manovich, L. (2001) *The Language of New Media*. London: MIT Press.

Moring, T. (2007) Functional completeness in minority language media. In M. Cormack and N. Hourigan (eds) *Minority Language Media: Concepts, Critiques and Case Studies* (pp. 17–33). Clevedon: Multilingual Matters.

Ó Laoire, M. (2001) Language policy and broadcast media: A response. In H. Kelly-Holmes (ed.) *Minority Language Broadcasting: Breton and Irish* (pp. 63–68). Clevedon: Multilingual Matters.

Williams, G. (2007) From media to multimedia: Workflows and language in the digital economy. In M. Cormack and N. Hourigan (eds) *Minority Language Media: Concepts, Critiques, and Case Studies* (pp. 88–106). Clevedon: Multilingual Matters.

Index